THE CHINA FREEDOM TRAP

The China Freedom Trap, My Life on the Run © Toronto, 2023 Dolkun Isa

First Edition published in Canada, United Kingdom and United States
Published by Optimum Publishing International.

All rights reserved. No part of this publication may be reproduced in any form or by any means whatsoever or stored in a data base without permission in writing from the publisher, except by a reviewer who may quote passages of customary brevity in review.

LIBRARY AND ARCHIVES CANADA CATALOGUING IN PUBLICATION
Title: The China Freedom, My Life on the Run
Dolkun Isa, author

Subjects: Human Rights, Genocide, Religious Freedom,
Transnational Repression
Description: Optimum Publishing International Canada edition

ISBN 978-0-88890-343-3 (Paperback)
ISBN 978-0-88890-352-2 (ePub)

Jacket and Interior design by Jessica Albert

Printed and bound in Canada.
Marquis Printing

For information on rights or any submissions, please e-mail to
Optimum: deanb@opibooks.com
Optimum Publishing International
Dean Baxendale, President & CEO
Toronto, Canada

www.optimumpublishinginternational.com
www.opibooks.com
Twitter @opibooks | Instagram @opibooks

THE CHINA FREEDOM TRAP

MY LIFE ON THE RUN

DOLKUN ISA

CONTENTS

DEDICATION	vi
ACKOWLEDGEMENTS	ix
ABBREVIATIONS	xi
CONTRIBUTOR FOREWORDS	xii
Nury Turkel	xiii
Sir Geoffrey Nice	xvii
Sophie Richardson	xxv
Ambassador Kelley Eckels Currie	xxvii
INTRODUCTION	1

1 FROM ACTIVIST TO TERRORIST — 7
Frankfurt detention, 1999 — 12
China brands me a terrorist — 16
My response to China's allegations — 18
Violation at Geneva — 22

2 INTERPOL'S LONG ARM — 29
Deported from Washington, D.C. — 29
The Victims of Communism Award — 41
Deported from Turkey — 47
Suddenly shut out of Taiwan — 53

3 MY BORDER PROBLEMS ESCALATE — 60
A diplomatic struggle — 64
A safe return, at a cost — 72
More border troubles — 75

4 UNDER CONSTANT PRESSURE — 83
Saudi Arabia: Surveillance in the Sacred Land — 83
Predicament in Northern Cyprus — 91

5 INSIDE INTERPOL 103
Regaining freedom: My Red Notice lifted 107
The president of Interpol disappears 116
The lingering ghost of the Red Notice 119

6 CHINA'S HIDDEN HAND INSIDE THE UNITED NATIONS 122
Expelled from the UN 125
China's mischief at the UN 128
Shaming China at the UN 133
A tense debate 139

7 THE CONCENTRATION CAMPS 152
Presidency of the WUC 154
Facing a Chinese agent at the UN 161
Concentration camp debate 165

8 THE PRICE OF ACTIVISM 168
Deported from Turkey—again 168
My mother's death 175

9 THE WORLD RESPONDS 180
The Uyghur cause in the diaspora 187
China's evil influence in Germany 190
The Uyghur Tribunal 196

EPILOGUE 203

APPENDIX A: THE BATTLE FOR FREEDOM CONTINUES 205
Key Achievements in 2022–2023 206

APPENDIX B: REBUTTAL TO THE CHINESE PUBLIC SECURITY MINISTRY'S "TERRORIST" ACCUSATION 232

ENDNOTES 247

DEDICATION

I am dedicating this book to two heroic women who have deeply impacted my life. These women both paid heavy prices for me. One is my mother, Ayhan, and the other is my wife, Mahire.

My mother died in a Chinese concentration camp. She paid the price for being my mother. All mothers are great, of course, but mine was a very strong and determined woman, whose only crime was to support my activism. When I was convicted in 1988 of leading a student movement and expelled from the university, many people—even my close friends and relatives—did not dare even to greet me. In those days when I began to feel completely isolated, my father and mother became my close friends, companions, and supporters.

In 1994, at the airport in Beijing before I boarded my flight to Istanbul, my mother hugged me and cried, "When will we see you again, son?" Her farewell words to me were, "Don't worry about us. We are happy for you. Think of your people and keep going on the path you believe in."

In 2003, the Chinese government labelled me a "terrorist" and circulated my picture in newspapers and on CCTV for weeks. Police came to our house in Aksu and forced my parents to disown and reject me, but my stern mother refused them. She said, "I

DEDICATION

will not give up on my own son. If you want, put me in jail and punish me, but my son is not a terrorist."

The endless interrogations, pressure, and threats from the Chinese police never broke my mother. She never complained, and she never said, "Son, think about us and stop your activities against China." The Chinese government put my faithful mother in a concentration camp at the age of seventy-eight and killed her. Her only crime was being my mother and being Uyghur. The Chinese government took revenge on my mother for not being able to stop me. I learned from Radio Free Asia that my heroic mother died on May 17, 2018, in that camp. I don't even know where she is buried or whether she has a grave. Nothing I do could be better than what my selfless mother did for me.

My wife, Mahire, is another hero. She is neither an activist like I am nor an active energetic figure with great ambition. She is a simple woman, a mother of two, but she has accompanied me through the thirty years of my life as an activist. When she embarked on her journey with me, she may have hoped for a quiet, peaceful, and happy family, but I could not give her the beautiful life she wanted because my life in exile has been full of trouble and conflict. Since I spent most of my time travelling, I couldn't take care of my family and children. She has been both mother and father to our children. To financially support our family, she has worked very hard. And, during our twenty-seven years in exile, she has not had the opportunity to visit her homeland or her parents.

Except for binding herself to me with pure love, this heroic woman has committed no crime. She has suffered for being the wife of a "terrorist." She has paid the price for being my wife, but she has never regretted it. China's accusations against me were a trap set in my path. As China's black hand stretched out all over the world, I was detained at the borders of many countries as I travelled to publicize the Uyghur cause. Several times I was in serious danger of being deported to China, even though I had become a German citizen. Every time this happened, my wife reached out to German embassies, begged lawyers for help, and tried her best to save me from captivity. She spent many sleepless nights waiting for my safe return. She has been the most loyal friend and confidante in my life; I wish I could have been a better husband to this heroic woman and a better father to our two children.

ACKOWLEDGEMENTS

On the occasion of my fiftieth birthday, my closest friends recommended that I write my biography, as for many years publishers had shown an interest in telling my story.

Starting in 2016, however, as the situation in East Turkistan worsened and a genocide unfolded, my responsibilities became heavier. To wake up the international community about what was happening and represent the World Uyghur Congress as its president became my duty. In this pressing situation, it was impossible for me to pick up a pen, gather my thoughts, and write a book.

But my friends and publishers didn't stop trying to convince me. At the very least, they wanted me to write about my experiences after China used an Interpol Red Notice to label me a terrorist, leading to my detention and expulsion from many borders and countries and the subsequent international press coverage, which demonstrated both China's growing international influence and its impact on individual nations and international bodies. Writing about my experiences as a falsely labelled and detained terrorist interested me, so I started this journey. Due to time and capacity constraints, however, there were many times when I wanted to give up halfway through the project, but with the help of many friends I was able to complete it.

Without the valuable efforts and help of these individuals, this book would not have been possible. I want to sincerely thank my long-time friend and schoolmate from Xinjiang University, author Ekrem Hezim, who helped me with the writing. Thanks are also due to Miriam Teich and Zumretay Arkin, who worked hard to edit the book, and Abdumuqtedir and Dr. Muhammed Imin, who assisted with the translation, as well as all the other friends who supported me during this journey.

This book is the result of my own efforts and the collective work of these individuals.

I would also like to highlight the enormous amount of work and effort by many people who worked on the second edition of the book, namely my editor Maura Blain Brown for her patience and my publisher, Dean Baxendale who has truly done it all to get this endeavour started.

I finally want to thank my esteemed colleagues and dear friends, Sophie Richardson, Nury Turkel, Sir Geoffrey Nice and Kelley Currie for their tremendous support over the years and for their kind contributions to this important book.

ASPI: Australian Strategic Policy Institute
CCP: Chinese Communist Party
CCF: Commission for the Control of Interpol's Files
CERD: Committee for the Elimination of Racial Discrimination
ETUE: East Turkistan Union in Europe
CAI: EU-China Comprehensive Agreement
EEAS: European External Action Service
GLAN: Global Legal Action Network
ICIJ: International Consortium of Investigative Journalists
NED: National Endowment for Democracy
NIA: National Immigration Agency
OHCHR: Office of the UN High Commissioner for Human Rights
OIC: Organization of Islamic Cooperation's
RFA: Radio Free Asia
STP: Society for Threatened Peoples
UNPFII: United Nations Permanent Forum on Indigenous Issues
UPR: Universal Periodic Review
UNPO: Unrepresented Nations and Peoples Organization
UAA: Uyghur American Association
UFLPA: Uyghur Forced Labor Prevention Act
UHRP: Uyghur Human Rights Project
VOC: Victims of Communism Memorial Foundation
WAOTY: World Assembly of Turkish Youth
WMD: World Movement for Democracy
XUAR: Xinjiang Uyghur Autonomous Region

CONTRIBUTOR FOREWORDS

THE WORLD CAN NO LONGER REMAIN SILENT

by Nury Turkel

In the pages that follow, you will embark on a journey through the life of Dolkun Isa, a man whose story is a testament to the resilience of the human spirit and a stark reminder of the grave injustices faced by the Uyghur people in East Turkistan. Dolkun has dedicated his entire life to seeking justice for his people, and as I pen this foreword, I cannot help but marvel at the courage and determination of my dear friend and colleague.

As co-founder of the Uyghur Human Rights Project in 2003, I, too, had faced the darkness that Dolkun and his organization confronted, fighting to give the Uyghur freedom cause a voice at a time when parliamentarians, Congress, and world leaders sought to get along with the Chinese Communist Party in the hopes that it would one day change its stripes.

This proved folly, and Uyghurs and Tibetans suffered immeasurable persecution and both cultural and systemic genocide at the hands of the regime. Its authoritarian influence only continues to grow, as we were recently reminded when Hong Kong citizens protesting for the rights afforded to them under the

Sino-British joint Declaration were crushed by Beijing's Hong Kong Authority.

Dolkun's narrative begins in a land often forgotten, East Turkistan, where the Uyghur people have endured decades of oppression under the Chinese Communist Party's rule. Born during Mao's "Cultural Revolution," Dolkun grew up in a time of repression and purges, witnessing the imprisonment and execution of countless Uyghur intellectuals and patriots. Despite the adversity, he found his identity and purpose while attending Xinjiang University, and from there, his journey as an activist and advocate for his people took flight.

From organizing pro-democracy student demonstrations to running an underground publishing house, Dolkun's activism drew the attention of the Chinese regime, branding him a "murderer," "criminal," and eventually a "terrorist" on Interpol's Red Notices. This ominous label hung over his head for twenty-one long years, making every step he took in the free world a potential move towards imprisonment and extradition. Yet, through it all, Dolkun never lost hope. He continued to speak out against the atrocities committed against the Uyghur people despite constant threats and intimidation.

Dolkun's struggles were not confined to the borders of China; they followed him even when he sought refuge in foreign lands. Despite becoming a citizen of Germany, the Chinese authorities relentlessly pursued him, attempting to silence his voice and erase his advocacy. His journey reflects the sad reality that the long arm of the Chinese Communist Party can extend far beyond its borders, influencing countries to shut their doors to those who dare to speak out against its brutal regime.

Throughout this book, Dolkun exposes the true nature of the Chinese Communist Party, a force that poses a threat to not only the Uyghur people but to all of humanity. He shines a light on the genocide and cultural erasure inflicted upon the Uyghur people, forced labor, religious persecution, and the destruction of mosques and historical artifacts. His experiences stand as a stark warning to the world, urging us to recognize the danger the CCP poses to our democratic values, human rights, and international stability.

As you read through the harrowing accounts of Dolkun's life on the run, facing stalkers and intimidation, enduring detainments, and uncertainties, I urge you to reflect on the message that echoes through every chapter of this book. Dolkun's struggle is not just his own; it is a struggle for freedom, justice, and the preservation of human rights that resonates with all of us who believe in the inherent dignity of every individual.

The world has a moral obligation to heed the cries of the Uyghur people and to stand against the tyranny of the Chinese Communist Party. As you turn the pages, I hope you will be moved to act, raise your voice, and join the fight for the freedom and dignity of the Uyghurs and all those oppressed by authoritarian regimes.

Dolkun's organization is nominated for the 2023 Nobel Peace Prize for advocating and championing the cause of the Uyghurs and all oppressed peoples. Even if it doesn't win the prize, it has accomplished so much over the past few years, and it is because of this dedication we should all pay tribute to Dolkun and his team at the World Uyghur Congress.

In sharing his story, Dolkun challenges us to confront uncomfortable truths and never forget the lessons of history. Together, we must ensure that the world is not silent in the face of oppression and genocide, that we uphold the promise of "Never Again," and always strive to build a world where justice and freedom reign supreme for all.

NURY TURKEL is an attorney and award-winning author of *No Escape: The True Story of China's Genocide of the Uyghurs.* He is a congressionally appointed Commissioner and former Chairman of the United States Commission on International Religious Freedoms. He is also a senior fellow at the Hudson Institute and Notre Dame Law School. He is a co-founder and Chairman of the Board of the Uyghur Human Rights Project.

THE TORMENTED CAN ONLY BE FREE IN A DEMOCRACY

by Sir Geoffrey Nice

Two or three years ago citizens of the countries of the West knew little—most knew nothing—of the Uyghurs of Xinjiang.

Dolkun Isa, in this book, shows how hard it has been to fill this knowledge gap, despite the Uyghurs being the major ethnic people of the People's Republic of China's (PRC's) largest region—Xinjiang, their homeland. And this is despite them being long-term oppressed ethnic people.

To broadcast knowledge of, and generate support for, his people—persecuted by the PRC for very many years—Dolkun Isa had to make the hardest possible choices: between supporting the oppressed by mobilisation of world opinion on the one hand and protecting his family on the other. He might have safeguarded his family by doing nothing: doing nothing about the universal rights of man—more particularly the Rights of Uyghurs—as set in the 1948 Declaration of Human Rights to which the PRC is a party; doing nothing about freedom of speech for his fellow Uyghurs;

doing nothing about the lawful wish of his fellow Uyghurs for the independence of Xinjiang from the PRC.

Instead, with his mother's approval and his wife's support, he stuck to the cause he started as a student. When he parted from his mother—decades ago—they may each have feared they would never meet again. They didn't. She died in a PRC camp. His father's death came simply without any account available to Dolkun Isa of how he died, why and where. As for his two brothers, they have received long prison sentences.

What dread choices to face? Those of us living in safer places, without the creeping and all-enveloping restriction of an implacable surveillance state controlling our movements, our practice of religion, our knowledge from books or media and even our thoughts can have no idea how we might have faced such a state?

Dolkun Isa faced the state of the PRC full on, he kept looking forward and he never gave up. *His* mission—to develop an activist international movement for the Uyghurs—meant travel; and travel meant crossing borders, giving the PRC the chance, time and again, to imperil him. First, when they had forced through, without any cause, a 'Red Notice' on him; after the notice was cancelled, even without the power to threaten and intimidate individuals and to persuade other states that such a notice holds.

The retelling of his life is a thrilling read, no more so than when he was forced to contemplate the PRC reclaiming him from South Korea to a prison, privations, torture and a probable death that finally—almost—balanced the prospect of his worldly success against the benefits of self-ending life itself. On this and all other occasions he battled through—with the help of the many he acknowledges as his saviours—and never gave up.

But there was a problem with getting through to the regular world citizen who, in democracies, vote for the regular politicians who form regular governments that decide whether or not to support a persecuted ethnicity. And governments, even of well-

THE TORMENTED CAN ONLY BE FREE IN A DEMOCRACY

intentioned citizens, can often be blinded and deafened by the power of commerce or the need for national security to still the better consciences of their voters. This, for long enough, may have been the reality for all who suffered human rights breaches at the hands of the mighty PRC.

The knowledge-gap problem for the suffering Uyghurs face was not unique. Practitioners of Falun Gong in the PRC, and concerned activists on their behalf, had been recording for at least 15 years how their fellow practitioners had been systematically detained and murdered for their human organs to stock the PRC's commercially and professionally successful transplant business. Internationally respected research revealing what was happening was always found 'insufficient' by governments approached for support.

The China Tribunal—a people's tribunal—was established to explore allegations of this grossest imaginable crime of 'forced organ harvesting' as it is known—killing order in order to sell hearts, livers, cornea etc. for transplantation. Its composition and procedures differed from most previous people's tribunals by those involved *not* being that concerned about Falun Gong and the Tribunal's members in particular being, intentionally, people who knew little or nothing of relevance to the Tribunal's investigation. The Tribunal's sole purpose was to fill a gap in public knowledge and to do no more. Were the worldwide allegations made about forced organ harvesting of the Falun Gong and others, allegations that governments declined to accept, in fact accurate?

China Tribunal Members heard evidence about the Uyghurs as well as about practitioners of Falun Gong. They heard about Uyghurs having been victims of forced organ harvesting—and of other oppression more generally. An approach was made while the China Tribunal was doing its work in general terms by a group of diaspora Uyghurs for assistance and advice. But that first approach—of course well-intentioned—was without focus or leadership. Those members of the China Tribunal—Nick Vetch,

Counsel to the Tribunal Hamid Sabi and I—are concerned that maybe something *should* be done about the gap in world knowledge of the Uyghurs and of their being persecuted felt we could *not* help a group that lacked clear leadership. Effective "civil society" activities require clear leadership by whoever seeks assistance or by an NGO with clear activist policy and intentions. Vague intentions by a disparate group usually get nowhere.

A later approach led by Dolkun Isa of the World Uyghur Congress (WUC) was different. There was a well-coordinated, well-led group of those concerned with Uyghur persecution. They and their leader could understand, from the start of discussions, why the Tribunal members could say—and mean—that they were not *that* concerned about the Uyghurs in the same way as the earlier China Tribunal formation was not *that* concerned about the Falun Gong—in the sense that they were no more concerned about these groups and their suffering than they may be, as non-specialist citizens, about the suffering of oppressed Rohingya Muslims or Nigerian Christians. Dolkun Isa and his team accepted, when they commissioned the formation of a new Tribunal, that the Tribunal would start from scratch with a blank piece of paper and might well not bring whatever result they hoped for.

That is a big decision for someone as properly committed as Dolkun Isa was and is and only a true leader might see the value of this approach. He saw the value. Just as the ETAC, the NGO managed by Susie Hughes, had been able to do for the Falun Gong, albeit in both cases only after some serious internal questioning, I have no doubt.

Unlike ETAC—which had funds and simply had to decide whether to spend them on the China Tribunal, Dolkun Isa had to raise funds for witness travel, translation of statements, hire of venues for hearings etc. The Tribunal members and all senior staff worked entirely *pro bono* but also *could not*, even if inclined, put money in—they had to be entirely neutral and without any financial interest if their Judgment was to attract respect. The total sum

THE TORMENTED CAN ONLY BE FREE IN A DEMOCRACY

to be raised was minuscule by the standards of any international court: the cost of a couple of days of trial hearings. But substantial for the expatriate Uyghurs who would have to accept Dolkun Isa's judgement and follow his advice. Once funding was underway by WUC, the Tribunal was able to help, but only by creating crowd-funding mechanisms and seeking other public philanthropy.

Nick Vetch, Vice Chair of the Tribunal, and I recruited the Tribunal Members. Hamid Sabi, Counsel to the Tribunal, ran the operation of evidence gathering and evidence presentation. Dolkun Isa's WUC was the first source of witness and other evidence. Meetings between WUC and the three of us required trust on both sides. Trust that evidence would be gathered and presented fairly and be representative of *all* evidence not in any way slanted. Trust that we the Tribunal would bend to no pressure—one way or the other—and be objective.

It is important to recall that there could only be informality in everything. The Tribunal was not just informal but ungoverned; there was no superior body to whom WUC could complain if they thought we erred. Likewise with WUC. If they corrupted evidence or rehearsed witnesses or did anything else to 'flavour' the record we could do nothing. All on both sides recognised this without needing to say it. The experience—looking back—was immensely encouraging of what can be done where there is no driving force apart from finding a better truth (us) and working for one's fellows (Uyghurs—them).

And there was a stated difference between us: Once our Judgment was delivered we would do little or nothing more. The Judgment would be for others to use as they might think fit. It was not for us to become activists in a cause we did not support in that way *before* our work started. This difference was understood and accepted. It required detailed reservations about social encounters and social mixing until the Judgment was delivered (and even then only minimal "outside work" meetings happened).

The Tribunal members—as they understood before they started work—could get little beyond a mention on a CV for working hundreds of hours *pro bono*. But they were all of such a senior professional level that such an addition to a CV would be otiose. So nothing in this work for the members but the satisfaction of the work itself.

Allegations about the Uyghur's suffering included that there had been and was genocide, always a troublesome charge because of its general use being "streets away" from the narrow legal definition the Tribunal had to apply. And the Tribunal was determined to be strict in the application of the law and equally determined only to find facts if proved beyond a reasonable doubt. Expert lawyers in written reports (only two of whom presented one report were prepared to rise from the printed page and speak to the Tribunal in public) mostly took bold steps in their reports to make general findings of genocide. Our chosen top-level lawyers who would have instructed the Tribunal on the law just a judge directs a jury, were disabled (for good personal reasons) from helping once the Tribunal and noted pro-Uyghur and anti-PRC persons and bodies had been sanctioned by the PRC. So we turned to our counsel team and one trustworthy outside lawyer. But their advice was less clear and emphatic and they were less responsive to the questions about the law from the Tribunal than the top-level lawyers might have been. The Tribunal members had, of necessity, to do some legal research themselves. This led to the Tribunal applying a most conservative and cautious understanding of the law by which to direct themselves. Might this lead to there being *no* finding of genocide? And would this inevitably bring sadness to the activist Uyghurs who saw the term in a commonplace way and who had invested trust in us?

The Tribunal met in plenary sessions and discussed fact and law from the ground up—that "blank piece of paper"—and reached their conclusions.

THE TORMENTED CAN ONLY BE FREE IN A DEMOCRACY

The Judgment, delivered in the fairly grand surroundings of Church House Westminster—took 2 ¼ hours to read, without a break. The hall was silent throughout and Dolkun Isa and one other Uyghur from WUC were in the front row.

It often feels mean for someone delivering a judgment to hold back the conclusion in which the central parties have the greatest interest until the very end. Why not spell it out at the start? On this occasion, that possibility had to be resisted because it was essential that those considering the Judgment should hear in detail—if only ever to consider it the once—the reasoning of our conclusions, whichever way they went. And so, once Torture and Crimes against humanity *were* found proved—beyond a reasonable doubt—the Judgment turned to genocide.

Dolkun Isa—as this book shows—has over very many years suffered terrible anxieties as well as physical suffering of many kinds. Did the Tribunal have to add to his already full chest of worry by leaving for two hours the conclusion on genocide? There was no pre-release of the Judgment to anyone, not even our own team, and as the genocide decision approached Dolkun and his WUC compatriot held hands and was very clearly *very* anxious. Looking over the Tribunal's desk it was both touching and heartening to see—not because of what *was* to come but because that essential separation of tasks between WUC and the Tribunal, functioning without formality, had worked. They had no idea what would be said. All in the process had played their parts.

The Tribunal found:

> "on the basis of evidence heard in public, the Tribunal is satisfied beyond reasonable doubt that the PRC, by the imposition of measures to prevent births intended to *destroy* a significant part of the Uyghurs in Xinjiang as such, has committed genocide."

Dolkun's hand held his companion's; energy and emotion will have flowed between them.

This small part of Dolkun Isa's story is worth telling because the problem facing the Uyghurs—still living in the PRC or now as diaspora—is immense and the work of the Tribunal can only at the very best be a very, very small bit of a long-term laborious, uphill endeavour that will last for decades and maybe for lifetimes.

Parts of the problem—say the continuation of the camps and the criminal acts committed in them—may be addressed if present activist work reduces the worst human rights abuses simply because the PRC has *some* concern about its public international image. But the rest of the problem—tragedies of many kinds for the Uyghurs, their culture and their very existence as an ethnic group—will remain unless and until there is a significant change in the PRC regime. Regime change is not within the gift of the international governments that WUC and other Uyghur groups seek to persuade of the rightness of their cause. It is certainly not within the power of NGOs anywhere on their own to achieve.

These unhappy but necessary observations make the book's survey of Dolkun Isa's work the more impressive. The honourable and correct integration of his work with that of the Tribunal reflects his overall integrity and his determination to make good use of what may help his people. Uyghurs reading this book may feel hope as long they enjoy the leadership of such strength and character. For the rest of us, Dolkun Isa demonstrates how the future of the world's varied and glorious people so often depends on the virtues of a few good people at any one time.

SIR GEOFFREY NICE

Chief Prosecutor for the International Criminal Tribunal for the Former Yugoslavia (ICTY); Chair of the Uyghur Tribunal (2022) and the China Tribunal (2019)

THE INTERPOL RED NOTICE WAS DEVOID OF MERIT

by Sophie Richardson

When in November 2012 Dolkun Isa and I first met in person, it was a moment of partial celebration. The United States had concluded that INTERPOL's "red notice" against him was devoid of merit, finally creating the opportunity for him to travel to Washington. By that time I had been aware of his work on behalf of Uyghurs' human rights for several years, and the difficulties he had faced as a result of the Chinese government demonizing him. So I was surprised by his good cheer. "One step at a time," I recall him saying.

There have been many steps—forward and backward—since that moment. It would be another six years before INTERPOL itself finally withdrew the baseless designation that had profoundly marred Dolkun's life as an advocate. And while that long overdue decision was welcome, it came at a moment of far greater concerns: rapidly deepening Chinese government repression in the Uyghur region of China, coupled with the Chinese government's growing global influence, deployed to thwart accountability. As this book goes to press, Dolkun is leading the charge to achieve a modicum of justice for Beijing's grave international crimes against the Uyghurs.

His degrees in physics and political science may have prepared him for a life of gravity-defying obstacles thrown in his path by powerful actors; this book tells the story of how he has surmounted those. From South Korea to Turkey, from the United Nations to European parliaments, he has challenged ignorance and efforts to exclude him, turning them into critical international support for Uyghurs and other communities persecuted by the Chinese government. He has stared down efforts to humiliate and demonize him. He has paid a tremendous personal cost, reflected not only in this book's moving dedication to his late mother, Ayhan, and his wife, Mahira, but also in the chilling description of learning of his brothers Yalkun's and Hashtar's enforced disappearances and his father Mehmet's death.

And yet Dolkun has never wavered. Whether navigating the riptides of geopolitical rivalries simply in trying to procure a visa, forging solidarity with other communities persecuted by the Chinese government, or building a global democratic movement outside China, Dolkun has demonstrated extraordinary courage and leadership. It has been a tremendous honor to learn from and work with him, and this book will inspire and comfort those trying to challenge the grave threats to human rights from Xi Jinping's government—and to secure respect for rights and democracy worldwide.

SOPHIE RICHARDSON
China Director, Human Rights Watch

THE UNITED NATIONS NEEDS TO STEP UP

by Ambassador Kelley Eckels Currie

In late March 2018, I received a message from Sophie Richardson at Human Rights Watch that our mutual friend Dolkun Isa was having issues with his registration to attend an upcoming UN event, the Permanent Forum on Indigenous Issues (PFII). This was not a particularly unusual message: in fact, it was something that came up every time Dolkun tried to attend a UN meeting. Previously, there was not much I could do to help beyond posting on Twitter or asking the State Department to do their job, but this year was different. I had recently joined the U.S. Mission to the United Nations (USUN) in New York as the Ambassador to the Economic and Social Council (ECOSOC) and a Deputy to Ambassador Nikki Haley, which meant that I was the person responsible for making sure the UN granted Dolkun access to the conference. I quickly checked in with the U.S. mission in Geneva, where Dolkun's credentials were being reviewed and made sure they were on the case. They assured me his application was in order and they were closely monitoring the office responsible for registering Forum participants. A week or so later, Dolkun received a letter from the Forum confirming his registration; he booked his ticket to New York and we set up a meeting in my office at USUN.

On the first day of the Forum, I was pleased to welcome Dolkun to my office and get an update from him on the increasingly dire situation facing the Uyghur people living in China. Our office had been closely following reports of massive securitization of the Xinjiang region since the arrival of Chen Quanguo as the party secretary there. As the former party secretary of the Tibet Autonomous Region, Chen dramatically escalated the level of repression, deploying a high-tech surveillance grid, rapidly growing the police presence, expanding political education in monasteries, and using all the tools available to the party-state to weaken the underpinnings of Tibetan culture. Since his arrival in Xinjiang, Chen had doubled down and expanded on these "strike hard" strategies. Dolkun and I discussed these troubling developments, especially reports of the detention of large numbers of Uyghur and other Turkic Muslim males over the age of 16 on specious charges of "terrorism." We talked about how the UN should be responding to the situation, and their failure to do so.

When it was time for him to go to UN's badge office to pick up his credentials for the Forum, I walked over with him so we could continue our conversation. As we waited in line, we chatted about Dolkun's goals for the Forum. When Dolkun approached the counter, I stood off to the side, checking in with my office and catching up on email. When I looked up after a few minutes, I saw Dolkun was still at the counter engaged in a very animated conversation with the UN official behind the counter. When I approached to ask what was happening, a UN security guard blocked my path and asked me what my business was. I showed him my UN badge and explained that was accompanying Mr. Isa to get his badge in case there was any issue, which apparently there

THE UNITED NATIONS NEEDS TO STEP UP

was. I asked what the problem was, as Mr. Isa was in possession of a letter from the Forum indicating his registration had been accepted and inviting him to attend the session in New York.

A series of frantic phone calls and consultations ensued among the badge office staff and security officers, after which Dolkun and I were informed that he was not able to get a badge due to a "security issue." I politely but insistently asked the security office to explain the nature of this "threat" and why they could not issue him a badge. In response, we were told we needed to speak to the UN's Department of Safety and Security (UNDSS). For over an hour, we engaged in a standoff at the badge office. I called our mission security chief Kenny Greenblatt and asked him to contact UNDSS. As the host country for the UN, USUN has an excellent working relationship with them and is in constant contact to resolve a host of security-related issues related to the UN, the 193 diplomatic missions, and thousands of UN and diplomatic personnel in the New York City area. When Kenny got back to me, it was with disturbing news: UNDSS said that Dolkun had been flagged as a "terrorist threat" and would not be able to get a badge. There was no question the Chinese government was behind this spurious accusation.

USUN subsequently learned that the Chinese Mission to the UN had told UNDSS that Dolkun was the subject of an INTERPOL "Red Notice." Rather than check with INTERPOL—a UN agency—UNDSS put a flag on Dolkun's name based solely on China's false allegations. Even though USUN provided UNDSS verification from INTERPOL that Mr. Isa was not, in fact, subject to a Red Notice, they still refused to lift the flag. USUN provided copious amounts of documentation that had been submitted as part of Mr. Isa's application for a ten-year multiple entry visa to the United States (which he was granted), our own internal investigations into Mr. Isa as part of a multi-nation effort to get the fraudulent Red Notice removed, and evidence of the Chinese government's routine use of false terrorism charges to silence political dissidents. As Mr. Isa is a German citizen, the German mission to the UN also actively weighed in on his behalf.

Ultimately, over the course of nearly two weeks, we had multiple meetings with both UNDSS and the Office of Secretary-General Antonio Guterres on this matter. In the end, UNDSS refused to issue Mr. Isa a badge without direct instructions from the Secretary-General. The U.S., German, and Chinese Permanent missions all engaged directly with Guterres on the matter. I heard from one contact in the Secretary General's office that the Chinese Permanent Representative had screamed at Guterres over the matter, threatening him and the UN with repercussions if Dolkun was given a badge. Our missions stood firm but as the situation dragged on, it seemed that Guterres was running out the clock—delaying his decision until it was too late for Dolkun to attend the Forum. With two days left, we received word that Dolkun could pick up his badge, but by that time he had already returned to Germany—a fact we were sure the Chinese were tracking. Fortunately, we were able to convince him to turn around and come back. On the last day of the Permanent Forum on Indigenous Issues, I finally escorted Dolkun Isa into the UN headquarters building. He arrived in time for the final session of the Forum, at which he rose to give a statement, only to be shouted at by Chinese participants.

Throughout all of this, Dolkun remained calm, determined, implacable, and unflappable. He never got angry, no matter how many times he had to send another copy of his German passport to the UN or respond to other, absurd requests for information. He knew the drill because he had been through it so many times. I knew that it had to wear on him: the punching down by a member of the UN Security Council, the perversion of institutions that were meant to protect human rights, the cowardice by prominent

THE UNITED NATIONS NEEDS TO STEP UP

world leaders, the inherent racism and deep injustice of constantly being forced to prove to others he and his community were not terrorists. But if it did, he never showed it. He remained steadfast, focused on how he could raise awareness about his community and the worsening situation they faced in Xi Jinping's increasingly authoritarian party-state. I had known about and known Dolkun for many years, but this incident in New York was the first opportunity I had to spend so much time with him and see firsthand the depth of his character, his self-effacing way of dealing with adversity, and his incredible resilience in the face of challenges that would overwhelm most of us. Again, these were things I knew he possessed in an academic sense, but to see it in action brought home to me what a special person he truly is.

When Dolkun asked me to provide a foreword for his book, I was deeply honoured and a little nervous. Then he sent me his first draft. As I read through the pages, it was filled with accounts of incidents I thought I remembered well: the appalling incident in South Korea; the visa refusals and immigration harassment he faced from liberal democracies; the seemingly endless fight to clear his name; the losses he has suffered of family. And again, seeing these events through his eyes and reading about them through his words, I was struck by what kind of person Dolkun Isa is and who he has become. I would go so far as to say he is a leader who has been forced to lead, and he has suffered because of that choice—being submitted to attacks by the most powerful and remorseless authoritarian country on the planet, and repeated humiliations and disappointments on the part of those countries that claim to stand for human values. Dolkun's story is important because it not only exposes the dangers of China's growing influence in the world, but also because it shines a light on the weaknesses of our own liberal democracies—the corruption, and corruptibility of our systems and how China uses our open societies, market fundamentalism, and assumptions about freedom against us.

It is an honor to call Dolkun Isa my friend. I am proud to have worked alongside him to highlight China's dangerous ambitions to subjugate the Uyghur people and undermine human rights worldwide. This is Dolkun's story: both a cautionary tale and a tale of the triumph of human dignity.

AMBASSADOR KELLEY ECKELS CURRIE

Former U.S. Depute Ambassador to the United Nations and United States Ambassador-at-Large for Global Women's Issues

INTRODUCTION

Despite living in the free world, I have been made to feel imprisoned for much of my life. Despite being a citizen of a European country—a country in which freedom, democracy, human rights, freedom of speech, and the rule of law are meant to be governing principles—I have continued to face injustices. I've been deprived of my freedom. My dignity has been trampled upon. I've been detained and interrogated. Many unfortunate events have befallen me in the free world that I longed for, believed in, and in which I hoped. They happened in Western countries that are governed by the rule of law. Despite these humiliations, or perhaps because of them, I have persevered with one objective: activism on behalf of and representation for the Uyghur people of East Turkistan, a people being forced to renounce their national identity and religious beliefs, and who face cultural and physical genocide. More than three million of them are currently imprisoned in concentration camps. In my quest for justice for my people, there were times I wanted to give up everything and end my life. When I was deported to Germany from Washington, D.C., I hoped my plane would crash, thereby ending my misfortunes. When I was detained in Seoul, Korea, and faced extradition to China, I knew then, without hesitation, that taking my own life would be better than being in the hands of the Chinese. The incidents that drove me to such thoughts and that have irrevocably altered my life were all the result of the treacheries of the most oppressive and autocratic regime in the world, the Chinese Communist Party (CCP).

How did I become the number one enemy of this gigantic country? I still struggle with this question. I grew up in a land far from the attention of the world, a land often forgotten. This land, East Turkistan, was placed under the occupation of Communist China in October 1949, when the People's Liberation Army troops marched into the country, effectively ending its autonomous rule. They turned this great land into a Chinese province, called the Xinjiang Uyghur Autonomous Region.[1]

I was born in Aksu in this region in September 1967, eighteen years after the Chinese communist invasion of East Turkistan. Mao's Cultural Revolution was raging in China and East Turkistan. Thousands of bright intellectuals, religious scholars, and wealthy people were imprisoned. Thousands of patriotic heroes were being murdered for "nationalism" and "treason." It was a time of darkness and oppression.

Before I enrolled at Xinjiang University in 1984 at the age of seventeen, I barely understood anything about my identity, nationality, or the relationship between the Uyghurs and the Chinese state. During my time in university, I was able to find myself, discover my national identity, cultivate my worldview, and own my ideology. This was a great gift. I became more interested in our history and learned that the oppression inflicted on the Uyghurs wasn't our destiny set by God as I had naively thought but was the result of an unjust occupation. I understood that I could play a role in transforming the tragic reality of my people, starting with education. Just as learning about my identity inspired me, I knew it could do the same for my people. Seventy-

THE UNITED NATIONS NEEDS TO STEP UP

five to eighty per cent of Uyghurs were illiterate and lost in a deep sleep. I wanted to wake them up.

That was the beginning of my activism and its personal consequences for me. From 1985 to 1988 I was active in student politics, founding the Student Union for Science and Culture and organizing hundreds of students, sending them all across East Turkistan to teach classes on topics ranging from the Uyghur alphabet to constitutional rights and the Autonomous Law. In June 1988, we organized a pro-democracy student demonstration in Urumchi attended by around five thousand students. As a result, I was expelled from the university before graduation and ended up on the Chinese regime's blacklist. After my expulsion, I started a small business in my hometown, and ran an underground publishing house.

When I moved to Beijing in September 1990, I studied English and Turkish for two years, and in 1992 opened a restaurant, but in May 1994, because of my ongoing activism I had to flee overseas, leaving behind my family, my friends, and my country. I never dreamed that this would be the last time I saw my parents or that I would one day become the enemy of a powerful country like China, labelled a criminal and a terrorist on Interpol's Red Notices.

After I left East Turkistan, I settled first in Turkey and later in Germany, where I became a citizen. Even there, however, the Chinese authorities pursued me. Because of my activities on behalf of my people, in 1997 the Chinese regime put me on Interpol's list of Red Notices, which is essentially an arrest warrant that branded me a "murderer" and a "criminal." These notices are sent to member countries of Interpol around the world requesting that the individual named in the warrant be extradited by law enforcement and surrendered to the requesting authority for possible legal action. After the bombings of the World Trade Centre in New York and the Pentagon in Washington, D.C., on

September 11, 2001, the Chinese authorities added another label: terrorist. Oppressive regimes can make you a criminal and even a terrorist overnight. And the life of a criminal and a terrorist is not an enviable one.

The Interpol Red Notice, which remained in place and hung over my head for twenty-one years, was my death warrant, given the ever-present danger of being extradited to China. It led to detainments in Switzerland, Turkey, South Korea, Italy, and the United States. With the terrorist label I considered myself lucky to survive death, butt I always believed that freedom and justice aren't free but are won by striving for them. I was downhearted when I faced severe consequences, but I never lost hope. I grieved, but I never gave up. Finally, on February 21, 2018, the threat that was my constant shadow was removed.

When I was a terrorist, all doors were closed to me. I was a man consumed with worry about his future. Now, I've become a freedom fighter and an advocate for human rights and democracy. I've received international awards and accolades from institutions that previously shut me out. I've testified and spoken at the parliaments of countries that formerly treated me like a criminal—states and institutions that were world leaders in international politics and economics, such as the U.S. Congress, the European parliament, various national parliaments around the world, and even the United Nations human rights mechanisms. Now I am able to share my experiences and the experiences of my people with them and expose the true nature of the Chinese communist regime.

Today, since there is no longer an Interpol Red Notice hanging over my head, I should be able to travel everywhere in the world as a free man. But that still is not the case. Although China's evil hands have been cut off by Interpol, its reach and influence in many parts of the world are persistent and relentless. Due to pressure from the Chinese regime, the doors of many countries

THE UNITED NATIONS NEEDS TO STEP UP

are still shut to me. Even regional powers like Turkey and India have not opened their borders to me.

Many countries and individuals remain ignorant of the threat of the Chinese communist regime. Many others recognize the threat but are helpless, indebted to China, and unable to act. Yet it is becoming evident that the CCP isn't a threat just to the Uyghurs, but is a plague on humanity, our democratic values, our human rights—and world politics as we know them. The CCP is already attempting to alter our liberal institutions by making its crimes and state terrorism legal, just as it legalized the erosion of democracy in Hong Kong by passing the National Security Act[2] in 2020. As a result, autonomy in Hong Kong is lost today.

After Xi Jinping's rise to power as president of the People's Republic of China in 2013, the CCP changed its assimilationist and discriminatory policy in East Turkistan to an openly genocidal one. In 2015, it passed the the Counter-Terrorism Law to legalize its crimes against humanity in East Turkistan legal. In 2016, it began to build concentration camps in East Turkistan disguised as "re-education centres," and locked up millions of Uyghurs, Kazakhs, and other Turkic Muslims. Hundreds of thousands of Uyghur children have been separated from their parents. The people in concentration camps are being made to renounce their national identities and are forced into hard labour and slavery. Hundreds of thousands of Uyghurs' organs are being harvested and sold. They are also being persecuted for their faith. Since 2017, thousands of mosques have been demolished, and thousands of Qurans burned. The CCP has publicly declared war on Islam, calling it "an ideological virus [that] must be eradicated."[3] Even cemeteries and seven- and eight-hundred-year-old artefacts have been destroyed. Sadly, the Muslim world remains silent, and some Muslim countries have even supported the CCP's crimes.

The world was silent during the Second World War when the Nazis slaughtered six million Jews. After the war, the Nazi crimes were criticized, and we promised: "Never Again." Seventy years later, the CCP is slaughtering the Uyghurs, and the world is still silent.

I have dedicated my career over the past thirty and more years not only to the struggle for the freedom of the people of East Turkistan but also to wake up the world to the criminal and terrorist threat that the CCP poses to humanity.

This book, based on my personal experiences, is a continuation of my life's work, an effort to illuminate and bring awareness to the dangers of the CCP. It will tell you the interesting stories of a person who has faced great injustice in the free world, and who has become a victim of larger ideological struggles between freedom and violence and democracy, and dictatorship. What sets my story apart from those of activists like Nelson Mandela or Mahatma Gandhi is that it takes place entirely in the free world and in centres of Western values. My story is also ongoing. I can't tell you how the story ends, or what will happen in my life in the future. As China's evil hands continue to reach further and penetrate the West, my future remains uncertain. Hopefully, after reading this book, you will understand that yours does too.

Just before my book was printed, I successfully returned from a work trip to Taiwan. To my great surprise, I was finally let in after a seventeen year travel ban. This victory, although small, is worth celebrating. After almost two decades, despite enormous pressure from Beijing, I still showed them their influence could only be so strong.

CHAPTER 1
FROM ACTIVIST TO TERRORIST

I didn't know I was a terrorist wanted by Interpol until 1999, five years after I had fled my homeland for Turkey in 1994. Perhaps telling my personal history as an activist will help to explain why China wanted to tell the world that I was a terrorist.

In 1984, at age seventeen, I enrolled in the physics department of Xinjiang University in Urumchi in East Turkistan, which the Chinese had renamed the Xinjiang Uyghur Autonomous Region. One year later, in December 1985, a group of students led a large pro-democracy demonstration on campus. My participation was a turning point in my life and had a huge impact on my world view. I began to think more deeply about the injustice, discrimination, and marginalization my people were facing, and how I could correct it. A voice deep inside me told me I couldn't stay quiet. It prompted me to do something. I had long conversations with my friends. I concluded that one of the most critical issues and enablers of this situation was the ignorance and lack of education inflicted upon my people. Almost 75 to 80 per cent of Uyghurs were illiterate. There were no schools in many villages. An illiterate nation couldn't grasp the nature and depth of the oppression it faced, and this lack of awareness and understanding meant they couldn't work to change it. The Chinese regime had inflicted ignorance upon the Uyghur people as a way to control them, and it was working.

Thousands of Uyghur university students spent their summer and winter breaks idle. It was important to mobilize them and organize classes to improve their literacy and knowledge. I felt it was crucial to do something, to start somewhere so, after several months of hard work, in December 1987 at Xinjiang University, I and several others founded the Student Union for Science and Culture. I was elected president. As a first step, we mobilized a few hundred students to teach them the Uyghur alphabet and educate them in their native language. It was quite successful. Yet even though the activities were legal and consistent with government policies, we faced pressure and obstacles from the government, experienced injustice in society, and realized that the Chinese regime's discriminatory policies functioned in a broader context.

On June 15, 1988, Erkin Tursun,[4] the treasurer of the Student Union for Science and Culture, and I had an intense, but ultimately illuminating, debate with Mr. Janabil, Party Secretary of the Xinjiang Regional Committee of the Chinese Communit Party (CCP), and other high-level Chinese officials, including the head of the Education Department, Jiang Yang; the head of the Finance Department, Mehmud; and the Director of the National Planning Committee, Tohti Eli. We spent five hours discussing the discrimination faced by Uyghurs in the education system and the inequality in their daily lives, but it was a discussion that went nowhere. So we returned to the university and started a strike, which eventually turned into a larger pro-democracy student movement in Urumchi. I was placed under house arrest that night. After a three-month investigation, Waris Ababekri, the secretary-general of our organization, and I were expelled from the university.[5] I spent the next two years working in small businesses between Aksu, Urumchi, and Beijing. I convinced some Uyghur businessmen to open a foreign-language training school in 1990 in Aksu, but the authorities denied the application. Eight months of effort to open a school had failed.

Then, in September 1990, I moved to Beijing and attended English and Turkish classes at Beijing Foreign Studies University. I met my wife, Mahire, during this time, and we married in June 1992. Mahire was working as an Arabic-Chinese interpreter in Beijing after graduating from the Arabic language department at Shanghai Foreign Language University, and I opened a restaurant. Life was normal. Then, things started to change. After I opened the restaurant, the Beijing police began harassing me, and I was questioned on several occasions. "Why do so many foreigners come to your restaurant?" was a frequently asked question. In fact, there were at least ten other Uyghur restaurants on the same street, all of them with foreign customers.

Eventually, I learned through a friend that the Chinese security bureau had been investigating me, looking for evidence that I had created an international information exchange centre in Beijing under the guise of opening a restaurant. The friend who warned me also encouraged me to leave China as soon as possible. I got a fake passport, which only my wife knew about, and started making arrangements to leave the country. However, I faced a bitter choice. My wife was pregnant with our first child, Dilfire. I could either take the risk and stay in Beijing until our child was born or leave China quickly and miss the birth. My wife preferred my safety and asked me to leave right away. After deep thought and contemplation, I agreed to leave.

I arrived in Turkey on May 22, 1994, after a stopover in Warsaw. It was the second day of Eid Al-Adha, one of Islam's two main holidays. During my time in Turkey from 1994 until 1996 when I left for Germany, I studied for a Master's degree in political science at Gazi University in Ankara and organized demonstrations and conferences, among other activism work. Although there were only sixty to seventy Uyghur students in Turkey at the time, with limited means, we organized academic conferences, memorial ceremonies, and demonstrations.

I founded the East Turkistan Student Youth Union with my friends and organized ceremonies to commemorate the Uyghur student movements of 1985 and 1988. In June 1995, we held the first-ever ceremony to commemorate the thirtieth anniversary of the death of one of the founders of the Islamic Republic of East Turkistan, Muhammad Amin Bugra. The Turkish government wasn't happy about all these activities and events since the Chinese government had been putting more and more pressure on it. Suddenly Turkish intelligence agents started paying me visits from time to time.

In July 1995, I travelled with a delegation to the Issy-Kul region of Kyrgyzstan to attend the World Assembly of Turkish Youth. We met Uyghur youths from Kazakhstan and Kyrgyzstan and planned to organize a World Uyghur Youth Cultural Day with them. In Central Asia, where Chinese influence was weaker, we had more freedom to organize such events, but as soon as we got back to Turkey we began preparations for the World Uyghur Youth Cultural Day. The first gathering was held in Almaty in October 1995.

My wife arrived in Turkey in February 1996 on a student visa. Financial difficulties and political pressures were squeezing us, as the Turkish economy wasn't doing well. It was then that Omer Kanat, a leader of the East Turkistan Union in Europe, suggested I move to Germany.

Problems with my passport provided another reason to move to Germany. My application for Turkish citizenship had been rejected, and when my passport expired after three years, the Chinese government wouldn't renew it. Although going to demonstrations holding the blue flag of East Turkistan and involvement in other anti-China activities were not banned in Turkey, there were still many obstacles for us. With no other way to get residency and a work permit in Turkey, there was little choice but to move to a country where I would be safer. Moreover, Germany was home to the East Turkistan Union in Europe, the one Uyghur organization in Europe whose existence made me hopeful for the future of our political movement.

I left Turkey in June 1996, arrived in Munich, and claimed asylum. My claim was accepted within six months.. In November 1996, I was one of the co-founders of the World Uyghur Youth Congress. The East Turkistan National Congress and the World Uyghur Youth Congress, the two largest Uyghur organizations in the diaspora until 2004, were also located in Munich.

After the Second World War, the United States established Radio Free Europe in Munich to conduct their media war against the Communist world. They opened an Uyghur service there, too. For these reasons, Polat Qadir, Satar Bulbul, Ghulamidin Pahta, Erkin Alptekin, Ms. Zeynep, Enver Can, and Omer Kanat went to Munich to work at Radio Free Europe.

Germany was also the only country in Europe where you could find Uyghurs and Uyghur organizations. The East Turkistan Union in Europe (ETUE), founded by Erkin Alptekin, was the first Uyghur organization established in the West. It was also the only Uyghur organization in Germany. After the dissolution of the Soviet Union in 1991, the newly established independence of the Central Asian republics brought hope to the Uyghurs, and many Uyghur youths began coming to Germany from Central Asia, Egypt, and Pakistan. Munich thus became the first centre of Uyghur political activism in the West.

I eventually became a German citizen in 2006, As a citizen, I always believed in the power of German law and personal security and felt safe. This was a common feeling among immigrants who settled in Germany. It was an environment that made us feel we could freely protest China's atrocities in East Turkistan.

After my arrival, I and several others, including Omer Kanat, who had played an important role in my decision to seek asylum in Germany, Asgar Can, Perhat Muhammet, and Abdulhakim Idris—who were all working at the ETUE—invited Uyghur youth from around the world to come to Germany in November 1996, where we hosted the World Uyghur Youth Cultural Gathering. Identifying a need to create a political body for Uyghur youth, we also founded the World Uyghur Youth Congress at the same time. Our goal was to advocate for our people and raise awareness about China's oppression of the Uyghurs. At the time, very few Europeans knew about our people, let alone about their plight. And almost no one truly understood China. Despite these activities, I never imagined that China, a fast-developing country in the 1990s, would be very concerned with a person like me. But an unexpected incident would prove me wrong.

FRANKFURT DETENTION, 1999

In December 1999, I was invited to a conference at the U.S. Congress in Washington, D.C., by a leading Chinese democracy leader, Wei Jingsheng. Delegate from Hong Kong, Taiwan, Tibet, South Mongolia, and the Uyghurs would be participating. Since I was not a German citizen yet and relied on a refugee travel document that required me to apply for a visa to travel to the United States, I went to the U.S. Consulate General in Frankfurt (there was no visa office in Munich). There I learned for the first time that I was a "criminal" under an Interpol Red Notice that had been issued against me.

I had never been to the United States before, but I had some friends and schoolmates there with whom I had led Uyghur students at the June 15, 1988 pro-democracy protest against the Chinese regime. As I had not seen my friends since I was expelled from the university. I wanted to attend the conference to be reunited with my friends and to look for opportunities to advocate for the Uyghur cause in the United States.

I travelled to Frankfurt with my friend Otkur Mamtimin and applied for a visa at the U.S. General Consulate. We waited almost an hour. While we were waiting outside the office, a security officer came out, frowning and cold-eyed. "Why is he frowning at me?" I asked my friend. I knew something was wrong. The man went back into the office and returned ten minutes later, still frowning.

"Stand up, let's go," he said.

"I am waiting for my passport. Where should I go?" I asked.

"Go, go out!" he yelled. We left the building. There were two German police cars waiting.

The security staff at the U.S. Consulate spoke with the German police for a few minutes. I overheard the German police saying, "We cannot arrest him for no reason." I was shocked and had no idea what was going on.

Two German police officers tried to reassure me, saying, "There might be a misunderstanding. We need to go to the police station. We want to clarify something." Nodding my head, I got into the police car. They didn't allow Otkur Mamtimin to go with me but gave him the address of the police station and told him to use public transportation or his own car. The calmness of the German police eased my worry.

At the police station, however, the first question I was asked was "Did you kill someone? How many people did you kill?" Although asked with a smile, the question was disturbing.

"Me? Did you know how many people I killed?" I retorted, also smiling, and shook my head. "There must be a misunderstanding," said the police officer. "Maybe someone with a similar name. Please wait, and we will check." His question—"Did you kill someone?"—rang in my ears as I waited. "What is happening?" I asked myself. "I have never killed anyone or anything in my life, not even a chicken!"

I listened as the police made several calls. The word "Interpol" was repeated several times. As I understood it, Interpol was an international police organization that only went after the most vicious criminals and fugitives—people who had committed terrible crimes. I couldn't fathom how I could be associated with such people, or with Interpol.

Two hours passed. The police were still making calls, and Mamtimin arrived as I was pacing inside the police station. . I was just anxious to get my travel document back before the U.S. Consulate closed.

Finally, the same police officer returned, but he was angry now. He showed me a picture and asked, "Is this you?" The change in his tone was apparent and indicated trouble. The picture he was holding was a photograph of me as a teenager from more than ten years earlier. I wondered, "Why do they have my picture from my country (East Turkistan)?"

"He looks like me," I said, lightly. "If this is you, you will be arrested now," the officer told me. I didn't know what to say in my defence. He showed me an arrest warrant that had my parents' names and my address in Aksu. It was obvious there was no misunderstanding. Finally, I understood the seriousness of my situation. I understood China was behind this. But how? And why?

It was a long time since I had been expelled from university for leading a student demonstration, and my activism in Turkey founding organizations and organizing demonstrations was not large-scale enough to attract China's attention. My activities with my friends since founding the World Uyghur Youth Congress in Germany in 1996 should not have been enough to alarm China. Our financial resources were limited, and our influence at the

FROM ACTIVIST TO TERRORIST

United Nations and the European Union was not very strong, certainly not compared with what it is today. Yet China had noticed.

The officer placed the arrest warrant in front of me. I was surprised to see that China had put me on Interpol's list of Red Notices in 1997 and more surprised to see the charges: "murder, criminal gang activity, robbery . . . ." This was serious. I called my lawyer in Germany, Dr. Albrecht Göring.

I waited almost six hours at the police station. The police didn't officially arrest me, but neither did they let me leave. They searched the documents I had used to apply for asylum and everything related to my political activism against China from the time of my arrival in Germany. They held meetings and discussed what to do with me.

Finally, the officer returned, and this time his tone was friendlier. "You led a student demonstration in 1988 protesting China. The CCP issued an arrest warrant for you in 1997. But you sought asylum in Germany in 1996, and you were accepted. Interpol's Red Notice is not applicable if an asylum claim is accepted in Germany. You will be safe in Germany and all the other countries in the European Union (EU). If you travel to the United States, they might arrest you at the border, but they will deport you to Germany, not China. You should not be travelling to third-world countries, though, especially countries that have an extradition agreement with China," he said.

The officer kept talking. I was stunned. We were planning to expand the World Uyghur Youth Congress to the United States, Canada, Turkey, Central Asia, and other parts of the world. With my travel restricted, the future of the movement was uncertain.

Clearly China was attempting to prevent our activism from expanding in the world. As for me, I had been travelling for two years without knowing I was considered a terrorist subject to an arrest warrant, although fortunately, until that point I had not faced danger in any country to which I travelled.

"When and where did I commit murder?" I asked the officer. He looked at the Interpol document. "It is written here that it was in June 1996," he said. "I was in Germany in June 1996," I told him, but he just shook his head.

With this development, my plans to visit the United States were cancelled. My lawyer told me Interpol's arrest warrant would not be valid in Europe, and that I shouldn't worry. Yet I was incensed by China's accusation that I was a serial criminal who had committed murder and robbery. Such baseless accusations by the CCP against people in East Turkistan was not new, but their use of Interpol to reach someone in the free world was alarming.

CHINA BRANDS ME A TERRORIST

At the time of my Frankfurt detention, I had no idea of the full impact of this arrest warrant on my life. But after the September 11 attacks in the United States in 2001, the Chinese government effectively exploited the subsequent international war on terror. Before 2001, the Chinese regime called Uyghurs "ethnic separatists," "separatists," and "radical religious activists." After 2001, we could be "terrorists" too.

In 2002, the Chinese regime declared an unknown group, "the East Turkistan Islamic Movement," a terrorist organization. Unfortunately, the United Nations and the United States did not understand the Chinese regime's true intentions, and they acknowledged the East Turkistan Islamic Movement as a terrorist organization. The Uyghur community in the diaspora was deeply disappointed. The consequences of such an acknowledgment by the UN and the United States were obvious to us. As expected, in 2002 following the terrorist designation, the Chinese regime started a war on "terror" in East Turkistan and carried out mass murder and arrests in the name of fighting radicalism. Thus, the international war on terror launched after September 11, 2001, became an effective tool to legitimize China's crackdown on Uyghurs and exploit the fears of the international community. For me personally it meant that in 2003, China successfully added a new claim, "terrorist," to the charge of murderer on the arrest warrant I first learned about in Frankfurt in 1999. For my own safety and the future of my work, I would eventually have to publically respond to China's false and nefarious charges.

Although I left Turkey in June in 1996 and claimed asylum in Munich, I went back to Turkey whenever I had a chance to visit the many friends and acquaintances I had made during my stay there. Until December 2003, I never had any problem entering Turkey for these visits. China was watching, however, and determined to silence me.

I had gone to Istanbul on December 13, 2003, to attend a ceremony to remember Isa Yusuf Alptekin, one of most tireless leaders of the Uyghur movement,[6] on the eighth anniversary of his passing. Uyghur activists and leaders of Uyghur organizations from around the world arrived in Turkey for the ceremony. But on the morning of December 15, 2003, the Chinese government, encouraged by the support of the United States and the United Nations in acknowledging the East Turkistan Islamic Movement as a terrorist movement and bolstered by the success of its increased suppression in East Turkistan published through its Ministry of Public Security a list of "terrorists." The list, which was intended to crush dissidents overseas, named four Uyghur organizations and eleven Uyghur activists. Two of the listed organizations were in Germany and included the World Uyghur Youth Congress and the "East Turkistan Information Center." Three of the listed Uyghur activists were also in Germany. I, of course, was among them, and with that, I became a terrorist overnight, in addition to my other crimes of murder, robbery, gang crimes, and organizing an explosion.

I didn't hear about the list until a few hours after it appeared. I got up a bit late that morning, and was having breakfast when my long-time friend and fellow activist Abdulcelil Turan called. Sounding anxious, he told me to come to his home. "Did something happen?" I asked. "We will talk when you get here," he said. I was at another friend's house in the Asian side of Istanbul but left immediately for the European side and soon arrived at Abducelil Turan's home.

Around twenty of my friends were waiting, and everyone was looking nervous. I soon discovered why: I was on China's list. The four organizations were the East Turkistan Islamic Movement, the East Turkistan Liberation Organization, the World Uyghur Youth Congress, and the East Turkistan Information Center. I was the third individual named on the list. International media outlets started calling before I even had time to process the sudden news. Baffled by the announcement, I called Dr. Albrecht Göring, my German lawyer. He had already heard and told me to return to Germany immediately. My friends in Europe and the United States, worried that Turkey could extradite me to China if it was promised a big deal from the CCP, also urged me to leave Turkey as soon as possible. I didn't agree with that concern, but I decided to go back to Germany anyway and took the first plane I could, on December 16.

MY RESPONSE TO CHINA'S ALLEGATIONS

Whenever I was asked, "Why does the Chinese government accuse you of terrorism?" I always made sure to set the record straight. The truth is, I had never touched a gun, or even seen one in person. I'd only ever seen guns and violence in movies. To

FROM ACTIVIST TO TERRORIST

slander a person who has never been associated with terrorism with false claims only proves the evil of the Chinese regime.

But those were private questions. When China publicly called me a murderer and a terrorist, I had to respond.

In its list of terrorists, China had not only named me, but made numerous allegations, completely fabricated, against me and the World Uyghur Youth Congress. It was very important to respond to their statements in detail, showing what empty lies they were. On December 20, after my return from Istanbul and following discussions with the leadership of the World Uyghur Youth Congress, I issued a statement in which I categorically denied being a terrorist and all the other claims China made against me.

In my lengthy statement, I listed each individual charge by China and my response. I began, however, by pointing out that the Chinese had for years mischaracterized the activities of the Uyghur people seeking freedom, human rights, and self-determination as "separatism," "fundamentalism," or "extremism" and had cracked down on them severely. I noted also that China had specifically seized the global war on terrorism as an excuse to denounce and transform the Uyghurs' peaceful resistance against government oppression into terrorism, using it as an excuse to imprison thousands of innocent Uyghurs and torturing and executing many. It also disregarded the international community's criticism of this behaviour towards the Uyghurs and had capitalized on the acceptance by the United States and the United Nations willingness to blacklist the East Turkistan Islamic Movement as a terrorist organization in 2002. I pointed out that now China was using "slandering tactics," including the statement of December 15, 2003, that named me a terrorist.

I began my detailed response to each of the accusations by denying that the WUYC was known by any other name and stating that the three other listed organizations were "fabricated out of thin air by Chinese authorities." I also strongly denied that the World Uyghur Youth Congress (WUYG) was a terrorist organization as China alleged, stating firmly that we opposed terrorism in any form and existed solely to alert the world to the "state terrorism and human rights violations" perpetrated by China against "Uyghurs, Tibetans, and even Chinese people."

In its statement China accused the WUYC, and me specifically, of organizing criminal gangs and committing violent acts of terrorism, including, "theft, robbery, and explosion," and accused me directly of participating in other unnamed terrorist activities. My response was direct and simple: I denied all of the charges, especially since China had produced no evidence to back them up. To support my statement, I provided details of my student activism, including my part in organizing the June 15, 1988, pro-democracy protest in Urumchi that had led to my expulsion from university. I noted that I had thousands of witnesses to the true nature of this activity and the thirteen-page notice of my dismissal from university to support my claim.

In more fabricated charges, China stated that I was the vice-president of the Eastern Turkistan Liberation Organization and that I helped its leader, collaborating in violent terrorist activities and overseeing the organization's activities in Germany. All of these were lies that I strongly denied, since I didn't know the group and had only heard of its alleged leader. Another charge was that I was part of another organization I had never heard of, with plans to assassinate "Party, government, and military leaders" in Xingjiang and to destroy infrastructure by explosions and create armed border disturbances. These were serious but totally unfounded charges, and I not only firmly denied them, I stated that I had never heard of the named organization, which I believed the Chinese government completely fabricated in order to discredit the WUYC as a terrorist organization. It even claimed that the WUYC was the mastermind behind two bombings in Xingjiang in 1993, even though the organization was not even founded until 1996.

FROM ACTIVIST TO TERRORIST

Our sources of funding also came under attack, with China claiming that the WUYC "mainly resorts to theft, robbery or other criminal means for funding." I categorically denied this charge in my statement, as the WUYC relied entirely on "donations and membership fees by patriotic Uyghurs living in Europe, mainly in Germany" as a legally registered organization in Germany and monitored by German authorities. I also denied that the WUYC had any members inside China.

Seeking to discredit the WUYC in any way it could, China went on to claim that we had international ties with fictitious terrorist organizations and that our recent Third World Uyghur Youth Congress had been supported by this group and its leader. Again, I firmly denied the charge, noting that the gathering had been openly covered by international media, and that Estonia, the host country, had explicitly rejected pressure from China to cancel the meeting.

The WUYC was also charged by China with helping "East Turkistan" terrorists to seek asylum. My response was that we had never helped terrorists but had helped refugees "avoid persecution for their involvement in political activities inside China and apply for refugee status from the UNHCR (United Nations Human Rights Commission) before being sent to democratic countries such as Sweden, Norway, and Canada."

The final part of China's list was directed specifically at discrediting me. I categorically denied a number of fictitious relationships with the alleged terrorist organizations China had named in its statement. The Chinese list specifically claimed that I was head of a terrorist organization and as such was the "target of an Interpol red notice," charges which I firmly rejected as untrue, pointing out that Germany had independently investigated and rejected China's allegations against me. The statement also tried to tie me again to a fictitious organization and deliberately confused my peaceful and legal activism with terrorist bombings in which I had no part. In strongly denying China's allegations I made the point that China wanted to discredit me because it feared the emergence of "a unified international Uyghur movement . . . that can represent the voices of Uyghurs at international forums."

I finished by asking "Germany, the United States and all other democratic countries and international organizations" not to take China's allegations at face value but to investigate for themselves." We were being attacked by China's slanders. I hoped the world would not only disbelieve them, but would come to our assistance.[7]

The UN, the European Union, Germany, and the United States didn't acknowledge this list. It didn't work in Turkey, either. However, when China added "terrorist" to the list of alleged crimes committed by me and requested my repatriation from Germany, the German Intelligence Service took notice. Fortunately, I was able to provide them with documents recording my activism since attending university. After learning the details, extent, and scope of my activities, they said, "Now we see why China accused you of terrorism," but they were a support to me in my many detentions and exportations arising from China's false claims against me.

The Chinese authorities never gave up demanding my repatriation from Germany, but Germany continued to reject their demands, citing lack of evidence. According to *Der Spiegel*, a weekly magazine in Germany, the German police even sent people to Urumchi in the beginning of 2004 to verify the claims against me. Finding no evidence of my "crimes," they realized China's claims were baseless.

VIOLATION AT GENEVA

Geneva is the capital of human rights. In the 2000s, the condition and even the existence of the Uyghurs was not well known in Western countries, so as the leaders of the World Uyghur Congress, several of us decided to start our advocacy for our people at the United Nations headquarters in Geneva. We didn't have even a fraction of the opportunities and privileges that other international organizations did. We had limited representation and financial resources, and no symbolic figure that could draw support or considerable political influence like the Tibetans had in the Dalai Lama. Despite this, Geneva became a frequent destination for us to advocate for our voiceless people suffering under Chinese oppression. The Tibetans assisted us. At UN meetings, we worked hard to let everyone know the simple facts: there is a people called the Uyghurs, and they are facing eradication by the ruthless Chinese communist regime. We used to get so excited when Tibetans would reference "Uyghurs" in their addresses, or when an article about Uyghurs was published in the media. Our movement was small, so every mention and moment of exposure was a big deal.

Of course, advocacy in the diaspora did not start in the 2000s. The prominent Uyghur leaders Muhammad Amin Bugra and Isa Yusuf Alptekin, who were forced to immigrate to Turkey after China's invasion of East Turkistan in 1949, started the advocacy movement in the 1950s in Turkey. They dedicated their lives to their nation's freedom. Unfortunately, their advocacy work never grew beyond Turkey, and their hope to bring the Uyghur plight to the world's attention was not realized.

The first person who had the chance to speak for the Uyghur people at the UN, and thereby bring the movement to Europe, was Erkin Apltekin. He had started cooperating with Tibetan organizations under the Dalai Lama's leadership at the end of the 1970s. Since the Uyghur cause was still unknown to the world, he essentially worked alone before some Uyghur youth arrived in Europe in the 1990s.

THE CHINA FREEDOM TRAP

In November 1999, the Second General Assembly of the East Turkistan National Congress took place in Munich. In 2004, two umbrella organizations, the World Uyghur Youth Congress and the East Turkistan (Uyghuristan) National Congress merged to establish one united and representative body of the Uyghur movement in exile, called the World Uyghur Congress (WUC). Erkin Alptekin was elected its president and I was elected secretary-general. We travelled to Geneva regularly to attend meetings of the UN Human Rights Committee. We also collaborated with Tibetan organizations and organized demonstrations in front of the UN building.

In April 2005, an unexpected incident took place in front of the UN headquarters in Geneva. Fifteen members of the WUC had taken an overnight minibus from Munich to Geneva to attend a session of the UN Human Rights Committee and organize a demonstration with the Tibetans to protest the Chinese government. Until then, I had been attending such meetings at the UN without any issues. This time, however, the UN refused to issue me an accreditation. The Secretariat did not provide an explanation except to say they were waiting for an answer from their supervisors.

With the members of the Tibetan organization, we held a demonstration for four hours. In my speech, I exposed Chinese atrocities against the Uyghurs and Tibetans. We shouted slogans in Uyghur, Tibetan, English, and Chinese to express our anger at the Chinese regime. Demonstrations like this brought us together, raised awareness, and were an important part of our activism against China.

After the demonstration, our group intended to leave the same day. Many of the Uyghurs who took part had taken a one-day leave from their work. The trip would be long—six hundred kilometres—and we needed to leave for Munich early enough in the day to accommodate the time it would take for such a journey.

FROM ACTIVIST TO TERRORIST

As we were about to leave, two cars suddenly arrived and surrounded our minibus. They were not police cars. The men who got out of the cars were not in police uniforms, either. "We are here to check your IDs," they told us. We were used to this, as it was common for German police to stop people for ID checks. Uyghurs used to face such police stops frequently, too, so our group wasn't overly concerned. We all showed our IDs. They didn't pay attention to the others' ID, but the man who checked mine told me to get in their car. "Where are you taking Dolkun?" my friends asked. "Do not interfere," they replied. They took me in their car, turned on the police signal, and drove off.

I learned that the men who detained me were Swiss national security agents. They escorted me into a building, searched me, and took my belongings before locking the door and leaving me humiliated. However, my anxiety and sadness were quickly overcome by fatigue. In my concern to arrive on time for the meeting and demonstration, I hadn't slept the night before. Then we shouted so loudly and exerted ourselves all day demonstrating, so we didn't eat. I was so exhausted that I fell asleep on the chair as soon as the agents left the room.

About an hour later I awoke to the sound of the door opening. Two men entered the room. My head felt heavy, and I was in a bad mood. My face was pale. I could feel my frustration rising, but tried to subdue it since there was no point in shouting at them. "Dolkun, calm down," I told myself. "These are just people following orders. There is no sense in confronting them. Hundreds of thousands of Uyghur youth like you are suffering, being tortured in Chinese prisons. And hundreds of thousands of Uyghur youth are being forced into hard labour, working on plantations and farming in the Taklamakan Desert. Never forget them." I also reminded myself that these officers were not like the Chinese police. They wouldn't beat or scold me. I figured they had come to tell me there had been a misunderstanding and would let me go. I tried to calm down, thinking this would probably be like the time I was detained in Frankfurt in 1999 when I had gone to the U.S. Consulate seeking a visa, and believed it was related to China's arrest warrant at Interpol.

The interrogation lasted for four hours. I was asked about every detail of my life from my birth to that day. Then they took my fingerprints and pictures of me standing in front of the wall, essentially treating me like a criminal.

There was a quarrel during the interrogation. "Why are you detaining me? Are you executing an order from China?" I asked. They didn't respond.

"Are you Chinese?" one of them asked.

"No, I am a Uyghur."

"Your travel document says you came from China."

"There are not only Chinese people in China. Do you know Tibetans?"

"Yes."

"We are just like Tibetans, an occupied nation. There are fifty-five ethnicities in China other than the Chinese."

I explained about the Uyghurs and the situation of East Turkistan. They looked at me as though they were hearing about this for the first time.

While I was in detention, the Society for Threatened Peoples, the Unrepresented Nations and Peoples Organization (UNPO), and other international organizations immediately issued statements saying, "Human rights are being violated at the human rights meeting," and criticized the Swiss government for my detainment.[8] Journalists started calling and interviewing me. Some journalists contacted the police, too. This made the agents interrogating me anxious. My lawyer, Dr. Albrecht Göring, contacted the Swiss authorities and told them I was innocent, threatening legal action if they did not release me.

After almost an hour, the men who had questioned me brought in the interrogation log and told me to sign it. The log was in French, even though the interrogation had been in English.

"I don't understand French. I can't sign something I don't understand," I said.

"Don't you trust us?" one of them asked.

"Did you trust me? How can I trust you when you didn't believe me?" I asked.

"Then what should we do?"

"You need to translate this into English. I will read it and sign it if everything is fine."

"Then we will look for an interpreter. Until then you need to stay here. We don't know when we can find an interpreter. It might be tomorrow."

I was furious. I couldn't wait for them to find an interpreter. I couldn't wait any longer to leave this place. The sleeplessness and exhaustion were torturous, and almost twenty people who couldn't leave without me were waiting outside. "Whatever it is, I just need to sign it and get out of this place," I told myself, and signed the log.

I was released. But the experience was not something I would easily forget. We had to prevent such an incident from being repeated in the future, especially if I was going to continue travelling to Geneva for activism. More than that, it was unacceptable to allow my rights to be violated, and to be violated so blatantly in Geneva, the centre of human rights, or at the UN, the protector of free speech.

Erkin Alptekin wanted the Swiss government to be made accountable. As then-president of the WUC, he sent a letter to the Swiss ambassador in Berlin. He said the WUC was a legally registered organization in Germany, the Chinese authorities were making false claims against it, and it was wrong for the Swiss authorities to believe such allegations and act upon them, interrogating the organization's secretary-general for four hours. He demanded that the Swiss government answer for this incident.

After two weeks, we received a reply from the Swiss Embassy. The letter said the case had been referred to the Swiss Federal Department of Foreign Affairs, and they would respond after consulting with the Department of the Interior. After two months, the Foreign Affairs Department sent us a letter saying there had been a misunderstanding and they wanted to apologize for it. They wrote, "Geneva is the world's capital for human rights and a city in which everyone's human rights are guaranteed. We welcome Mr. Dolkun Isa to visit Geneva whenever he wants."

I carried this letter with me whenever I went to Geneva. It became a protective document I felt could prevent any disturbance with Swiss police. Since I wasn't a German citizen in 2005 and was still using a refugee travel document, I knew it was possible Switzerland had a secret extradition treaty with China, and if they did, Swiss authorities could detain and extradite me to China. Luckily, this never happened. I went to Switzerland many times every year, attended UN meetings, and presented reports, all without further incident. But I often faced such incidents in other democratic countries.

CHAPTER 2

INTERPOL'S LONG ARM

DEPORTED FROM WASHINGTON, D.C.

Although I cannot say when my homeland is going to be free, I firmly believe we will one day be liberated from Chinese occupation. Just like in the Central Asian countries, I always hope something, maybe a miracle, will happen—the political atmosphere will change—and my country will be freed. Since the Chinese communist army invaded East Turkistan in 1949, the East Turkistan peoples have led hundreds of different uprisings and resistance movements, and had paid a heavy price. Our creator, Allah, would never let the oppression the Uyghur people suffered and the blood they have sacrificed be in vain. It was this conviction that prevented me from applying for German citizenship even after nearly ten years of living in Munich. "I will go back to my free country with the same identity," I always thought. The incidents in Frankfurt and Geneva made me think twice.

As an activist and the secretary-general of the WUC, I was receiving invitations for conferences and other events around the world. I didn't have any problems using my refugee travel document in Europe, but it prevented me from attending conferences outside Europe owing to visa requirements and security concerns. After the Geneva incident, I decided to be more proactive in obtaining German citizenship, a process that typically takes around six months to a year when all the conditions are met. Although I applied in 2004, I didn't get an answer for almost two years.

The December 2004 issue of *Der Spiegel* tells this story:

> The security authorities are now also benefiting from the good relationship between Berlin and Beijing. Two terrorism experts from the Federal Criminal Police Office will travel to China's Uyghur Autonomous Region Xinjiang in the next few days. They want to sift through material from the Ministry of Public Security against alleged Uighur [*sic*]terrorists who are fighting for an independent East Turkistan. The background: Beijing has declared four groups of Uyghurs to be terrorist organizations because they are "attempting to divide China with violent activities in Xinjiang, in other parts of China and in some other countries." Two of the suspected organizations have their headquarters in Germany— the World Uyghur Youth Congress and the East Turkistan Information Center; [the] World Uyghur Congress took place in Munich in mid-April. Beijing repeatedly calls on the German authorities to ban such activities and to arrest leading officials.⁹

Der Spiegel didn't provide the exact details of what happened, but the report proves that German intelligence went to Urumchi to investigate the claims made against me. I thought this would mean they would conclude that I was innocent and was being victimized by the CCP and their lies. I assumed there would be no issue with me getting German citizenship. But there was no reply to my application.

Two years later, in 2006, the German Intelligence Service interviewed me. They told me the Chinese authorities had learned about my application for German citizenship and pressed Germany not to grant it. "Dolkun Isa is a terrorist. His citizenship application must not be approved. Germany should not employ double standards on terrorism. We protest granting Isa German citizenship," the Chinese government had said.

They repeated such requests every three to four months. The German government became really annoyed. Every time the Chinese government sent such a request, it would be received at the Federal Ministry of the Interior. The ministry would then forward the request to the Federal Intelligence Service, which would have to investigate. This process was repeated multiple times, every time China sent a request. The Intelligence Service was fed up.

"Why don't the Chinese just leave you alone?" an agent from the service asked me once. He said that after every investigation they told the Ministry of the Interior "We didn't find anything the Chinese government reported." The Germans didn't understand this madness, but they felt they had to do their job. This was likely the reason why my citizenship application was delayed until 2006.

After I received my German citizenship in June 2006, I no longer needed a visa to travel to the United States. But my troubles were not over. I flew to Washington, D.C. on September 19, 2006, to attend a conference organized by the Asian Freedom Coalition. After my nine-hour flight, I landed at Washington's Dulles International Airport and immediately, and unexpectedly, faced humiliation and insult to my dignity.

I was stopped at passport control and sent to a different exit. I wasn't told why. I was detained for four hours while my friends were waiting for me. It was my first time visiting the United States, and I couldn't wait to meet my friends there after all these years, but I couldn't even call them and explain the delay, since my phone was out of service. Concerned, I asked the officers if I could use their phone to call my friends. They angrily denied my request. "Sit and wait!" said one officer.

After almost five hours, a commissioner started questioning me.

> I am an officer of the United States Immigration and Naturalization Service, authorized by law to administer oaths and take testimony in connection with the enforcement of the Immigration and Nationality laws of the United States. I wish to take your sworn statement regarding your application for admission today.
>
> **Q:** Do you understand what I have said to you?
> **A:** Yeah, if you speak a little bit more slowly, I understand.
> **Q:** Any statement you make must be given freely and voluntarily. Are you willing to answer my questions at this time?
> **A:** Yes, I can answer.
> **Q:** Do you swear or affirm that all the statements you are about to make are true and complete?
> **A:** Yes.
> **Q:** What is your true and correct name?
> **A:** Dolkun Isa.
> **Q:** Have you ever used or been known by any other name?
> **A:** Nah.
> **Q:** What country are you a citizen of?
> **A:** Germany.

Q: What country are your parents a citizen of?
A: China.
Q: Do you have any reason to believe that you are a citizen of the United States?
A: I beg your pardon?
Q: Do you believe that you may be a U.S. citizen?
A: No, I already have German citizenship.
Q: Did you present this German passport #[xxxxx], along with I94-W #[xxxx], to an immigration inspector and apply for entry into the United States as a visitor for business?
A: Yes, it is mine . . . for a conference.
Q: What conference do you plan to attend?
A: Asian Freedom Coalition conference.
Q: Have you attended this conference before?
A: This time it is in the United States, before it was in Germany. I attended before.
Q: What organization is sponsoring this conference?
A: Wie Jingsheng Foundation. It is a democratic China opposition leader.
Q: How long have you been affiliated with the Chinese opposition?
A: It is, it is . . . twelve years. Actually, since 1988. I was a student leader at that time.
Q: Are you affiliated with any other groups related to Chinese opposition?
A: Wie Jingsheng, we have relationships with Amnesty International, Human Rights Watch, International Campaign for Tibet . . .
Q: Are you employed in Germany?
A: Yeah.
Q: What is your occupation there?

A: Leadership training project. We are human rights leadership trainers. This is supported by an organization from America, the National Endowment for Democracy.
Q: How long have you lived in Germany?
A: Since 1996. More than ten years.
Q: How long have you been a citizen of Germany?
A: This year, 2006, June.
Q: Did you ever apply for entry to the United States, or for a U.S. visa?
A: You mean, a previous visa? Yes, I have.
Q: Do you have a previous visa from the US?
A: About two years ago, I was invited to another conference in America, but we were told then we had to obtain permission from the State Department.
Q: Did you apply for a visa?
A: Yes, I applied.
Q: Was your visa application approved?
A: No answer. No rejection, no approval.
Q: So, you applied for a visa, but you did not receive a visa? Is that correct?
A: Yes.
Q: Have you ever been arrested anywhere in the world?
A: No.
Q: Would you like to contact your embassy?
A: The German Embassy? If necessary, yes.
Q: It's not necessary. It's simply the right of every traveler to America. Would you like to contact your embassy?
A: If I'm not in any trouble, then no.
Q: Do you have anything you would like to add?
A: No.

Q: You have been found inadmissible to the United States per Sections 212(a) (7) (B) (i)(II) and 212 (a) (3) (B)(i)(V) of the INA, to wit: you are a non-immigrant without a valid, unexpired non-immigrant visa, and you are a member of a foreign terrorist organization. Do you understand?
A: I thought that it meant I had to have a visa and then have it canceled. I didn't know I was denied a visa. I don't agree. I am not a member of a terrorist organization.
Q: Do you understand you have waived all of your rights to review or appeal our decision as to your admissibility?
A: Yeah, okay.
Q: Do you understand you must obtain a valid, unexpired visa from an American Embassy or consulate for all future travel to the United States?
A: I understand.

The commissioner finally said, "We are not letting you enter America. Do you want to talk with your embassy?" I was taken aback. Did they mean a Uyghur Embassy, the German Embassy, or the Chinese Embassy? I had only got German citizenship three months earlier. My nationality was Chinese in my refugee travel document, and I had become accustomed to this, since it had been my reality for more than ten years of travel. I never had a "my embassy." "Which embassy did you mean?" I asked. "The German Embassy," the officer said. "Yes, if you are not letting me enter America, then I want to talk with the German Embassy," I said.

I called the German Embassy. It was past nine in the evening, but fortunately, there was still someone there to answer my call. I told them what happened, and that I didn't know why I was being refused entry to the United States. The embassy staff took my passport number and other details and told me they would contact me soon.

Later, I learned that the German Embassy contacted the German Ministry of Foreign Affairs and the U.S. State Department. My friends were fearful. They contacted officials at the U.S. Congress and the State Department. They worked hard to try and get approval for my entry to the United States, but ultimately, they couldn't prevent my deportation to Germany. Included in the State Department's blacklist was the Chinese regime's notice calling me "a terrorist on Interpol's Red Notices."

My German citizenship didn't help me. Two officers came, told me to remove my belt, took the laces from my shoes, and emptied my pockets. Then they locked me in a dark room. Their treatment of me was deplorable.

There was a small red lamp hanging from the ceiling. It was so dim that it was impossible even to read. There was a toilet. There was no bed or place to rest except an iron chair.

"I want to call my embassy," I said. The officer refused and shook his head. There was nothing I could do to occupy myself in the cell. My watch was confiscated so I didn't even know the time. I couldn't stop thinking, "Is this America? The country I yearned for, had so much hope in? If even the United States is being deceived by China, what will become of the world?" Only three months earlier, the National Endowment for Democracy (NED) had approved the WUC's funding request and I was appointed the manager of the project. I showed the officers the NED documents, but it didn't help.

I was outraged at the Chinese regime. I knew this was related to the Interpol Red Notice and was the fault of the CCP. And I was outraged with the world for not realizing China's evil. When the CCP wants to get rid of someone, they twist, slander, fabricate, and exercise their influence to harm that person in any way they can, not allowing them even a moment of peace.

Nevertheless, I had no choice but to stand strong against their injustice and humiliation.

I awoke to the irritating sound of the iron door opening. It was morning. An officer entered, frowning. "Did you want to have breakfast?" he asked. I was hungry, since I hadn't eaten in twenty hours, but I remember thinking, "If I tell him I'm a Muslim and don't eat pork, it will probably just add to his suspicion that I am a terrorist." "Yes, I want to have breakfast, but I'm a vegetarian," I said.

He brought me juice and bread with some vegetables, but there was a piece of bacon on top of the vegetables. My hopes of satisfying my hunger were gone. I just drank the juice.

Another twenty hours passed in detention. I was desperate. I beat on the door and yelled, "Why don't you just deport me? What are you waiting for?"

"Don't yell, keep quiet and wait!" the guard shouted, anger in his voice. People say police in Bavaria have a bad temper, but I would say the police in the Washington, D.C. airport are much worse. I received no compassion from them. I was very disappointed in the United States.

The police eventually took me to the boarding gate for my flight. Everyone seemed to be glaring at me as if I were a criminal. I was wearing a T-shirt and pants. I had no belt, no laces in my shoes. The police were guarding me like a criminal. My dignity was lost. As if this was not enough, after all the passengers had already boarded the plane, the police escorted me to a seat in the back, marching me past the rows of other passengers. It felt as though they were saying, "Did you see this bad guy?" Now everyone was looking at me, shocked. I was humiliated. The police didn't give me my passport. Instead, they gave it to a crew member and told him to return it to me in Frankfurt. They took all my belongings and checked them in with the cargo.

We landed in Frankfurt after nine hours. I got my passport back and then waited two more hours for my flight to Munich. Without my bags, I didn't even have money to buy coffee during my layover.

The weather in Frankfurt was ugly that day. Except for me, no one was wearing a T-shirt. I felt uncomfortable, as though everyone was watching me.

As soon as the plane landed in Munich, airport staff called my name over the loudspeaker and asked me to come to the exit. Two police officers were waiting for me. They took me to their office and asked me why I had been deported. They checked my passport and called the head of the police. "There is nothing wrong with your passport. You're a German citizen. You can leave," they said. I was struck by the compassion of the German police after my experience in D.C. The contrast was so stark.

When I went to claim my bags, my luggage hadn't arrived yet. "Your baggage is still in Frankfurt. It will arrive in two hours," the staff told me. I didn't want to go home in a T-shirt, so I waited. But after two hours, the baggage still hadn't arrived. Giving up, I told them to send me my things later and left the airport.

It was early in the morning. I had no money to buy a metro ticket, so I took the metro without one. It was drizzling outside, and people were wearing heavy coats. Anyone seeing me would have thought I was mad, but I didn't have the energy to think about that.

I was hallucinating. Hungry, cold, and still reeling from my experience, I was exhausted, mentally and physically. I ran into my neighbour on his way to work. "What happened to you, Dolkun?" he asked, noting my dejection. "Nothing, I was jogging," I replied. "Hmm, but your clothes are so light, and it is so cold," he said.

I was lucky to arrive at home before my wife left for work. My keys were in the delayed luggage and my cellphone battery was dead.

I rang the doorbell. My wife opened the door and stepped back, her eyes wide. Two days earlier I had left for the United States wearing a sharp suit. Now I was standing in front of her looking like a beggar.

"What happened, Dolkun?"

"Nothing, get me something to eat."

The U.S. Consulate's refusal of my visa application in 1999, their calling German police to detain me, and this denial of entry in 2006 meant my case was not a small issue in America. My friends made many efforts to remove my name from the U.S. blacklist that claimed I was a threat to U.S. national security. They even met with members of Congress. But we didn't succeed for six years. When a government agency blacklists someone, other departments register the blacklisting in their own systems and treat the person based on that information. But it didn't work the other way around: you could manage to get your name removed at one department, but it didn't guarantee other departments would automatically remove it from their lists. I needed to remove my name at the State Department, the Department of Homeland Security, and other security agencies. It wasn't easy and required a lot of time and effort.

Then-congressman Tom Lantos, congressman Frank Wolf, president of the NED Carl Gershman and vice-president Louisa Greve, and my friends Omer Kanat, Alim Seytoff, Rishat Abbas, and Rushan Abbas attempted to have my name erased from the blacklist many times. But it took years to completely remove it. Finally, I gave power of attorney to Nury Turkel, a Uyghur who had emigrated to the United States and become an attorney and human rights activist. He represented me and worked to resolve this issue. We submitted hundreds of pages of documents, and he met with officials at the State Department and national security agencies numerous times.

On November 6, 2012, Nury Turkel called to tell me the issue had been resolved and that I would be hearing good news in a few days. The next day, the U.S. Consulate in Munich called and asked me to come in. After a short meeting with the visa officer, he stamped a ten-year visa on my passport. It was one day after President Barack Obama started his second term.

I immediately told my friends in the United States the news and arranged a trip. They wanted to commemorate the East Turkistan National Day on November 12 together. I left for Washington on November 9. At the airport, I was once again sent to a different exit, but the customs officials were friendly this time. They asked some questions and let me go. Meanwhile, friends and colleagues Omer Kanat, Nury Turkel, Alim Seytoff, Ilshat Hassan, Zubeyre Shemsidin, Abdulhakim Idris, Rushan Abbas, Louisa Greve, and Kilic Kanat were waiting for me at the airport. We hugged each other. Although we had met at conferences and events in Europe, this reunion in the United States felt different. We were emotional, feeling as though we hadn't seen each other in many years. The next day, on November 10, the Uyghur American Association held its annual election, and Alim Seytoff was re-elected president. On November 11, we held a ceremony to commemorate the two East Turkistans that were re-established in 1933 and 1944. I met many old friends, including schoolmates from Xinjiang University. I also met with members of Congress, U.S. government officials, and the media. After various disappointments over the years, the United States was finally welcoming me, seemingly with open arms.

Still, the dangers of a growing Chinese power—concerned with infiltrating U.S. institutions—lurked around the corner. I was concerned that the U.S. government was only seeing what

China could offer and ignoring the threat it posed. There was no one listening to our warning: "China is going to destroy the whole world."

THE VICTIMS OF COMMUNISM AWARD

After my entry ban was lifted, I visited the United States frequently as the chair of the Executive Committee of the World Uyghur Congress. In January 2016, I received an unexpected letter from the Victims of Communism Memorial Foundation (VOC) in Washington, D.C. They were giving me their Human Rights Award, to be conferred at a ceremony on March 30.

Though I knew nothing about this award or why I was considered for it, I was thrilled that my struggles for Uyghur rights were being recognized by a foundation in the United States. Almost ten years after my deportation, I was going to receive an award for freedom on U.S. soil.

The award ceremony was held at Capitol Hill on March 30. Several House Representatives, laureates of the "Truman–Regan Medal of Freedom," staff of the VOC Memorial Foundation, journalists, and some Uyghurs living in Washington, D.C. attended the ceremony. The foundation's executive director, Marion Smith, delivered an emotional speech talking about my background, why I was being given the award, and the atrocities the Uyghur people were facing. Then, the chair of the foundation, Dr. Lee Edwards, called me and my wife, Mahire, to the stage to receive the award. It was a triumphant moment. A person like me, labelled a "terrorist," listed on Interpol's Red Notices, was receiving an award for human rights and freedom.

Taking the award from Dr. Edwards, I was proud. "Dolkun Isa received this award for his sacrifices for democracy, freedom and [the] human rights of the Uyghur people," Dr. Edwards said. Inscribed on the award was the following:

Presented to Dolkun Isa, in recognition of his advocacy efforts for a peaceful solution to end Uyghur persecution in the People's Republic of China by the Victims of Communism Memorial Foundation, Washington D.C., March 30, 2016.

"This award was given to the Uyghur people," I said in my speech, which is reproduced below.

Washington, D.C., March 30, 2016

Remarks by Dolkun Isa, executive chairman of the World Uyghur Congress

It is a true distinction to be here today. I want to thank the Victims of Communism Memorial Foundation for this recognition of my life's work and for continually remembering the suffering of the Uyghur people under Chinese communist rule.

John Paul the Second once said communism "fell as a consequence of its own mistakes and abuses" and that it had "become a powerful threat and challenge to the entire world."

The Uyghur people are among the millions of victims of communism's abuses. Eastern Europeans were too and are rebuilding their nations under democratic systems; however, the captured nations of China still brave the injustices of communist rule. Chinese communism still endures to challenge world peace [from] militarization of the South China Sea to arming brutal dictators.

In our overlooked struggle, the Uyghur people stand firmly with the democratic peoples of the world who seek a conclusive end to the poverty and cruelty of communist repression. This honor not only shines a light on the Uyghurs' resistance to communism, but also clearly states we will not stop our work until we consign this destructive ideology, in the words of the Victims of Communism Foundation, to "the ash heap of history."

My role in this work began when I was a student at Xinjiang University. In 1985, I protested China's devastating nuclear testing program in East Turkistan and in 1987, several friends and I formed the Student Association for Science and Culture. We encouraged Uyghur students to carry out outreach activities across East Turkistan. We wanted to spread the word of cultural and scientific progress among our people; but the communist authorities were threatened by a grassroots mobilization of Uyghur people and forced us to end our activities.

Later, on June 15, 1988, I helped organize a protest calling for equal rights. From that day, I was placed under house arrest. In September 1988, while in my final year of study, I was expelled from Xinjiang University as a result of my part in the demonstration. My right to an education was taken away because I demanded justice and challenged discriminative policies. Large numbers of Uyghur students who attended the rally were later sent to remote areas on completion of their studies and are still victimized by the Chinese communist regime even today.

This injustice set in motion a chain of events that led me to the free world and eventually to my work with the World Uyghur Congress, which advocates for the freedom of the Uyghur people. However, China is unending in its persecution and aims to silence human rights activists, even overseas. Today, the Chinese government sees me as a "terrorist," and the government has issued a warrant for me through Interpol. As a result, I have been arrested or refused entry in countries vulnerable to Chinese pressure.

These accusations are made to discredit my work. I firmly advocate for a peaceful resolution to the Uyghur issue and reject violence, and this threatens China. The Uyghurs are a people of peace and development. They refuse the ideologies of extremists that threaten the welfare of humanity. These principles make the Uyghur issue not a Uyghur problem, but a Chinese government problem. A condition generated by systematic denial to Uyghurs of fundamental human rights and freedoms. Concerned people should not yield to Chinese narratives that deflect scrutiny of its record in East Turkistan.

It is not surprising that Chinese officials work hard to conceal events in East Turkistan as the Uyghur people face gross human rights violations on a daily basis. A number of agencies have detailed a broad range of rights concerns regarding Uyghurs, including: enforced disappearances; jailing of political dissidents, journalists and webmasters; repression of independent religious leaders; forced abortions; destruction of cultural heritage; restrictions of movement and formidable obstacles in obtaining a passport; tight controls on freedom of expression, particularly on the Internet; marginalization of the Uyghur language in education and society; pressures exerted on foreign governments to deport refugees; targeted surveillance; and suppression of non-state-sanctioned religious association and assembly.

Although I am physically free from the pressures and threats of the Chinese communists, my soul is weighed down by the suffering of my fellow Uyghurs still forced to live under the discriminatory policies of the autocrats in Beijing.

Many of these policies have been enacted under the guise of anti-extremism and counter-terrorism campaigns. Laws prohibiting normal religious practice at home, or wearing clothing tied to one's own culture are now regarded as extremist. The collective punishment of the entire Uyghur community in East Turkistan has only continued, leading to a climate of fear and helplessness.

Underlying all of these restrictive policies is the Chinese Communist Party that wishes to assimilate the entire population, but Uyghur communities have been resistant. Examples in the past reinforce this. The Soviet Union's attempt to assimilate populations under their control led only to a strengthening of culture in opposition to the central government. In China, the same is true. Attempts to eliminate practices that are fundamental to Uyghur culture will not succeed and have already strengthened the feeling in many Uyghurs that their culture must now be held onto even more tightly.

Assimilation is not the answer to the current conflict in East Turkistan. It is one of the fundamental abuses John Paul the Second mentioned.

I want to express my deep admiration to the Victims of Communism Memorial Foundation for its recognition of the dire conditions faced by Uyghurs. In a time when China's economic prowess is increasingly silencing criticism of the Chinese government, even in democracies, this strong statement of support counts more than ever. The honor of accepting the Human Rights Award is a further expression of solidarity with the Uyghur people and on behalf of all Uyghurs, I extend our friendship in return.

This award is given to the Uyghur people.

Thank you.

The *Washington Times*, *Voice of America*, Reuters, and many other U.S. media outlets reported on the ceremony. They stated that the Chinese government was extremely agitated and tried to stop it from happening.[10]

The Chinese ambassador in Washington, D.C., Cui Tiankai, demanded that the State Department withdraw the award and reinstate the ban on my entry to the United States. The State Department responded that the United States was a country ruled by law, that freedom of speech and freedom of assembly were guaranteed, and that they couldn't interfere in an organization's decision.

Chinese foreign ministry spokesman Hong Lei expressed anger about the award, saying I was a wanted man in China for serious crimes, including murder. "The giving of this award by the relevant organization to a terrorist like Dolkun Isa, who has carried out multiple crimes, is to profane and sully human rights and the rule of law," Hong said at a daily news briefing.

An important reason the Chinese government was so angry was that the ceremony was scheduled on March 30, the same day

Xi Jinping, Chair of the CCP, was scheduled to visit Washington, D.C. I don't know if this was a coincidence or on purpose.

After an exciting, celebratory week in the States, Mahire and I returned to Munich on April 4. My friends were waiting for me at the airport, holding flowers. They congratulated and hugged me. It was a warm, happy scene. A week later, Erkin Alptekin organized a celebration for me, inviting the Uyghur community in Germany.

DEPORTED FROM TURKEY

In the years 2004 to 2006, after the Chinese government had announced on December 15, 2003, that I was a "terrorist," the Turkish Consulate in Munich continually refused my visa applications. When I asked for the reason, they said "Your issue is complicated. The Chinese Consulate is messing with us a lot. We can't approve your application without consent from Ankara."

Only after I received German citizenship in 2006 was I able to travel to Turkey to spend a vacation with my family, as the German passport didn't require a visa to enter Turkey. I went again in 2007 and 2008. All of these trips were uncomplicated, and I began to feel a sense of peace with my trips to Turkey. That is, until the World Uyghur Congress organized worldwide demonstrations and calls to boycott the Beijing Olympics in August 2008. In response, the Chinese regime prepared a new blacklist of Uyghur activists, which they provided to governments around the world, including the Turkish government, claiming we were "separatists and terrorists, wanting to bring trouble to the Beijing Olympics." China demanded action from countries like Turkey and published this blacklist in their state-sponsored newspaper, the *Global Times*. I was, of course, on the list.

THE CHINA FREEDOM TRAP

On August 22, 2008, I arrived at the Antalya Airport in Turkey ahead of a planned vacation with friends and faced a new reality.

"You are banned from entering Turkey," the passport control officer said.

"Why?" I asked.

"We don't know the reason. The Turkish interior ministry decided to ban you from entering Turkey."

"Since when?"

"Since 2006."

"Sir," I said, smiling, "I entered Turkey in 2006, 2007, and even in February of this year with this passport. Look at the stamps, please."

"Those were misunderstandings. You shouldn't have been able to enter Turkey after 2006," the officer said.

"Is it even possible for there to be misunderstandings? Three to four times? I think we have a misunderstanding now."

The argument didn't help. The police locked me up in the Antalya airport detention centre and told me that I'd be deported to Germany the following day. My friends in Turkey spoke to police officers and government officials, but nothing worked. Twenty-five hours later, I was deported to Germany.[11]

Upon my return to Germany, I sent letters to the Turkish Foreign Ministry, the Turkish Embassy in Berlin, and the office of the General-Secretary for European Union Affairs. I told them all that I had studied in Turkey, loved Turkey—probably more than a Turkish citizen—and that I'd been defending Turkey in international gatherings, and asked how could someone like this be banned from Turkey while many people, even those who had burned the Turkish flag in Taksim Square, were able to travel there freely. I said I couldn't understand this and requested an explanation. No one responded—and they never would.

After a few months passed, in December 2008 I went to Berlin to attend a meeting. I wanted to take the opportunity while I was there to meet the Turkish ambassador in Berlin. Ambassador Ali Ahmet Acet welcomed me. We talked for an hour, and I presented a report on the situation of the Uyghur people. There were many questions. I told him I had been banned from entering Turkey. "How come? I never knew," the ambassador said, surprised. "I sent you a letter," I replied. He said he hadn't received my letter, so I told him everything that had happened. The ambassador told me he would get in touch with the foreign ministry and personally resolve the issue.

I spoke with the ambassador once every few weeks at first; his secretary even called me asking for a copy of my passport and other information. The secretary told me the ambassador was working urgently to resolve my issue, so I was optimistic. However, as time passed, they stopped answering my calls and didn't respond to letters. It seemed they had forgotten me.

A four-day international conference called "Cultural Diplomacy" that I attended in Berlin in May 2011 gave me an opportunity to make inquiries at a higher level. Many former presidents, ambassadors, diplomats, and politicians attended the conference, including the former Turkish Foreign Minister, Yasar Yakis, who was an advisor to President Erdoğan at the time. Mr. Yakis knew of the Uyghurs well and had helped many of them when he was an ambassador to Saudi Arabia and Egypt. I thought he might be able to help me when I told him that I was banned from entering Turkey. He was surprised, said there must be a misunderstanding, and told me he would be personally dealing with this issue. He asked me to email him the relevant information and said I should remind him from time to time. We kept up correspondence for a few weeks. But like Ambassador Ali Ahmet Acet, Mr. Yakis also disappeared after some time.

My friends in Turkey met many high-level officials and party leaders in Turkey about the ban. Many of them promised they would resolve it and made some efforts in the beginning, but most of these efforts later stopped.

Although I knew the Chinese government was behind the ban, I wanted to know the pretext the Turkish government was employing to keep me out of the country, and how long the ban would likely last. Lawyers advised me that such bans were usually valid for five years, and that I should try going to Turkey then. So, in July 2014, I bought a Turkish Airlines ticket that had a stopover in Istanbul on my way to and from Tokyo. I thought I might use the five-hour layover as an opportunity to test the ban. When I went to passport control, the border officer took my passport calmly, but his face changed as he looked at the screen. He asked if I had another identity document, and I shook my head no. He took me to an office and told me to wait there. After about forty minutes, a police officer came in.

"You are banned from entering Turkey," he said.

"Why? Since when?" I asked, as though I knew nothing.

"Since 2006. You were deported once," he replied.

"Yes, it is true. I heard the ban would be lifted after five years," I responded.

"Who told you this? Your ban has no time frame—it is unlimited. Do you know a minister or someone in the parliament? Try to talk to them," he said. "There is a flight to Tokyo in three hours; you will return there. It has already been arranged."

I was startled. I had just arrived in Istanbul after an eleven-hour flight from Tokyo. If I returned there, I would need to fly another eleven hours to get back to Germany. This was the worst possible outcome.

"What? I have nothing in Tokyo. I'm on my way to Munich. It's just a stopover—look at my ticket!" I exclaimed, my voice quite loud. "What are you doing here then? Stopover passengers should go to the second floor. This is an entry point," the officer retorted angrily.

"How would I know? I just followed the crowd," I said. Although that wasn't true, I had done so for a purpose.

"Well, now you have to go back where you came from. This is the rule. We've already arranged it," the officer said. I was infuriated and, raising my voice, shouted, "Call your manager, I want to talk to him." Another police officer entered as I was shouting.

"What is this noise about? Sir, calm down, what's the problem?" he asked. I told him I was a German citizen on my way from Tokyo to Munich and showed him my boarding pass, repeating that I had mistakenly come to passport control instead of the transit area.

"Usually, you would need to go back to where you came from. Since you're going back home, maybe we can make some changes. Please wait," he said, and left the office.

As the departure time for the flight back to Tokyo was approaching, and there was still no news, I began to worry. "Will I be deported to Tokyo?" I worried. Almost an hour passed before the officer came back.

"We solved your problem. We're letting you fly to Munich. But you can't leave this office until departure time, which is in two hours. We will escort you to your plane half an hour before and will keep your passport until then," the officer told me.

I was relieved, but wary, sensing that something unexpected could happen at any time. Time passed slowly, and the two-hour wait felt like forever. Finally, a police officer and an airline employee escorted me to the gate and returned my passport. Arriving back in Munich, I decided I should never attempt to test the ban again, although I continued to try to find other ways to lift it.

In January 2015 in Berlin, I presented a list of eight requests of the Uyghur people to then-Turkish Prime Minister Ahmet

Davutoglu, taking the opportunity to tell him about my entry ban. The prime minister said he would help, but this assistance never materialized.

On February 16, 2018, I had a chance to briefly meet Turkish Prime Minister Binali Yildirrim and Turkish Interior Minister Suleyman Soylu during the Munich Security Conference. I submitted reports outlining the requests of the Uyghur people in Turkey and reminding them of their brotherly responsibility towards the Uyghurs. I also submitted a written explanation about my entry ban in Turkey, but they never responded.

In short, no one seemed able or willing to solve this issue. Turkey had closed its doors to me on August 23, 2008, and ten years later, it was still unresolved.

But why?

No Turkish leader answered this question. It was obviously Chinese pressure, but no one wanted to admit it. Maybe they were ashamed to say, "Turkey is afraid of China."

Most Uyghurs feel that Turkey is their second homeland. Uyghurs and Turks share common roots and a close culture. It is true that Turkey welcomed many Uyghurs refugees who had nowhere else to go, including those who fled China's death threats. The Turkish people's sympathy and brotherly love was a solace to the Uyghur people , but the Uyghur people expected much more from Turkey. Recep Erdoğan condemned the Chinese government after the Urumchi Massacre on July 5, 2009,[12] and called it a genocide. This bold step from Turkey brought great hope to the Uyghur people, who believed Turkey could be their saviour. However, Turkey's position didn't last long. During elections, Erdoğan mentioned East Turkistan cities Urumchi and Kashgar, implying that he hadn't forgotten the Uyghur people. However, after he won the elections, Turkey's stance on the Uyghur issue changed drastically.

Of course, there are Kazakhs, Kyrgyzs, Uzbeks, Turkmens, and Azerbaijanis in Central Asia who are also brethren to the Uyghurs. They all got independence in the 1990s. But the Uyghurs don't expect the same level of help and support from them as they don't have the power Turkey has. Those countries also understandably fear China so much that they've extradited Uyghurs who sought refuge in them, and still do, to this day. For this reason, among the Turkic republics, Turkey is considered the most important and safest country for Uyghurs. Uyghurs have always hoped Turkey would play a key role in defending them internationally. Unfortunately, Turkey has thus far remained neutral. It may be time for us to admit we're expecting too much.

SUDDENLY SHUT OUT OF TAIWAN

From October 27 to 29, 2006, I travelled to Taiwan to participate in the eighth General Assembly of the Unrepresented Nations and Peoples Organization (UNPO).[13] The Uyghurs, along with the Taiwanese, were one of the founding members of the UNPO in 1991, and Erkin Alptekin played a significant role in the establishment and development of the organization. He also worked as its secretary-general and president. Between 2017 and 2022, I served as UNPO's vice-president, and the WUC is a member organization of the UNPO, representing East Turkistan.

The eighth General Assembly was called by the Taiwan Foundation for Democracy. High-level officials and ministers in Taiwan participated, and the foreign ministry of Taiwan arranged a banquet for the participants. The assembly went off without a hitch, ending peacefully.

This was my first time travelling to Taiwan. I attended the assembly with Alim Seytoff, then-chairman of the Executive Committee of the WUC.[14] At the time, I served as the secretary-general. During our one-week stay in Taiwan, we not only participated in the UNPO General Assembly, we also accepted interviews from the media and reported on the situation in East Turkistan. With the invitation of Chinyun University's Central Asia Research Center, we also delivered talks to university students.

At the time, Dr. Erkin Ekrem was teaching at Chinyun University as a visiting professor on a one-year contract. In the evenings when we were free, we got together with Dr. Ekrem. We debated the similarities and differences between Taiwan and China. Taiwan was a Chinese-speaking country, but it wasn't like the People's Republic of China. The life people had in Taiwan under democracy, including freedom, dignity, and peace, wasn't available in Mainland China. It was obvious from the daily lives of Taiwanese people that Taiwan had learned and applied Western values. "Democracy, freedom, and human rights are suitable for Chinese people too!" I told my friends, seeing life in Taiwan. The country left a really positive impression on me on my first visit. When I accepted interviews with journalists from Radio Free Asia (RFA) back then, I praised Taiwan.

A few years later however, in July 2009, something unusual happened. Taiwanese journalists started calling me. "Are you in Taiwan? Can we interview you?" they asked. "I went to Taiwan once in 2006 and I've not been back since then. Why did you want to interview me?" I asked. The reporters answered, "There is news spreading in the Taiwanese media that 'the terrorist Dolkun Isa has arrived in Taiwan with fourteen terrorists. He is trying to carry out terrorist activities in Taiwan.' We wanted to investigate this."[15]

I was shocked. I didn't know why and how such news had spread in the media. When I visited Taiwan in 2006, Chen Shuibian of the Democratic Progressive Party was Taiwan's president. His party was a proponent of Taiwan's independence. In 2008, the Kuomintang (the Chinese Nationalist Party) won the election, and Ma Yingzhou ruled the country. It was during his presidency that the rumours about me had first appeared in the Taiwanese media.

I told the journalists that I was in Germany, that I didn't travel to Taiwan, I wasn't a terrorist, I had never had any intention of carrying out criminal activities in Taiwan, and I was in fact disgusted at any kind of violence carried out in other people's lands. After this, news about me began to increase in the Taiwanese media. There were reports that I wanted to visit Taiwan but wasn't allowed by the Taiwanese government to enter the country.

In September 2009, when *Ten Conditions of Love*, a film about the life of the former president of the WUC, Rebiya Kadeer, was going to be streamed in Taiwan, Ms. Kadeer was invited to Taiwan. However, the Taiwanese government refused to give her a visa. This created a buzz in the Taiwanese media, and the issue of Uyghurs' visits to Taiwan as well as the Uyghur crisis became hot topics across the country. The issue even attracted the attention of some international media outlets. As a result, questions on whether to let Uyghurs, especially WUC staff, enter Taiwan caused debates in the Taiwanese parliament and its government agencies.[16]

Media reports at the time described the debates in the Taiwanese parliament as quite tense. The Democratic Progressive Party asked serious questions of the ruling party, the Kuomintang, including "Why isn't Rebiya Kadeer allowed to enter Taiwan? Why isn't Dolkun Isa allowed to enter Taiwan? Dolkun Isa visited Taiwan in 2006 . . ." The Taiwanese Minister of the Interior answered, "Dolkun Isa is a man on Interpol's Red Notices. Rebiya Kadeer will be able to enter Taiwan as WUC's president if Dolkun Isa resigns as the organization's secretary-general, or if Rebiya Kadeer resigns as the president of the WUC." They were very clear: my Red Notice was the problem. This was the pretext Taiwanese authorities used to prevent Rebiya Kadeer and I from visiting Taiwan.

After this incident, I received many invitations to conferences in Taiwan, including the Asia Pacific Religious Freedom Forum in February 2016. I wanted to participate in this conference, as I knew it would be a great opportunity for me to expose China's religious persecution of my people in East Turkistan. But it was also important to consider my safety, in light of the rumours about me that had spread a few years earlier in Taiwan, the unstable political climate after the change in government, the fact that Taiwan was a hub for the CCP's spies, and the constant threat to Taiwan from China. These factors required my careful consideration.

Although I didn't require a visa to visit Taiwan as a German citizen, I asked my assistant to send a letter to the Taiwanese Representative Office in Munich anyway. I told them I wanted to visit Taiwan on a visa and asked them if I would be able to enter the country. The Taiwanese Representative Office offered to look into the issue, but I didn't hear from them for quite some time. I asked again, but still there was no word. When I asked for the last time, they replied, "Please contact the National Immigration Agency (NIA)." We sent a letter to the Taiwanese NIA, but they didn't reply either.

The Taiwanese journalists who learned that I would not be attending the Asia Pacific Religious Freedom Forum approached me to ask why. I remember telling them this:

> The Taiwanese authorities should know that I'm not a threat to Taiwan's national security. When I visited Taiwan in 2006, I came back with a good impression, and nothing bad happened. Maybe the Kuomintang (the Chinese Nationalist Party) holds a grudge against the Uyghurs and the people of East Turkistan. In 1944, the people of East Turkistan fought the Kuomintang army and won, establishing the East Turkistan

Republic. The Kuomintang (Chinese Nationalists), just like the Chinese Communist Party, views East Turkistan, Tibet, even the Mongolian Republic as part of China. Their nationalistic ideology is strong. Although there are differences in ideology between the CCP and the Kuomintang, they are the same when it comes to their national interests. The Kuomintang views the Uyghurs, Tibetans, and Mongolians the same way Communist China views them. The success of democracy and freedom in Taiwan doesn't mean the nature of the Kuomintang has changed.

Later, the Kuomintang lost the election and the Democratic Progressive Party, under the leadership of Tsai Ing-wen, formed a new government. However, the democratic government's stance on me didn't change: they still didn't allow me to visit Taiwan. After I became president of the WUC in 2017, I was again invited to several conferences there, but the Taiwanese Representative Office in Munich continued to ignore my questions. Their answer was always the same: "Please contact the NIA; only they can solve this issue."

In October 2018, I met Jhy-Wey Shieh, the Taiwanese ambassador at the Representative Office of Taiwan in Berlin. I told him I was invited to a conference in Taiwan but couldn't get a response from the Taiwanese government about whether I could enter the country and asked for his help. The ambassador asked me to send him documents about the Interpol Red Notice and assured me he would investigate and give me an answer after contacting the president's office. Yet, despite these assurances, he never sent me an answer.[17]

Hsu Szu-chien, a Taiwanese representative to the UNPO, became Taiwan's Deputy Minister of Foreign Affairs in July 2018. I met him in October 2019 in Prague during Forum 2000[18] and again during the Halifax International Security Forum in Canada in November 2019 and talked with him about whether I could enter Taiwan. "I am discussing this issue with the president. It's a bit complex, and I need some time," he told me. Hsu Szu-chien is now the deputy director of the National Security Council of Taiwan. In October 2020, I had an another opportunity to discuss the matter with him when we both spoke at an online panel during Forum 2000. During the session, I asked Hsu Szu-chien jokingly, "When will you solve the problem of my entrance to Taiwan?" He just smiled and didn't answer.

Many government officials and members of the Taiwanese parliament worked to solve this issue. President Tsai Ing-wen's Ambassador-at-Large for human rights and democracy, Maysing Yang-Huang, was one of them. She met President Tsai Ing-wen and the leaders of the National Security Council of Taiwan to discuss my issue but did not get a positive reply. The Taiwanese government consistently denied me entry to Taiwan. As a result, Maysing Yang-Huang resigned from her post on November 11, 2019, protesting the Tsai Ing-wen administration.[19]

The same day, she sent me the following email explaining her resignation: "The government didn't respect Taiwan's basic principles of freedom, democracy and human rights, didn't fulfill their promise and bowed to the pressure and threats of China. Not allowing Dolkun Isa to enter Taiwan is a typical example of that," she said.

I received many letters and messages from government officials, human rights activists, and journalists in Taiwan expressing their disapproval of the administration and anger at its abuse of justice by bowing to Chinese pressure. They told me they felt ashamed to be Taiwanese.

The issue of my admittance to Taiwan remains unresolved today. Being banned from the country and thereby deprived of raising the East Turkistan crisis in conferences there didn't disappoint me as much as it might appear. If Turkey, which has a population of eighty million Turks, closed its doors to me, it was understandable that Taiwan—a small island facing China's cannons and under constant threat of Chinese invasion—would take such an approach. Nonetheless, as I had been playing an active role in helping Taiwan gain UN membership and fighting the Chinese regime in the UNPO as allies, and considering their democratic values, I hoped Taiwan would welcome me. I still hope Taiwan won't become like Hong Kong one day or like East Turkistan later.

CHAPTER 3
MY BORDER PROBLEMS ESCALATE

My detention in South Korea was totally different from the other detentions I had experienced. There, my life was at stake as I was on the brink of ending up in the hands of the Chinese.

The Taiwan Foundation for Democracy invited the former President of the WUC, Erkin Alptekin, to the three-day World Forum for Democratization in Asia to be held in Manila in October 2007. As Alptekin's health didn't allow him to travel, he suggested I attend the forum in his place, which I did. Two years later, in September 2009, the Taiwan Foundation for Democracy planned another forum, this time in Seoul, South Korea. I received an invitation in July 2009. The foreign ministry of South Korea collaborated with the country's human rights organizations, and around one hundred and fifty activists from different Asian countries planned to attend. It was a great opportunity for me to present the Uyghur crisis before many international organizations.

My wife, Mahire, expressed an interest in coming with me, as she was a fan of the South Korean movies and songs that were becoming popular among Uyghurs. She had never asked to accompany me before as she wasn't very interested in politics,

MY BORDER PROBLEMS ESCALATE

so I agreed and asked the organizers of the forum to arrange a hotel for the two of us.

I began receiving requests for interviews from South Korean journalists ahead of my trip. As news about the forum and its participants was already being reported in the media, journalists wanted to interview me to learn more about the Uyghur people. I told them about the Chinese atrocities in East Turkistan, including most recently the massacre that China had carried out in Urumchi on July 5.

On September 15, Mahire and I took a flight with the Emirates airline from Munich to Seoul. We had a four-hour layover in Dubai. As we landed in Seoul, I suddenly had a troubling thought. "What if something bad happens at South Korean Customs?" I needed to tell my wife about this. "I think we should go through Customs separately. Let's go to different counters," I suggested. "Why?" she asked, surprised.

"Anything could happen. If I have a problem at Customs, you will be stopped too. It is better we go to different counters."

Mahire was alarmed, and her eyes grew wide.

"The organizers of the event are waiting for us at the airport," I told her. Here is their address and phone number. This is the address for the event. Some Uyghur youths studying in South Korea said they will be coming to the airport too. Here is their number. This is the German ambassador's phone number. If I get stopped at Customs, contact these people," I continued, handing her a piece of paper.

"Why are you scaring me?" she asked, despondent. "Maybe nothing will happen," I said.

She took the paper quietly. I could see she wanted to tell me I was overthinking things. "Whatever," I thought. "It is better to be careful and take precautions." After being deported from the United States and Turkey, I made a habit of taking the contact information for the relevant German Embassy on my trips outside Europe.

When we arrived in Seoul, we separated at passport control as planned. Passing through quickly, Mahire waited outside, keeping an eye on me from the window. I gave my passport to the border officer. He took it and turned to his computer, then looked up at me suddenly, as though he had received a shock.

"Please wait here," he said.

I realized instantly that trouble lay ahead. But I didn't imagine the magnitude of the events that would follow, that my life would be at stake, and that I would be the cause of a diplomatic struggle involving Germany, the United States, South Korea, and China.

"Have you ever been to South Korea?" the border officer asked when he returned.

"No, this is the first time," I said.

"You need to wait, maybe one to two hours," the officer said. I called my wife. "I think I'm going to have a problem here. Go out and meet the people who came to welcome us. Tell them I've been stopped at Customs. I'll call you later," I told her.

The South Korean police took me to a separate room to wait. After two hours, they announced, "You can't enter South Korea. We'll be deporting you to Germany."

"Why?" I asked. The police didn't respond; they didn't want to explain. I recalled the painful scene in the Washington, D.C. airport when I was deported to Germany. I recalled the day I was deported from Turkey. I winced, anticipating the same hurt, discomfort, and insults.

I had learned from those experiences that regardless of the country, being told to wait at Customs means that trouble is certain. I also learned that there was little point in arguing with the police, and if I did, I would be mistreated. I tried to hold out hope that they would deport me to Germany as soon as possible—which would be better.

MY BORDER PROBLEMS ESCALATE

I called my wife. "They're not letting me enter South Korea. I'll be deported to Germany, I don't know when. Please contact the German Embassy and tell everyone at the airport what happened," I told her.

Mahire contacted the German Embassy. The embassy staff told her not to worry, they would contact the South Korean foreign ministry. In the meantime, all the forum attendees learned what had happened, and my story was all over the news.

The border police told me I would be taking a flight to Germany through Dubai in five hours. I was so relieved to have a flight confirmed, and to know I wasn't going to be locked up that I wasn't even upset about not being able to attend the forum, visit South Korea, or stay with my wife.

I updated Mahire and told her not to worry but to enjoy her vacation in South Korea and said I would call when I got on the plane. She was disappointed, but she was also accustomed to such incidents.

As the time for my departure neared. I counted every second. An hour before I was to leave, a police officer came in and told me to get ready. But then, with forty minutes left, a group of police came in. "You can't leave today. Our security service has questions to ask you tomorrow. You need to answer them," they told me.

Realizing that things were taking a bad turn, I called my lawyer in Germany, Dr. Albrecht Göring. "South Korean security officers don't have the right to force you into an interrogation. You're a German citizen, you have the right to refuse. Don't answer their questions, and if they pressure you, tell them to contact me," he advised.

I was locked up in a hall with about twenty people waiting to be deported. Being locked up in a democratic country again was something I couldn't accept. I was unsettled, and I was hungry—as a Muslim, I couldn't eat the food they provided. One by one the others left, but I remained, waiting. It was hot and smelly, with no place to shower or rest. I eventually slept sitting upright on a chair.

A DIPLOMATIC STRUGGLE

I awoke the next morning dejected and anxious, unaware of the many things that had taken place during the night while I was asleep. Intense communications between Germany and South Korea, secret meetings between China and South Korea, and harsh dialogue between the United States and South Korea had all happened while I slept in a cage.

The South Korean security services that wanted to interrogate me never came. I didn't know if my lawyer had talked to them or if it was the German Foreign Ministry or the German Embassy.

I learned later that as the World Forum for Democratization in Asia started, my detention at the Seoul Airport became a point of discussion. It quickly created a buzz in the South Korean media. Headlines such as "World Forum for Democratization in Asia has been trampled upon" blared out the news. Journalists started calling me. I didn't accept their interviews at first, as I didn't want to do anything that might escalate the situation.

Another day passed. I was restless. All the "detainees" in the hall had been deported, so I was left alone. The police couldn't answer my questions: they didn't know when I would be deported, or why I was still being detained. "We're investigating" was all they said. One of them would come in and glance at me every now and then. I became paranoid; the Korean officers looked like Chinese agents to me. "Are they Chinese agents?" I thought sometimes.

To me, the scariest possibility was being deported to China. I was certain I wouldn't survive that. The Chinese wouldn't just kill me, they would torture me for a long time, as is their practice, and then shame me before the whole world. They would subject me to extreme tortures, such as forced confession, as they have

MY BORDER PROBLEMS ESCALATE

done to many Uyghur activists. They would make me a lesson for other Uyghurs.

My second day in detention also passed without any interrogation. The police didn't have questions for me, but journalists, and my friends around the world, eager to check in, didn't stop calling. Getting information to them about my status was another matter. Ironically, my cellphone provider in Germany helped me out when they called to tell me that I had exceeded my limit of 1,200 euros and were about to suspend my line. "No, don't.," I told them. "Don't suspend it even if I spend 10,000 euros. I am having trouble in South Korea, and my line must stay open."

Since incoming and outgoing calls attracted very high fees, I asked the police for a phone I could use to stay in touch with my family and the embassy. The police gave me the number for their front desk. I gave it to my wife and told her to use it if she needed to reach me. Otherwise, I mostly avoided answering calls on my cellphone but kept it on, just in case. Everyone ended up learning the front desk number at the immigration detention centre, and friends, as well as journalists and human rights organizations started calling. The police were irritated that their line was constantly busy with my calls and by the second day were fed up.

"We have other things to do besides taking your calls all day. From now on, we will only take calls from your wife and the German Embassy," they told me. Of course I agreed and told my wife. But this didn't last long. Men called saying they were from the German Embassy. Women called saying they were my wife. Journalists used this tactic, too, to try to get interviews with me.

"How many wives do you have?" asked a police officer, exasperated.

Although the South Korean police didn't disturb me on the second day, many things were happening behind the scenes. The U.S. State Department, some congressmen, the German Embassy, and the German foreign ministry were all involved. I learned afterwards that officials from the U.S. and German governments took my detention in South Korea very seriously, intervening and pressuring the South Korean government enormously.

The German Embassy in Seoul was taking the situation most seriously. On the second day of my detention, the legal counsel to the German Embassy, Alexander Nowak, visited me at the airport. I told him everything, including that I couldn't take care of basic personal hygiene because I hadn't been able to take a shower for two days. He bought me new items and obtained special permission for me to shower.

On the second evening of my detention, some German Embassy staff paid me a visit to reassure me that Germany and South Korea had a great diplomatic and economic relationship and they would do everything they could to rescue me. They told me many countries were interested in my case, especially a third country, a neighbour to South Korea. They didn't say the third country was China, but implied that this "neighbour" was putting a lot of pressure on the South Korean government.

I learned from Mr. Nowak that the South Korean ministries of the Interior and Foreign Affairs, as well as the Immigration Department were discussing my case, but still hadn't reached an agreement. Eventually, I learned that the South Korean government had already promised to extradite me to China.

There is one thing I don't know to this day. How did China learn of my arrival in South Korea? Did it know I was coming in advance and request my extradition? Did South Korea inform China after seeing the Interpol Red Notice at Customs, or did China make the request after learning about my detention at the airport through media reports? Whichever it was, South Korea agreed to extradite me to China.

As they prepared for my extradition, South Korea began receiving warnings from Germany and the United States and other European governments making it clear that there would be

MY BORDER PROBLEMS ESCALATE

consequences for South Korea if they didn't change their stance. Marco Perduca, the deputy chair of the Italian senate and a close friend of mine, also sent a letter to the South Korean ambassador to Italy requesting they let me leave for Germany immediately and warned that it would be a stain on South Korea's democratic values if they didn't.

My detention at the Seoul airport became a hot topic in the German and European media. Amnesty International, the UNPO, Peoples Under Threat, the World Forum for Democratization in Asia, and Uyghur and other organizations issued statements condemning South Korea and calling on Western governments to protect me.[20] The European Union also intervened. There was immense pressure on South Korea, which had a difficult decision to make: either fulfill its promise to China and extradite me, or side with its traditional allies, break its promise to China, and release me.

Of course, it wouldn't be easy for South Korea to upset the United States, Germany, and the rest of Europe by siding with China. However, it would be a small sacrifice compared with the potential loss of huge Chinese investments and money. Germany, the United States, and maybe all the Western countries would have condemned South Korea for some time. But South Korea's crime would have soon been forgotten, leaving me as the only real, permanent victim. States can and do put aside humanitarianism for national interests when it is practical to do so, with few long-term repercussions. They will sacrifice freedom, democracy, and other purported values.

By my third day in detention, there was still no news from South Korea. Mr. Nowak came to visit me again. "We're making our last efforts. South Korea promised to tell us their decision at 5:00 p.m. today. They answered our calls this morning. But we haven't been able to reach them for the past two hours. If they don't answer us by 5:00 p.m., we're going to submit a Diplomatic Note to South Korea. But we hope it won't come to that point," he said.

I assumed Germany followed through with their plan to warn South Korea that it would submit a Diplomatic Note if I was not released, which would mean Germany was determined to rescue me. But they still couldn't make me any promises.

My friends, the leaders of the human rights that had become involved, and the diplomats who had assured me and encouraged me to stay optimistic on those first two days changed their tune by the third day, expressing defeat and helplessness. I realized the situation was escalating and becoming more threatening. Germany, the United States, and other Western countries are all trying to save me, " but what can I do here?" I asked myself. I decided to declare a hunger strike.

Journalists never stopped calling. I told one of them that I would be declaring a hunger strike if I wasn't released by 8:00 p.m. The news quickly spread to the world., and journalists' new question was "Did you start the hunger strike?" Meanwhile, the German Embassy sent me a message. "We're heading to the airport now; we will be there in organizations an hour. Don't do anything before we arrive," it said. I waited, losing hope.

The threat of extradition as well as, hunger and sleeplessness were strangling me, particularly the worry about what I would do if I were extradited to China. "I can't end up alive in the hands of the Chinese, no matter what" I told myself. The only solution was suicide, but it wouldn't be easy. I would need to break the window to throw myself from the building, but the window looked too strong to break. There was no rope with which to hang myself: even my laces and belt had been confiscated. I thought maybe I should hit the wall, with force. But what if I still didn't die? This wouldn't work either. It is one thing for a man to decide to commit suicide, but figuring out how to do it is something else.

"What if I can't kill myself and I end up alive in China?" was my constant worry. I remembered the stories of the heroes who had been captured alive by the Chinese. Their torture methods

MY BORDER PROBLEMS ESCALATE

were harrowing: pulling out your fingernails, forcing spicy liquids down your throat, ironing your back, hanging you from the ceiling, whipping you, making you sit in an electric chair, inserting cables into your genitals, cutting your toes off one by one. They will torture you until you lose consciousness; they will force you to say anything they want. Then, when they have everything, they need, they will groom you nicely and film you; you'll confess that all your rightful struggles during all those years of resistance were crimes, vicious crimes that couldn't be forgiven. You'll repent to the Chinese Communist Party, you'll tell the Uyghur people to just live their lives, be grateful for and obey the Communist Party, and disgrace the fight for our cause.

Then what?

China will send a message to the world, "See, we can bring a famous separatist like Dolkun Isa back to China, punish him, and make him repent!" This will bring great despair to those fighting for our cause. It will make them lose their spirit, become depressed. Then, China will simply dispose of you, kill you with an injection, or a blow, tell the world you had a stroke, send your body to your family, or bury you in some unknown place.

These thoughts were agonizing. I returned to thoughts of suicide instead. But *how*?

It was 10:00 p.m. when, suddenly, a group of people in black suits entered the hall. "Turn off your phone and come with us," one of them told me.

"Where?" I asked, alarmed.

"We're sending you to Germany. You need to cut off all communications with the outside world from now on. Turn off your phone, now!"

"Wait, I need to tell the German Embassy. I'll turn off my phone, but you should give me another one," I said.

They gave me another cellphone that I used to call Alexander Nowak. "These people are saying they'll send me to Germany, but you still haven't come. Should I wait for you?" I asked him.

"We've arrived at the airport," he informed me, "but we thought it would be better not to meet you. We could be followed. The *neighbours* (China) are staying vigilant. Just follow the people who came to get you—they're responsible for escorting you to the plane safely. Don't worry. Don't turn your phone on, don't talk to anyone, not even your wife. We'll wait until you leave. We'll be watching you," he instructed me.

His words comforted me. The men escorting me to the plane told me I would be flying to Dubai. "Why aren't they sending me directly to Germany? What if South Korea and China made a secret agreement? It is possible I'll be extradited to China when I land in Dubai," I thought. "Why don't you wait for a direct plane to Germany tomorrow?" I asked him.

"We don't know what's going to happen tomorrow. We've been told to return you right now. Our job is to make sure you safely leave South Korea today," he replied.

There were trains connecting the different airport terminals. The men escorting me to the departure gate, South Korean intelligence agents in plain clothes, entered one of them and told the passengers the train had broken down. The train emptied and we rode alone.

"Can I borrow your phone? I need to call the German Embassy," I asked an agent when we arrived at the departure gate and took his phone. I called Alexander Nowak. "I'm boarding the plane now. I have an eight-hour layover in Dubai. Is there a possibility I will be sold to the Chinese in Dubai? What if this is all a game? Why don't I wait for the direct plane to Germany tomorrow?" I asked.

"I have to ensure you safely leave South Korea today because the situation could change tomorrow. Your trip has been arranged

MY BORDER PROBLEMS ESCALATE

by the German Foreign Ministry. You won't stay long in Dubai, and people will be waiting for you there. Call the German Consulate in Dubai as soon as you arrive," he told me.

"So I can safely board this plane?" I asked again.

"Yes, rest assured," he replied.

The agents took a different route to the plane than the other passengers, communicating with each other using earpieces, and watching all around the gate. I saw there were other agents too, not just the five escorting me. They closed some passages for me to pass, looking very serious, as if they were protecting a top-level government official.

I felt like I was in a movie; it was surreal. Was it all a lie? Would they turn me over to the Chinese?

They took me to an office next to the boarding gate, stopped me at the door, checked the office to make sure it was secure, and took me inside.

The head of the South Korean immigration department arrived. "Mr. Dolkun, I'm really sorry you're leaving South Korea with such a bad impression. Had I known it would come to this, I would have let you enter, or just deported you. But your case escalated, and it transcended my authority. I couldn't do anything. Please forgive me," he said.

"What's happened has happened, sir," I said. "I believed South Korea was a democratic nation. I am disappointed, but I thank you for your apology. This isn't really important. What's important is that this will be a stain on South Korea's image as a democratic and rule-of-law nation."

The flight was delayed forty minutes waiting for me. As I was escorted to the plane, I was hesitant. I had no passport or boarding pass, nothing to prove where the plane was going. "How can I know for sure if this plane is flying to Dubai or Beijing, sir?" I asked an agent with me. He called another man over. "This man is responsible for you on this plane. He will be going to Dubai with you. Don't worry, Mr. Isa," he said.

Boarding the plane with me, the agent escorted me to my seat at the back. After telling me he would be in the front cabin if I needed him, he left.

The plane was full, but the seat next to me was empty. I figured this was a rule. The seat next to me was empty when I was deported from the United States, and from Turkey, too.

There was a woman seated across from me in the same row who looked Asian. I turned to her and asked, "Where is this plane going?"

She looked at me, dumbfounded. "Where do you want to go?" she asked a moment later.

"Dubai," I said.

"This plane is going to Dubai," she said.

"I was just kidding," I said, smiling.

Finally, I thought, I know I am in the right place. Had she said the plane was going to Beijing or Shanghai, I would have made a commotion to try to be taken off the plane.

I would rather go to China a dead man than end up alive in their hands. I put these thoughts aside and calmed down as the plane headed to Dubai. But I still didn't know what would happen there. Countries like Pakistan and the United Arab Emirates live at the mercy of China. They can sell you for a small price. And like China, they don't care if the whole world condemns them.

A SAFE RETURN, AT A COST

The plane landed in Dubai at five in the morning. As everyone started leaving the plane, the man responsible for me turned up. "Mr. Dolkun, please wait until everyone has left the plane. You will be escorted from the plane then," he said.

MY BORDER PROBLEMS ESCALATE

When everyone had left the plane, two Arab men arrived to greet me. One of them said, "Welcome to Dubai, Mr. Dolkun Isa. I am a service manager at the Emirates, I will be responsible for your safe passage to Germany. Please come with me,"

I had flown from Seoul worrying that Chinese security agents would be waiting for me in Dubai. Seeing that the man was not Chinese, I followed him. During my stopover in Dubai en route to South Korea, the airport had been overcrowded, but this time, I was walking through a completely empty terminal. Suddenly paranoid, I thought I should pretend to talk to people, so I talked to the Emirates guy and found out he was Palestinian. When he discovered I was a Uyghur, he said our people shared a similar fate.

The manager took me to an Emirates Business Lounge. "Mr. Dolkun, your flight was supposed to leave in eight hours, but we were able to change it. You have two hours to boarding time. Please rest here and have some food. There is a bed in the other room if you want to sleep, and here is my business card. Please call me if you need anything." Then he handed me my passport and boarding pass and left.

"He locked me up here and now he could be going to get Chinese agents," I thought, and left the lounge. I bought a calling card and dialled the number Mr. Nowak gave me before leaving South Korea.

It was 5:30 a.m. A woman answered the phone. "Is this Mr. Isa?" she asked.

"Yes."

"Is something wrong?"

"No, nothing is wrong. I've just arrived. I just wanted to ask, do you believe I'll be okay at the airport? Will I arrive in Germany safely?" I asked.

"I believe everything will be all right. Your route has been arranged by the German foreign ministry. Don't worry, you will be under our watch until you fly to Germany. In case anything happens, just call this number," the lady said. She told me she was an official at the German Consulate in Dubai.

I calmed down and went back to the lounge. There were food and drinks. After four days, I finally had fresh food. All they gave me at the detention centre in the Seoul airport was a chicken sandwich; my stomach was practically empty.

I had lost connection with the world for more than twelve hours. The German Embassy and South Korean security agents had asked me to turn off my phone and not contact anyone until I landed in Germany, for my protection from China. No one knew where I was or whether I was safe or not, and my friends were probably anxious. I thought I should at least tell my wife that I had arrived safely in Dubai, but I still didn't want to risk turning my phone on. I later discovered that my wife, journalists, and human rights organizations had been calling the Seoul airport asking for me. When the police said there was no one there named Dolkun Isa, they had become really worried.

Finally, I boarded the plane to Germany, eager for the plane to take off as quickly as possible. Still feeling that someone could come take me away at any moment, my anxiety and distress were overwhelming.

As the plane began its take-off, I turned on my phone and sent a quick message to my wife—"I'm flying from Dubai to Germany"—before turning it right back off. After the disturbing experience in South Korea, my anxiety only began to ease once I landed in Munich.

Some time after this experience, a friend sent me some information about the incident that had been published on WikiLeaks.[21] It said that the day after I was detained in South Korea, five officials from the Chinese Ministry of Public Security arrived in Seoul and waited there to take me to China. South Korean authorities had informed China that a man on Interpol's Red Notices had been detained at the Seoul airport. China

MY BORDER PROBLEMS ESCALATE

demanded extradition, and South Korea agreed. But South Korea had to break its promise after pressure mounted from Germany, the United States, and other EU countries.

Later, I also met people from the German foreign ministry who told me they had leveraged all the power they could to rescue me at the last minute. They said, "If possible, please don't travel to Asian countries." According to them, South Korea had initially decided to extradite me to China, but feared pressure from the West. Those final moments before they reached their decision were critical to my being successfully freed from South Korea.

A few years later, in 2015, the World Movement for Democracy invited me to attend its Eighth General Assembly, scheduled to be held in South Korea. I wanted to see South Korea's reaction and wrote a letter to the South Korean Embassy in Berlin and to its foreign ministry asking them if I could visit South Korea. I didn't get a response for a long time, but I didn't give up trying. Finally, the embassy replied that it had given its answer to the German Embassy in South Korea, which sent me the news: "We cannot welcome Mr. Dolkun Isa to South Korea."

MORE BORDER TROUBLES

Around mid-November 2009, I received an invitation from the U.S.-based World Movement for Democracy (WMD) to participate in their sixth General Assembly, to be held in Jakarta from April 11 to 14, 2010. I had participated in the assembly in Ukraine two years earlier. Usually, around five hundred people from more than one hundred countries participated, including influential political figures, leaders of organizations, activists, experts, and government officials. This was an important opportunity to raise awareness of the Uyghur crisis but I was still traumatized by my trip to South Korea. If the incident that occurred in South Korea, a democratic nation, was repeated in Indonesia—a country over which China has even greater influence—it would have been impossible for me to escape. I had to think carefully about whether to take such a risk.

The WMD was founded with the initiative and financial support of the National Endowment for Democracy (NED), one of the organizations that had looked out for my safety in South Korea, so I agreed to participate. With five months left until the assembly convened, I thought I could look further into whether Jakarta would be safe for me, knowing I could cancel if necessary, keeping in mind the advice of the German foreign ministry not to travel to Asian countries.

Shortly after that, I received my flight tickets. I would be flying on Lufthansa, a German airline, with a stopover in Singapore on my way to and from Jakarta. I had many concerns. I didn't think it would be safe to make a stopover in Singapore, and I was still concerned about my security in Indonesia. I had to find answers. I sent a letter to NED asking for a direct flight from Germany to Indonesia, or one with a stopover in a European country. I also sent the invitation and my flight itinerary from NED to the German foreign ministry and asked for their advice.

The German foreign ministry replied the next day to say they would investigate and would let me know shortly. Two weeks later I received a letter: the German Embassy advised that I could participate in the meeting, but they could not guarantee my safety. It was up to me to decide if I was prepared to take the risk.

Having a German passport meant I didn't require a visa to visit Indonesia, but I still felt it best to check in with the Indonesian Embassy. I contacted their embassy in Berlin to explain my situation and asked for a visa to ensure my safety. They issued me a visa two weeks later with a letter stating I had no untoward record in Indonesia and would be able to travel there safely like any other German citizen.

MY BORDER PROBLEMS ESCALATE

Still concerned, I wrote to NED's president, Carl Gershman, and vice-president, Louisa Greve, sharing my worries, and explaining that as Indonesia wasn't like South Korea if I faced similar issues there the outcome could be terrible. They agreed to consider my situation.

At the time, China was reported to be spending billions of dollars to improve its international image and fight "separatists" overseas. Incidents of Chinese hackers stealing political and economic information from Western countries were rampant. Cybersecurity was in a bad state. As my communications with NED were via email, it wasn't impossible that Chinese hackers had learned about them. After discussing the issue with Louisa Greves, I emailed NED at the beginning of April 2010 that I would not be able to attend the Sixth General Assembly of the WMD owing to other important engagements. A representative from NED replied, saying, "I'm very sorry you won't be able to join us in Jakarta and look forward to catching up another time."

These emails were a ruse, a ploy to deceive the Chinese hackers and prevent China from learning my plans and plotting against me. After this, I communicated with NED solely by telephone and fax. They changed my flight ticket and faxed the new one. There were no direct flights from Germany to Indonesia, so I would stop in Amsterdam both ways, with no more risk of a stopover in Singapore. But the WMD still wanted to take extra precautions and decided someone should accompany me during the trip. In an exceptionally compassionate and impressive act, Mr. Gershman arranged for Louisa Greves to make a special trip from the United States to accompany me to and from Jakarta.

Louisa Greves arrived in Munich on April 9. She visited the WUC headquarters and had a short meeting with my staff before we flew to Amsterdam, where about twenty other travellers from Europe on their way to Jakarta for the WMD meeting were gathered at the airport. Some were my acquaintances, and many more knew Louisa. As we were all taking the same flight, we boarded together and headed to Jakarta.

However, instead of flying directly to Jakarta, we landed at the airport in Bangkok, apparently to fuel the plane, and were told that the passengers would have to get off while this happened. Becoming a little nervous because I had faced so many unexpected events in the past and Thailand was a neighbour to China and influenced greatly by it, I hoped my email ruse had worked.

We got off the plane and were seated in a hall to wait. While we passed the time drinking tea and coffee and talking, the incident in South Korea came up. When our fellow travellers learned that Louisa had come from the United States to accompany and protect me, everyone started looking out for my comfort and safety. One of our friends who had a business class seat even switched seats with me when we returned to the plane. That was the first time I ever sat in business class.

Before landing in Jakarta, we came up with a game plan. We prepared short texts to send the U.S. and German authorities and their embassies in Jakarta if I got stopped, collected the contact information of some influential international organizations and media agencies, and drafted messages to send to them. We also planned to stagger our places in line at passport control so two people would go before and after me, giving Customs officials the same story. Still, none of us knew what was waiting for us at Customs and if these precautions would work.

I grew increasingly anxious when the plane landed in Jakarta. In my travels within European countries, there were no passport checks. But whenever I travelled to a non-European country, I experienced anxiety as soon as the plane touched down. As I faced the most risk and hardship at passport controls, I was uneasy and worried about them, knowing that the Interpol Red Notice would appear there if it appeared anywhere. Passport controls reminded me of those awful days in Seoul, Washington, D.C., and Istanbul.

MY BORDER PROBLEMS ESCALATE

For that reason, the half-hour or hour at Customs always felt like an eternity for me. This time, I wasn't alone in my fear; my companions were also nervous, considering what had happened to me in South Korea just six months earlier. We didn't know much about Indonesia's laws and regulations, or their democratic system. If they faced pressure from China, would they dare to protect a fellow Muslim like me? Would they act as South Korea did? We didn't know. There was almost no Muslim country in the world that regarded the Uyghurs with brotherly love and loyalty.

We lined up at passport control. Although I was surrounded by my companions and counting every minute, I was still consumed with worry about being detained or turned over to the Chinese. The twenty minutes as I waited my turn felt like forever. Then the two companions ahead of me passed through and waited for me just around the counter as I handed my passport to the officer. I may have looked calm, but I was in a panic.

In the end, there was no issue, and my entry took just a few minutes. My passport was stamped, and I passed through successfully. As I turned the corner where my friends waited for me, we cheered with relief and excitement. Passersby looked at us with surprise. If my return trip had been as successful as this one, my Indonesian trip would not have been as memorable as it turned out to be.

The General Assembly opened on April 11 with a speech by Indonesian President Susilo Bambang Yudhoyono. Then former leaders of other countries, foreign ministers, and diplomats delivered their remarks. There were five hundred and fifty participants from more than one hundred countries, who in addition to the General Assembly, took part in workshops, debates, and discussion sessions.

I took this opportunity to organize an exhibit on Uyghurs and included documents, reports, and other materials to raise awareness of China's oppression. The exhibit attracted many people. I spoke with government officials and leaders of human rights organizations and had a particularly meaningful conversation with former Deputy Prime Minister of Malaysia Anwar Ibrahim. I felt this exhibit was successful in exposing China's heinous crimes against humanity.

We left Jakarta the day after the meeting ended, on April 15. Around fifty people from the meeting were taking the same plane with us. As we had all participated in the meeting together and already knew each other, there was a feeling that we were travelling together. They were all also stopping over in Amsterdam and leaving for their home countries from there. The energy was joyful and warm as we reminisced about the meeting. But two hours into the flight, panic ensued. I didn't hear the pilot's announcement at first as I was passionately talking with my companions, but it was serious: a volcano had erupted in Iceland, and as a result, European air travel was severely affected.

The plane made an emergency landing at Kuala Lumpur International Airport, joining the many other European flights that had already landed. Flights out of the airport were all suspended, so the airport was full of travellers. Everyone was waiting for news about when they could leave, and we were all powerless to do anything except wait. The volcano was still erupting, the news reported, and no one knew how long the situation would continue.

We decided as a group to stay at the airport hotel while we waited for news, but unfortunately, it was already full. Our next option was to go to a hotel in Kuala Lumpur, since, as no visa was required for European passport holders, we could all enter Malaysia easily. However, as I started to fill out the Customs form, a voice within me suddenly pleaded, "Don't go through this passport control, Dolkun!" Passing through passport controls was the most distressing and fearsome thing for me, and this just created new anxieties. "If China didn't know I was coming to Indonesia before, will they know now, when I leave?" I thought. Luckily,

MY BORDER PROBLEMS ESCALATE

I didn't have any issues leaving Indonesia. But the Interpol Red Notice could still show up as I passed through Malaysian Customs, and if it did, I would definitely have a problem.

In the past, Malaysia had extradited some Uyghur youths who had escaped from China, and China's influence in Malaysia was growing day by day. If I were detained at the airport and China learned of it, it was entirely possible Malaysia would hand me over to China. I knew I couldn't take such a great risk.

Deciding not to go into Kuala Lumpur, I tore up the form and told my friends I would be staying back at the airport. Louisa Greves and three other people from European countries also decided to stay back, since Malaysia required a visa for those holding refugee travel documents. Everyone else left for the city. I wanted Louisa to go with them as it there would be no place at the airport for her to sleep, but she insisted on staying. "I came from the United States to be responsible for your security. I have to accompany you until you safely reach Europe," she told me.

With nowhere to lie down or even sit in the crowded airport we found a quiet corner and spent the night sitting against the wall, napping on and off. The next day passed without any news, and we spent the time eating and drinking coffee at restaurants. Another day passed. The most difficult thing was sleeping seated against the wall at night, and I felt guilty that Louisa had to endure this hardship to protect me.

On the second day I went to an airport hotel and asked reception if they could at least find a room for the women among us. There was still no vacancy, but they promised to call if a vacancy opened up. Two hours later the call came: a double room was being vacated. We immediately booked it for Louisa and the other lady. Another room became vacant that night, so I took it and was finally able to shower and sleep on a bed after two days in the terminal.

On our fifth day in the airport, the news spread that air travel was going to be resuming shortly. Test flights were successful, and we received notice that if everything went well, we would be flying to Amsterdam the next day. We had landed on April 15 and would leave on April 20 after spending six long days at the Kuala Lumpur International Airport.

We arrived safely at the Amsterdam airport on April 21, although it was also crowded because of cancelled flights. We couldn't find tickets that day, but Louisa contacted NED and managed to get tickets for both of us for the same day. On April 22, I flew to Munich and Louisa left for Washington, D.C.

A year later, I learned that I made the right decision that day by choosing not to leave the airport in Kuala Lumpur. In August 2011, the Malaysian government extradited eight Uyghurs to China, and later it became even more dangerous for Uyghur refugees to enter the country. Although international organizations criticized the Malaysian government many times, another incident occurred in November 2017 when eleven Uyghur refugees escaped from a prison in Thailand and reached Malaysia after overcoming many difficulties. The WUC and other organizations sent two representatives to Malaysia to provide humanitarian aid and move the refugees to a temporary shelter. However, the Malaysian police soon caught the refugees, sending shockwaves throughout the Uyghur diaspora. Initially, the Malaysian government said it was going to deport the refugees to China. This generated backlash and criticism from the international media and many organizations; the United States and some European countries even sent warnings to the government. Shortly afterwards, in May 2018, there was a change in the Malaysian government, and Mahathir Mohamad became the country's new prime minister. His government rejected China's demands and announced it would not be extraditing the Uyghur refugees to China. In October 2018, the eleven Uyghurs left Malaysia and arrived in Turkey.

CHAPTER 4

UNDER CONSTANT PRESSURE

SAUDI ARABIA: SURVEILLANCE IN THE SACRED LAND

An invitation to attend the Mecca-based Muslim World League conference on anti-terrorism as a guest of honour in February 2015 led to another dilemma and an unsettling incident. Attending the conference would enable me to perform Hajj, one of the five pillars of Islam; a Muslim must perform Hajj (make a pilgrimage to Mecca) at least once in his or her lifetime if he or she is financially and physically capable. As a Muslim, I wanted to perform Hajj. However, I also had serious concerns over my safety in Saudi Arabia in light of my experience in South Korea. Also, since February wasn't the time of Hajj, I could only perform Umrah (which can be done at any time of the year). I decided to wait and think about it as the conference was still four months away.

According to the invitation this was going to be an international conference hosted by King Salman bin Abdulaziz and attended by high-level officials. As an Uyghur, I was a member of a little-known nation, and it was an honour to be recognized and invited to attend. This was also an invaluable opportunity to inform the Muslim world about the oppression being inflicted upon the Uyghur Muslims by China, a declared enemy of Islam. However, I had reason to hesitate. Saudi Arabia had been getting closer to China and it was also a country in which human rights weren't protected. Some of my fellow activists told me I should not miss such an opportunity; others advised against travelling to Saudi Arabia. I couldn't decide for some time.

Almost a month passed, and the Muslim World League was urging me to confirm my attendance. I finally replied that I would be coming and sent my passport to the Saudi Embassy in Berlin for the visa application. The embassy would conduct a background check on me, and if their security system was alerted to my Interpol Red Notice, they would definitely refuse my visa application, but the fact that King Salman was hosting the conference might improve my chances.

Obtaining a Saudi visa was rarely easy, given the numerous conditions and requirements. With the help of the Muslim World League, however, I received a code that I simply sent to the Saudi Embassy. They issued the visa in a week and returned my passport. I was surprised, however, to see myself described on the visa as "Vice-President of the World Uyghur Congress, Dolkun Isa." I had never seen anything like that before. I think no other country writes visitors' jobs on a visa.

Saudi-German relations were stable at the time. Nevertheless, I sent a photo of the visa to the German foreign ministry and asked for their advice. I told them that as a Muslim, I wanted to visit Mecca but still had to consider my security and was worried about a repeat of my trouble in South Korea and needed their advice. The ministry responded that they would advise me after contacting the German Embassy in Riyadh. It was the middle of December 2014.

The German foreign ministry sent a letter a few days later assuring me that since the conference was organized by the Saudi government, and I was invited as its guest, there would most likely not be any security issues for me. However, they also said there was no guarantee and I had to decide for myself. They advised me to contact the German Embassy in Riyadh in case there were any problems and asked to be informed of my final decision.

My friends in Saudi Arabia, whom I consulted as well, advised me to attend without hesitation, since I was a guest of the government. The Muslim World League had already sent a business class ticket that departed from Frankfurt on February 20 and returned on February 27 from Jeddah.

I took a train to Frankfurt on the morning of February 20 and boarded the flight for Saudi Arabia around 5:00 p.m. Maybe it was because I was going to the sacred land of Islam, but I was somehow excited. At the same time, my worries about Customs remained, preventing me from fully enjoying the comfort of business class. The plane landed in Jeddah around noon. The airport was bustling and overcrowded, making the Customs procedure even more uncomfortable.

It was difficult, coming from Germany, to adjust to procedures in the Arab world. The Customs officers were irresponsible, slow, and careless. They would chat while checking passports, sit and drink tea, forgetting about their job, and were extremely slow. There were only around five people ahead of me in line, but it took almost an hour for my turn. My persistent nervousness around the Interpol Red Notice didn't help matters.

When it was my turn, I handed my passport and the government invitation to the officer. The invitation proved its power. The Customs officer read it and suddenly his attitude changed; he began treating me with heightened respect. "Welcome, sir," he said, and completed the process in two or three minutes. I took a deep breath, relieved. My worries disappeared. Two people were waiting for me. "Welcome, Mr. Dolkun Isa," they said and took my bag as they escorted me to a car. We left for Mecca.

We were given a room at the Hilton Hotel next to the Masjid al-Haram, the great mosque of Mecca. The Kaaba was at our doorstep—we could see it from the hotel window. The people doing Tawaf could also be seen. Other Uyghurs had arrived for the conference: Nury Turkel from the United States, Abdusalam Alim from Australia, Muhammad Ali from Finland, Alishir Halilov from Kazakhstan, and Sirajidin Azizi from Saudi Arabia. Abdulsalam, a trained religious scholar, led me to perform Umrah. As he knew the history of Islam well, he explained the history and meaning behind every part of the ritual.

The conference began on February 22 with the Emir of Mecca delivering the opening remarks, followed by a congratulatory speech by the Saudi Minister of the Interior. More than five hundred people participated in the conference, including renowned Islamic scholars, government officials, and diplomats. We participated as the Uyghur delegation. Everything went according to plan, until the break.

As the Uyghur delegation were chatting among ourselves, a man approached, standing with us for a while before eventually leaving. He looked familiar, but I couldn't remember him. "Who is that man?" I asked Sirajidin Haji, who was sitting next to me. "That was Anwar. He left after seeing us." Now I remembered him. I actually knew him well but didn't immediately recognize him, as his appearance had changed a lot and I hadn't seen him in many years. He was from Aksu, the same city as me. He was also my wife's classmate for five years in Shanghai, where he studied Arabic. After graduating from university, he had found a job in the Chinese foreign ministry. He wasn't very involved in the Uyghur community in Beijing, but we still met from time to time at gatherings there.

Anwar was China's General Consul in Jeddah and was loyal to the Chinese government. I learned from the Uyghurs in Saudi Arabia that he wasn't a friend to them. As a Uyghur, to become a

Chinese diplomat he had to work for the CCP regime with the utmost loyalty and successfully pass its many tests. I had heard he was working in Saudi Arabia before. "Come on, Anwar. Why are you running away from us?" I thought of calling out to him. But as the Executive Chairman of the World Uyghur Congress, it wouldn't be right for me to speak to him. He would never be able to explain it to his boss and would lose the trust and credibility he had built over many years of loyalty to the CCP.

The conference continued. My Uyghur friend, Abdulahad Haji, who was a Saudi resident, bought me a SIM card that I used to make calls to arrange trips around the area. We wanted to take the opportunity of being in the cradle of Islam to visit the sacred sites. On the third day of the conference, Nury Turkel, Abdusalam Alim, Adil, and I travelled to Medina. Abdusalam taught us about the sacred sites between Mecca and Medina and about the life of the Prophet Mohammed (Peace Be Upon Him).

After we arrived in Medina, I started receiving SMS text messages in Arabic. I ignored them at first as I didn't understand Arabic. But then my phone and internet started cutting off. I showed the messages to Abdusalam so he could translate. "The telecommunications company says to contact them," he said. I decided to leave it for the day and deal with it later. The next day, when the company called, I handed the phone to Abdusalam. They talked for a while.

"Who is using this card? Who is he? The man who bought the card under his name has to contact us," the company said. I told Abdulahad Haji. We finished our visit to Medina that day and went to Jeddah, where Amin Abdul-Gafur, one of the wealthy Uyghur businessmen living in Saudi Arabia, had arranged a banquet for Uyghurs and other guests from abroad, and Uyghurs from Mecca and Medina. We met many people at this gathering and had the opportunity to discuss our work with them. But

Abdulahad Haji seemed to be in a bad mood, frowning and looking dejected. I asked him what was wrong.

"The telecommunications company was mad at me," he said. He told me they had asked him what kind of man he bought the SIM card for and why. There were lots of questions. The company told him they had been questioned by the state authorities.

I apologized to him for the trouble. After the banquet, we went back to Mecca. When I arrived at the Hilton Hotel, two men were waiting in front of the door to my room. I nodded and entered my room. It was 2:00 a.m. Why were they standing in front of my room at this hour?

Mecca was a bustling city at all hours. People moved throughout the city well past midnight. I couldn't sleep, and after 3:00 a.m. I went out to get a cup of tea, and when I opened the door, I saw that the two men were still in front of my room. Pretending not to notice them, I took the lift downstairs. They followed me as I got my tea and were watching me from afar as I went back upstairs to my room. They followed me again and resumed standing in front of the door, but never said a word. Were they watching me or protecting me? I didn't know. Anwar's approach to me in Mecca, my cellphone service being suspended, my friend's issue with the telecommunications company after buying me the SIM card, and now two men tailing me—it all seemed related.

When I left the room the next morning, the two men were still there. It was obvious the Saudi government had arranged for them to either watch or protect me. For the rest of the conference, they followed me wherever I went. It started getting annoying.

After making inquiries about the men through other channels. I learned that the Chinese government had protested my attendance at the conference to the Saudi government, saying, "You've invited a terrorist who is on Interpol's's Red Notices to a conference on anti-terrorism." The Saudi security authorities had therefore arranged for the two men to follow me but apparently to protect rather than watch me. I learned later that, years earlier, an Iranian scientist who had gone to Saudi Arabia for Hajj had disappeared, one of several such incidents.

I discussed it with Nury Turkel and other friends. I was a German citizen invited to the conference as a guest of honour by the government; if anything happened to me, the Saudi government would be held accountable. Maybe that's why they had to protect me. Or maybe the Saudi government arranged for the men to keep sight of me in case it had secretly agreed to extradite me to China. Whatever it was, I felt the surveillance was becoming a threat to me. Nury Turkel and I emailed the German foreign ministry to tell them what was happening.

The ministry replied soon after that they had contacted the German Embassy in Riyadh and the General Consulate in Jeddah and were reassured that nothing worrisome would happen to me. Regardless, I was told to stay vigilant and contact the German General Consulate in case of emergency. Although the reply calmed me down a bit, I remained nervous. The two men were following me everywhere. If the Saudi government had made a secret agreement with China, I couldn't hope to come out of this situation alive. In Saudi Arabia, it wasn't law but the words of the King, emirs, and princes that held power. If they were pressured or if an arrangement or deal was in their interest, the life of someone like me wouldn't matter much. If they wanted to take me away with a black bag over my head, no one would question it. It was a time when even Uyghurs who had been living in Saudi Arabia for many years were facing the consequences of Chinese pressure. In this context, the surveillance was a bad omen.

I lived with this constant stress from February 24 to the 26th, when I received a message from the conference organizers asking me to be ready at 5:00 the following morning to be dropped off at the airport to leave Saudi Arabia. I was instantly suspicious. "What if they take me somewhere else instead of the airport?" I contacted the German General Consulate in Jeddah right away, which agreed to send someone to accompany me until the plane took off. Still nervous, I asked my friend Muhammad Ali Haji, who had come from Finland, to accompany me to the airport. If anything happened, I thought, at least someone trustworthy would be there to witness it and know where I had gone. He agreed to come along. On the morning of February 27, we set out for the airport in the car arranged by the Muslim World League. Still suspicious, I worried, "What if this car is heading somewhere other than the airport?" I was relieved when we reached the airport and notified the German General Consulate that I had arrived. They told me they were also at the airport and would be watching until I passed through Customs and my plane took off safely. This was certainly comforting.

The only remaining obstacle now was clearing passport control. Having passed safely through Customs when I entered Saudi Arabia didn't guarantee my safe exit. The Chinese government didn't know I was coming to Saudi Arabia for the conference, or they surely would have pressured the Saudi government to prevent my participation or prepared a plot to arrest me at Customs. They only discovered I was at the conference when Anwar saw me in Mecca, which explained why they protested to the Saudi Foreign Authority on February 23. If pressure from the Chinese regime had worked on the Saudi government, I could be in danger passing through Customs on my way out of the country.

To my relief, however, I made it through the Saudi Customs without incident, and my fears that a police officer would tap me on the shoulder and say "Mr. Dolkun, please come with us, we have something to ask you" disappeared. I let the German General Consulate know that I was waiting for my flight. They simply asked me to message them after boarding, which I did. They still wished to be notified of my safe arrival, so, after landing safely in Frankfurt, I sent a message thanking them for their care of me on this and previous trips. If Saudi-German relations hadn't been better than Saudi-Chinese relations and had I not been the guest of honour of the Saudi government, things could have been different.

PREDICAMENT IN NORTHERN CYPRUS

From the end of 2016, communicating with and getting information and news from our homeland became exceedingly difficult. The reports we did receive were spectacularly alarming, and the world didn't seem to be reacting to what was happening in East Turkistan. As an active advocacy group for the Uyghurs in the diaspora, it was the WUC's duty to find a way to fight against the Chinese oppression that was increasing daily. After discussions with Dr. Erkin Ekrem, the head of the WUC research centre, we decided to call a conference for Uyghur elites and activists to study the current world situation and the Uyghur crisis. But deciding where to hold the conference was a challenge. There were important people in Turkey and Central Asia whose participation we wanted, but if we held the conference in Europe or the United States, it would take a long time for them to get visas. Turkey was likely the best option, but I was banned from entering the country.

We eventually decided to hold the conference in the Turkish Republic of Northern Cyprus. No one attending the conference would requir a visa to enter Northern Cyprus. The country wasn't recognized in the UN—or by any countries except Turkey—and had no diplomatic relations with China. And I had been to this island state for a vacation before with my family.

After quick preparations, we sent out invitations for the conference, which we called the first "East Turkistan Strategic Discussion meeting," to be held February 25 to 27, 2017 in Northern Cyprus. The WUC's assistant secretary-general, Dr.

Erkin Emet, was responsible for arranging the conference hall and hotel stays.

Nineteen people were invited, from Germany, the United Kingdom, Norway, Switzerland, Sweden, Turkey, Saudi Arabia, Kazakhstan, Australia, Japan, Canada, and the United States. Everyone asked for a leave from their workplaces, purchased flight tickets, and made preparations for the trip.

Three days before the conference, however, we ran into a roadblock. Dr. Erkin Emet, working with a company called Puzzle Travel, had signed a contract with the Acapulco Hotel, located by the beach in the city of Kyrenia. On February 21, Puzzle Travel notified him that the contract had been cancelled. When we asked why, they claimed their contract with the hotel had expired. Puzzle Travel refused to help us find another hotel and said they would refund our money. After that, they cut off communications with us. We realized politics must have been involved in this.

I was participating in the Geneva Summit when I heard the news. This issue with the hotel arrangements in Northern Cyprus made me nervous. As I had to be in Northern Cyprus by February 24, I wrapped up my work in Geneva early and decided to leave on February 22 to help sort things out, but there was no direct flight. I had to either stop over in Turkey or fly to the Republic of Cyprus and travel from there to Northern Cyprus by car.

I chose to stop over in Istanbul, and left Geneva on the morning of February 22. I waited in the Istanbul airport for more than three hours and arrived in Northern Cyprus that evening. Several friends from Germany and Turkey, Ascar Can, Abduljelil Turan, and Dr. Erkin Emet, had arrived the day before to try and arrange a hotel.

Since February was considered the off-season for tourism, hotels in Northern Cyprus were mostly empty, but we couldn't find one to host us. We tried the Acapulco Hotel first, but apparently they they didn't have any vacancies, leading us to believe they were pressured not to book with us. On February 23, after meeting with several hotels, we finally booked a hotel called the Lord's Palace.

On February 24. I was going over the conference agenda in my room after breakfast when Dr. Erkin Emet called and asked me to come downstairs. I saw three people in regular clothes standing at reception. Dr. Emet was explaining something to them. After greeting us coldly, they asked,

"Who are you? Where did you come from?"

"I'm Dolkun Isa. I came from Germany."

"We're from the police station. We've received a complaint against you guys. You need to come back with us to the station," one of them said.

"What complaint?" I asked, surprised.

"We'll talk at the police station," he said.

We realized they meant business and that we had no choice but to go with them. As we were about to leave, an important-looking man accompanied by hotel security appeared. He approached me, smiling, and shook my hand.

"I'm Mustafa, the under-secretary of the Northern Cyprus Foreign Affairs Ministry. Are you Dr. Erkin Ekrem?" he asked.

"No, Dr. Ekrem hasn't arrived yet. I'm Dolkun Isa."

"That's good. Please come with us, let us talk," Mr. Mustafa said. He told the police to wait outside as he wanted to speak with me. Then he led me to a sofa near reception. Dr. Erkin Emet sat with us, too. We talked for about forty minutes. Mr. Mustafa began:

"We've received a complaint that a group of terrorists [has] gathered in Northern Cyprus to call a conference. You may know, the Turkish Republic of Northern Cyprus is under embargo from the UN and other countries. We're a fragile state, [and] we have enough problems. We don't want any power to bring another headache for us. With these complaints, you can't hold the General Assembly in Northern Cyprus. Our government won't allow this."

"Mr. Mustafa, we don't know who made this complaint. No country except China and its supporters view us as terrorists," I explained, and went on:

"Our organization, the WUC, was founded in Germany and is a legal entity. We organize activities in and work with EU countries, the United States, the UN and the European parliament. We fight against Chinese oppression in East Turkistan, which is just like the Turkish Republic of Northern Cyprus. It also doesn't have representation in the UN and is a country under occupation. Uyghurs share a long relationship with the Turkish Republic of Northern Cyprus and hold a special love for it. The founder and President of the Turkish Republic of Northern Cyprus Rauf Denktaş and the Uyghur leader Isa Yusuf Alptekin were close friends. In the 1980s, Rauf Denktaş extended his friendship to Alptekin and helped many Uyghur and Kazakh students who came to Turkey to study in Northern Cyprus. Maybe for this reason the Uyghur people love Northern Cyprus; they wouldn't want to do anything to bring trouble to it.

"Now please ask us about the credentials of the people who have come for this meeting. Some of them are university professors in Turkish universities, while others are intellectuals and researchers who engage in political activism in Western countries. Some are journalists working in the media. Each of them are well respected in their own countries. No one here has any links to terrorism. Our gathering here is to discuss the future of our homeland and might also help raise Northern Cyprus's global profile. These people come from twelve countries in Asia, Europe, North America, and Oceania. You have received a mistaken complaint."

My phone rang while I was talking. Ilham Mahmut from Japan and Hidayatullah Oğuzhan from Istanbul had been stopped at Customs in Northern Cyprus. The border officers wanted to send them back.

"Mr. Mustafa," I continued, "Our people, who flew eleven to twelve hours to come to Northern Cyprus from Australia, Japan, the United States, and Canada, have been stopped at Customs. Our friends from Australia flew more than twenty-five hours. If these people are sent back to their countries, this incident will reach the international media. Do you think that would be good for Northern Cyprus's image?"

That made Mr. Mustafa nervous and after thinking for a while, said,

"I personally don't believe you're terrorists. But we can't ignore the news from Ankara. The decision of the Northern Cyprus government is clear. You aren't allowed to call a conference here, but you can take a tour, and then leave. If you agree, I will tell Customs to allow those who've been detained to enter the country."

Not having any other option, we agreed. Mr. Mustafa told us to contact him if we needed anything, and then left. But we still had to go to the police station. "Our orders are to talk to you," they told us. At the station, we told the police the same thing we told Mr. Mustafa. The police officers who had been cold to us at the hotel warmed at our sentiments.

The people who were stopped at Customs were allowed to enter the country, but they had a difficult time for five or six hours before being allowed in. Still, everyone arrived in Kyrenia on the evening of February 24. Now the question was how and where we could hold our conference meetings. Even though we had promised Mr. Mustafa, the conference was too important to take a tour and leave. And we were furious at the people who had made the complaint against us.

On the morning of February 25, we considered starting our meeting at the dining table over breakfast at the Lord's Palace. But the police officers were there and listening to us closely, and we didn't want to cause any friction with them. After breakfast, we went to the terrace and started our meeting, pretending we were having a regular conversation. Two police officers watched us from five metres away.

Almost an hour later, the police gave us a warning. "If you want to take a tour, we'll call a car for you." We decided to continue our meeting outside in a park or a restaurant and asked the police to call us a small bus that could accommodate twenty people. A minibus arrived shortly after. We took the bus and left Kyrenia for the capital, Nicosia. The police officers followed us in their car.

We continued our meeting on the minibus. When we arrived in Nicosia, we visited a historic site and then went to a park and sat at some tables at a teahouse. We continued our meeting pretending we were having tea while the police watched us from ten metres away. Although they knew what we were doing, they didn't want to interrupt us. In this secretive way we were able to complete our agenda for February 25 and returned to the Lord's Palace in the evening.

Holding our meetings on February 26 was a more challenging affair. As on the previous day , the police arrived at the hotel in the morning and waited for us in the cafeteria. While we were having breakfast, they approached to ask where we wanted to visit that day. "Let us tell you after we think about it for a little while," we said. After some discussion we agreed to hold that day's meetings on a ship in the White Sea. We thought we would be better able to escape police notice on a ship. But as it was winter, there was no sea tour. We told the police that we wanted to go anyway, and they contacted some companies to arrange a small ship.

The weather was clear that day but the cold sea air was torturous. Our tour shocked the locals. People at the beach looked at us like we were crazy. "How come they're going on a sea tour in the winter?" they must have thought. Over the roar of the ship's engine, we held our meetings and finished our agenda for that day.

Our meetings on February 27 continued in parks and restaurants and concluded our conference. A full three-day conference had evaded the notice of the government of Northern Cyprus. To prepare a roadmap for the future of East Turkistan, we discussed many topics: the changing world order, the situation of the Uyghurs and China, the positive and negative impact of current political conditions on the Uyghurs, how we could deal with the consequences of such impacts, and China's present and future. As a result of these discussions, we adopted a fourteen-clause resolution on the last day of the conference.

In July 2017, I received an invitation from Italian Senator Luigi Compagna. Working with the Nonviolent Radical Party, he was organizing a press conference in the Italian Senate to introduce the Uyghur crisis and asked me to participate. I was a member of the Nonviolent Radical Party, and good friends with its leader, Marco Panilla. Although he died in May 2016, Marco Panilla was a strong supporter of the Uyghur movement during his lifetime and organized many conferences about the Uyghurs and Tibetans in Italy and the European parliament. After my friend's death, my relationship with the party continued, and I happily accepted Senator Compagna's invitation.

The press conference was scheduled for July 26. I arrived in Rome on July 25 and checked into my hotel. The next morning, I visited the headquarters of the Nonviolent Radical Party, met the Party leader Mr. Maurizio Turco, and its representative at the UN, Ms. Laura Hart. Then at 10:30 a.m., we left together by foot for the Senate building. When we arrived ten minutes later, a group of twenty or so people were gathered at the entrance. I thought they were journalists, until they approached us.

"Are you Mr. Isa?" a man among them asked me in English.

"Yes, I am," I said.

"We're national security agents," he said, flashing his identification. "Can we check your ID, please?" I handed over my ID.

"Please come with us, we need to conduct a brief investigation," he said.

"What investigation?" I asked, displeased.

"We're doing our job, please cooperate. Come with us. We will bring you back here in half an hour."

"The press conference is starting at 11:00 a.m. You can do it after the conference," I said.

"We know, but you need to come now. If you don't cooperate, we will need to force you," he said firmly.

Mr. Turco spoke with the agents for a long time, but even the party leader's disapproval didn't work. The agents took me to their car, where I contacted the German foreign ministry and informed them what had happened.

We drove to a magnificent building, built in the Roman style, where I was taken inside to an office and told to wait. Although I asked the police officer who stayed back with me why I had been brought in for investigation, he said he couldn't answer, that he was just doing his job. Then we talked about other things. Police officers checked in every now and then. "Do you have any other name? Any other citizenship? Have you ever committed a crime? When did you move to Germany?" they asked, delivering me tea and coffee between questions. They were kind to me, but I was still uncomfortable and irritated with the trivial questions. I didn't know why I was being detained, but I suspected it had to do with the Interpol Red Notice. There could be no other reason.

After three hours, several police officers came in and took me to another department to take my fingerprints and picture.

UNDER CONSTANT PRESSURE

They were not harsh, but I was being treated like a criminal, just like in 2005 when I was detained in Geneva. I was escorted back to the same office and told to wait for a while and that I would be released soon.

Later, I learned that the German Embassy in Rome told the Italian authorities the Interpol Red Notice was a mistake and Germany didn't recognize it. The embassy demanded I be released immediately.

I was released after four hours. There was no point going back to the press conference as it had already ended. I had to fly back to Munich in three hours.

"Let us drop you at the airport," the police said.

"I can go myself, but thank you for your generosity," I replied.

"Then let us drop you at the Nonviolent Radical Party's office."

"No, I will go myself."

They insisted. I didn't understand their obstinacy, but I couldn't refuse their demand, as news of my detention had spread quickly to the media, .and journalists were waiting in front of the police station. I agreed to be dropped at the Nonviolent Radical Party's office. We left the building through the back door and got in their car. They drove off only after I entered the party building.

Not finding Mr. Turco and Laura at the office, I asked the secretary where they had gone. "What are you doing here?" the secretary asked in surprise. "They're waiting for you in front of the police station." On learning of my release, however, they came back from the police station to meet me. Senator Compagna was with them. At the press conference we held at the party headquarters, Senator Compagna criticized the Italian government, saying, "Italy bowed to China." The press conference at the Senate had been cancelled due to my detainment, and he blamed the Italian police. Italy hadn't yet signed the Belt & Road Initiative (BRI), a massive Chinese infrastructure project, but China's influence in Italy was quite strong, and Italy became the first EU nation to sign the BRI in 2019.

After the press conference, Senator Compagna said, "Mr. Isa, an inappropriate incident has happened in Italy. We all apologize. I kindly ask that you stay for one more day. I will be organizing a program at the Senate, and I hope you will leave after you attend it."

"That sounds great, I just hope I won't be detained again tomorrow," I joked.

"Nothing like this will ever happen again in Italy," he said in a firm voice.

So, I cancelled my flight to Munich to attend the program at the Italian Senate and planned to meet them in front of the Senate building in the morning before leaving for the hotel.

On the morning of July 27, when I arrived at the Senate building with Ms. Laura, Senator Compagna was waiting, looking pale and uncomfortable. I assumed there was trouble.

I was right. The Chinese government had protested my being admitted to the Italian Senate. "If Italy allows a terrorist like Dolkun Isa—who is on the Interpol Red Notices—to enter its Senate and speak, it will affect our diplomatic relationship, and we will remove our embassy from Italy," China warned. In the last decade, China's habit of threatening to cut economic and diplomatic ties had become an effective means of coercion in many countries—even European countries like Italy.

We held a press conference in front of the Senate building and criticized the Italian government for my ban from the Senate, saying that this action went against principles of human rights, democracy, and the rule of law.

Senator Compagna didn't forget the incident. On August 1, in the 870th meeting of the Italian Senate, Mr. Compagna delivered a written statement demanding an explanation from the Italian interior and foreign ministers. He also demanded to know who ordered my detention by the police for three hours; the legal basis for detaining me, a German citizen, while Italy was a member of the European Security Council; and if there were secret agreements between China and Italy.

My ban from the Italian Senate at the behest of China, and my detention by the Italian National Security agents became hot topics in the Italian media for a few weeks. I believe I wouldn't have received such coverage or made such an impact had I spoken at the Senate. But this way, many Italians learned about the Uyghurs and, more importantly, the Italian government realized their vulnerability to Chinese pressure.

Italy is known around the world as a pioneer in the textile industry. However, more than 70 per cent of the Italian textile industry has been bought up by Chinese companies. Although the products say, "Made in Italy," the manufacturers are Chinese companies, businessmen, and workers brought into Italy by those companies.

In 2020, when the COVID-19 pandemic spread from the Chinese city of Wuhan throughout the world, Italy became an early hotbed, and the European nation most affected by the first wave of the virus. Although there are different views about this, it is clear that one of the most important reasons for Italy's vulnerability was that 100,000 Chinese people went to Italy in February after the Chinese New Year. Many of them were infected with COVID-19, and they brought the virus to Italy.

COVID-19 awakened the Italian government as well as the people to the pitfalls of their ties to China, and public opinion reflected that discontentment. But as the virus spread to the rest of the world, becoming a global pandemic and causing infection and death in other countries, we witnessed the Italian government and people gradually forget their anger and discontent with China. Nevertheless, there is a growing debate among Italian politicians concerning China's threat to the world and Europe's democratic values.

In the years since being detained and interrogated by the Italian police, I've witnessed many changes in Italy and around the world. In July 2020, for example, I was invited to testify at the Italian Senate, and in October, I delivered a testimony at the Italian parliament at the invitation of its Foreign Relations Committee. Both testimonies were given online due to the COVID-19 pandemic.

On February 13, 2023, I was again invited to the Italian Senate, this time by Senator Giulio Terzi, the former Italian Foreign Minister and UN ambassador to New York for my book launch in Italian. Six years after I was arrested and detained by Italian police, I was back in Rome and successfully entered the Senate and presented my book. That was a proud moment.

CHAPTER 5

INSIDE INTERPOL

In China, giving and receiving bribes is a way of life. Even if you are a talented, educated, and distinguished person, you can't get a desirable job in China without participating in this practice. Bribery is everywhere in China. Like a plague, it has become part of the moral decay of Chinese society.

The CCP uses this immoral weapon widely in foreign policy. It's impossible to count how many people China has bribed in international bodies such as the United Nations, the World Health Organization, the European parliament, the Organisation of Islamic Cooperation, Interpol, the ruling elites of various governments, and high-powered officials in finance and technology. Decidedly, we can say there have been many. A member of the European parliament once told me, 'The Chinese diplomats are so shameless." He went on:

"They might have heard that we're helping the Uyghurs. Staff of the Chinese Embassy in Belgium asked to meet us many times. We wanted to know what their intentions were, so we finally agreed to meet. 'Let's become friends,' they said. I said, 'We're already friends.' They said they wanted to become closer. I said, 'Why not?' Then, they wanted to give me a Huawei mobile phone. I asked why they wanted to give me a phone. They said it was for our friendship. 'Friendship isn't built on gifts,' I told them. 'This is a small gift. If we become better friends, we'll give you extraordinary gifts in the future,' they said. Sensing more nefarious ends, I refused it."

This member of the European parliament refused the Chinese bribe. But how many others have not refused? What about in other European countries and the United States? We have no way of knowing.

Over the past two decades, China has practised "investment" politics in Africa, Central Asia, and South Asia and, to some extent, has successfully carried out an economic invasion of those countries. In this way, over the years they have created a collection of loyal vassal states. They have used similar principles to expand China's influence in the UN and other international organizations through financial aid and bribing important people with money and gifts.

China's influence in Interpol is one such problematic alliance. I knew of its consequences most personally and became determined to remove my name from Interpol's list of Red Notices as soon as possible. I had long conversations with my lawyer, Dr. Albrecht Göring, who agreed to help find a way and wrote letters to Interpol. But the letters were costly, and I couldn't afford to pay for them for long. I also contacted the German authorities, and they made efforts to help. Nonetheless, China's deep influence in Interpol prevented us from finding a solution, and after two years of trying, I finally gave up.

As time went on, it became obvious to the international community that Interpol was being exploited by China, altering its public image. Criticism of Interpol grew even stronger when it started processing arrest warrants for totalitarian countries and threatening their dissidents—even those who had become citizens of European countries. In 2016, German Chancellor Angela Merkel voiced her disappointment with Interpol and called for its reform. Various statements and articles criticizing Interpol were published. According to an investigation carried out by the International Consortium of Investigative Journalists (ICIJ), more than twenty countries were exploiting Interpol to go after political activists.[22]

My advocacy work sometimes required me to travel to Asian counties, as I received invitations to conferences from international organizations based in India, Japan, and Taiwan. But the Interpol Red Notice always inhibited my travels, and Japan became the only Asian country to which I was able to travel. When we held a conference in Japan in May 2012, I called the Japanese Consulate in Munich asking them if it was safe for me to go, recounting for them what happened in South Korea. "Japan isn't South Korea; you can travel here with peace of mind," they told me.

I had previously travelled to Japan in 2008 to attend a hearing in the Japanese parliament on human rights atrocities in East Turkistan. While there I met former Prime Minister Shinzo Abe, and some members of the Japanese parliament approached me about a visit that Chinese President Hu Jintao would be making to Japan a few days later. "Shinzo Abe is meeting Hu Jintao. He intends to mention the Uyghur crisis. Which specific issues do you think he should mention?" they asked. I outlined five issues, including the case of Uyghur historian Toxti Tuniyaz, who had studied in Japan and was arrested in Beijing upon his return to China.

The WUC's Fourth General Assembly in May 2012 in Japan had angered China immensely. China harshly condemned Japan, and the Chinese newspaper, *The People's Daily*, published an editorial criticizing Japan and calling out Rebiya Kadeer and myself. This had some impact on China-Japan bilateral relations.

Nonetheless, Japan didn't really care, and high-level Japanese politicians continued to publicly sympathize with the Uyghur crisis. Unfortunately, the same couldn't be said for India.

In April 2016, democracy activists from Tibet, East Turkistan, South Mongolia, Taiwan, and China planned to hold a conference in the Indian city of Dharamshala. Omer Kanat, Ilshat Hassan, and I received invitations, and I applied for an electronic visa, which was approved. Having learned my lesson, I thought I had better confirm with the Indian government in advance to ensure I wouldn't have any issues at Customs. I wrote a letter to the Indian Embassy in Germany asking the usual questions: "Can I enter India without any problems? Can you guarantee my safety?" I asked. Before I received a reply from the embassy, Indian newspapers learned I was coming to India and started calling me to ask if I was coming to India. "I'm thinking about it," I told them.

During this time, at a press conference, the Chinese foreign ministry spokesperson announced that "Dolkun is a terrorist on the Interpol Red Notices. We object to India issuing a visa to him. He should be banned from visiting India." As a result, the Indian Consulate in Germany sent me a letter revoking my visa. This became another hot topic in the media, and journalists called me for the next few weeks.

I made a statement to protest China's hegemony and voice my disappointment at India's lack of courage. I said I was profoundly disappointed in India, the largest democracy in the world, and a humanitarian country that had been supporting Tibet's case for sixty years. I wrote that it was a shame that a democratic and rule-of-law country like India had bowed to China's pressure and in so doing, tainted its image. This incident made headlines in Indian as well as Western media outlets like the *New York Times*.

Most importantly, the role my Interpol Red Notice played in the incident attracted the attention of international organizations that had become critical of Interpol. They began coming to me asking for materials and information about the organization. It looked like they were building a case.

REGAINING FREEDOM: MY RED NOTICE LIFTED

From the day I learned that I had been issued an Interpol Red Notice at the U.S. Consulate in Frankfurt in 1999 until my detainment in Italy and expulsion from the UN in 2017, everything that happened to me, all the misfortunes that befell me overseas, were because of the Red Notice. After many failed attempts to try and clear my name over the years, I had given up hope. There was no one to say "Dolkun, this is an injustice. China is persecuting you, Interpol is persecuting you; let us help you resolve this issue," and offer me a helping hand.

When the Chinese foreign ministry spokesperson used the Red Notice to protest my visit to India, he said "Dolkun Isa is a terrorist wanted under the Red Notices of Interpol and by the Chinese police. He should be brought to justice." These words captured the attention of human rights organizations that were becoming disgruntled with Interpol's injustices. Fair Trials International, a London-based criminal justice watchdog, was one of them.

This was the organization's second time contacting me. In April 2012, two years after I was deported from South Korea, an expert from Fair Trials, Alex Tinsley, contacted me to say he had become interested in my case after learning about me in the media. We had some calls and exchanged emails. But for some reason, we fell out of touch. Then suddenly, on April 29, 2016, I received an email from Fair Trials. The email said:

> Mr. Dolkun, we contacted you before and unfortunately, we weren't able to help you then. Now we've learned that you have been prevented from traveling

to India for the same reason. We believe now is the right time to work with you to resolve your issue. Although Interpol still has issues with its system, particularly with regards to arrest warrants initiated for political reasons, it has undergone reforms in recent years. We submitted a request to Interpol to conduct further reforms and to remove everyone who has been granted refugee status from its Red Notices. Regarding your case, the Commission for Control of Interpol's Files may review it and change their decision.

This was good news for me. "There are people who care about me," I thought. But I was still cautious in my optimism. It was possible the outcome would be the same even after a review. Nevertheless, I had to take this opportunity seriously. I had a full-day meeting with Fair Trials on Skype. They asked about my life story, and I told them all about my activism during my university days and after leaving China and that the Chinese government had submitted a case against me to , calling me a "robber and murderer," and in 2003 added that I was "a terrorist who had been involved in an explosion," further intensifying my case.

Fair Trials is an organization that aims to fight injustice and abuse of law around the world. One of its important areas of focus is to monitor Interpol and reform its constitution. After watching the organization closely, Fair Trials was becoming increasingly critical of the injustices committed by Interpol and was preparing an investigative report on it.

After I spoke to and exchanged documents with Fair Trials' legal and policy officer, Mr. Bruno Min, I became more optimistic and told them I was ready to work with them anytime. They sent me documents about Fair Trials and its projects and a contract authorizing them to represent me. I signed it and sent it back, and

Fair Trials began looking for ways to remove me from Interpol's Red Notices.

I didn't know much about how Interpol worked. To my understanding, when an individual or group committed a crime and fled to another country, the original country would ask Interpol to issue a Red Notice alerting other countries that this person was a fugitive. Interpol would investigate and decide whether to issue the Red Notice. Then, if it was approved, they would announce the Notice to the world, and all member countries would have an obligation to arrest the fugitive(s).

However, it wasn't like that. I later learned that Interpol didn't have a system or set of principles to investigate claims against individuals and organizations. Totalitarian states that wanted to eliminate dissidents or people who might be a risk to them could easily fabricate false crimes and submit them to Interpol, which would act upon the request without conducting an independent investigation. This was the true Interpol.

Of course, when the Chinese government finds such loopholes in international organizations, it tends to take advantage. If there is a small hole, they pick at it until it becomes big, then pick at it even more until the organization decays and its structure becomes totally meaningless. Maybe this was the secret to China's ability to exploit Interpol and manipulate its Red Notices with such ease.

Interpol's lack of a procedure to investigate and verify claims before accepting them made them complicit in injustices. Not just China, but also Russia, Iran, and Pakistan have all abused Interpol and exploited Red Notices as a tool to suppress their dissidents. In reaction to this, many countries, especially democratic ones, began ignoring Interpol Red Notices and making decisions about listed individuals and groups based on their own laws and the behaviour of the listed individuals in their countries. The tide against Interpol became stronger as international organizations witnessed many cases of Interpol Red Notices jeopardizing the lives and freedom of activists against totalitarian regimes.

In July 2011, CNN reporter Libby Lewis conducted an investigation that found twelve countries, including China, Russia, and Pakistan, had used Interpol Red Notices to suppress dissidents. The report included my name along with other "big" names such as the former prime minister of Pakistan Benazir Bhutto, the former prime minister of Kazakhstan Akechan Kazhegeldin, an Iranian dissident leader, and the owner of the Los Angeles-based TV program "Channel One," Shahram Homayoun.[23] Many other media outlets and human rights organizations published similar reports about Interpol, and many of them mentioned my case.

After several months of investigation, research, and collection of materials, Fair Trials submitted a request to the Commission for the Control of Interpol's Files (CCF) in Beijing on January 11, 2017, formally asking them to review my case and remove my Red Notice. I received Interpol's answer through Fair Trials on October 19, 2017. The CCF had investigated my case and contacted Interpol's office in Beijing—the National Central Bureau (NCB)—for their opinion, but it rejected the request. Beijing had been the one to request the Red Notice initially, so why would they agree to remove it?

Thus, the first attempt had failed. Although it was Interpol's obligation to respect other countries' legal integrity, I concluded that if Interpol had to get China's approval to remove my Red Notice, there was no way it would happen. But Fair Trials proposed to look for other ways and make a new request after collecting more evidence.

On August 19, 2017, during a vacation in Spain, Spanish police arrested Doğan Akhanlı, a German author of Turkish origin who had been issued a Red Notice at the request of the Turkish authorities. His arrest caused a political crisis involving Germany, Spain, and Turkey. Turkey demanded that the Spanish authorities extradite Doğan Akhanlı to Turkey. Germany called for Spain to immediately release Mr. Akhanlı and send him to Germany. After long discussions, a ruling from the Spanish court, and even the intervention of Chancellor Merkel, Doğan Akhanlı was released to Germany in October 2017.

His arrest and my own (in Italy) in July, as well as the arrests of two German citizens in EU countries, both a result of Interpol Red Notices, became a hot topic in the German press and among politicians.

Angela Merkel was adamant in her August 2017 declaration that Interpol had to be reformed, shining a spotlight on criticism of Interpol on the world stage. With the support of countries like Germany and calls from international organizations, Interpol's constitution of was amended, and some clauses were changed. One new clause said, "the processing of Red Notices and Diffusions are [sic] not allowed if a person sought asylum in a country and his/her asylum was accepted."

This clause was relevant to me and others like me. It wasn't that simple, though. Western countries didn't accept asylum claims easily: an asylum seeker was required to meet many conditions. Then, there was a verification process, where the situation and condition of the asylum seeker's country of origin was thoroughly researched. However, a claimant who had completed this process and had their asylum claim accepted could live peacefully and with their political rights guaranteed. When a country thus confirms someone's right to life, this should include their safety from any harm by Interpol.

Unfortunately, this clause no longer applied to me. I had already become a German citizen when it was put into effect. I wasn't an asylum seeker anymore, but a citizen of a country.

What now?

I wondered if there was a way of reframing my case. When the Chinese regime first issued their arrest warrant against me,

I wasn't a German citizen, but a person whose asylum had been accepted. Could we make this argument to Interpol?

I discussed it with Fair Trials. They asked me to translate from German to English and notarize all the documents I had used for my asylum application. I provided everything they asked for and also sent them the statement I had made in 2003 refuting the Chinese government's first use of Interpol to label me a terrorist. I also sent Dr. Albrecht Göring's correspondence with Interpol on my behalf after I was deported from South Korea in 2009. There were a lot of documents. With them, Fair Trials submitted a new request to Interpol in January 2018. At the time, however, we didn't realize how deeply China had infiltrated the organization.

While Fair Trials was working on my application, criticism of Interpol by the German government was gaining momentum, drawing attention to my case at the federal level.

In 2016, Frank Hartmann became Angela Merkel's Director of Bilateral Relations with the states of the Middle East, Africa, Asia, and Latin America. I had first met him in 2014 when he was the director of the Department of the Asia Pacific Region at the German foreign ministry; the cancellation of my Indian visa and the statement of the Chinese foreign ministry had attracted the attention of the German government, but especially Mr. Hartmann. From our first meeting, we developed a sincere and close relationship. We met several times regarding my issue with Interpol.

The German Chancellery Office, foreign ministry, and federal police worked together to fight my Interpol Red Notice. Mr. Hartmann was at the centre of this fight and kept in constant communication with me throughout. He believed from the bottom of his heart that I was a victim of a totalitarian regime and a man struggling to be a voice for his voiceless people. He did his utmost to end this injustice as quickly as possible.

INSIDE INTERPOL

Mr. Hartmann invited me to Berlin on August 2, 2017. We met at the Chancellery building. At his suggestion, we turned off our cellphones and left them in another office. Then he turned to me and said, "Have you ever seen your Interpol Red Notice?"

"I didn't see it properly. When I was first detained in Frankfurt in 1999, the police showed it to me quickly, but I don't know what is written in it," I said. He then put the Red Notice in front of me and for the first time I read it in detail.

After our meeting, I learned that the German authorities were acting to remove the Notice, but it was a complex process and wasn't something that could be done quickly. There were other avenues to resolve this issue. I could hire an international law firm and work with a group of lawyers. We discussed this option, but it would take more lawyers to work on such a large case, and would cost between 50,000 and 100,000 euros. I could not afford this luxury.

Mr. Hartmann told me he would do his best but couldn't guarantee an outcome. The German government was working to remove two men from Interpol's Red Notices. I was one; he didn't tell me about the other man. In the meantime, while waiting for a decision from Interpol, they were trying to get the German federal police to issue a letter saying, "The Interpol Red Notice on Dolkun Isa is deemed baseless by Germany and Dolkun Isa has no criminal record in Germany." Mr. Hartmann told me I could show this letter if I were detained overseas, and that it could be helpful. This gave me a sense of security.

The German national security apparatus had begun taking my case seriously after German embassies had to interfere on so many of my trips overseas. Every time China demanded my extradition, the German government refused, saying I had not committed a crime in Germany and that China's claims were not convincing, with insufficient evidence for the allegations made against me. The authorities conducted in-depth investigations, gathering documents about my activities in Germany and sending reports to Interpol to prove my innocence.

On November 6, 2017, Mr. Hartmann reported good news from the German interior ministry. Interpol had moved the Red Notice on me to the documentation department, which effectively concealed it within their system, meaning my file wouldn't show up in the systems of any country to which I travelled. This was a positive first step and meant I would likely be safe from situations such as my arrest in Italy. Nevertheless, I still didn't feel completely at ease.

With the efforts of Fair Trials and the cooperation of the German government, my case became an urgent issue during the time Meng Hongwei, the former Chinese Vice-Minister of Public Security, was president of Interpol. Meng's reign at Interpol would be a hurdle to resolving my case, I thought. Nonetheless, the secretary-general of Interpol responsible for its operations and overall management was Jurgen Stock, a former deputy chair of Germany's Federal Criminal Police Office–BKA. Besides, the CCF was an independent body that had the authority to make decisions regarding Red Notices.

Fair Trials submitted the request to the CCF to review my case. It was discussed at the next meeting of the CCF, which took place from January 30 to February 2, 2018. Based on the evidence and independent investigation by Interpol, the CCF concluded that I wasn't linked to any of the crimes the Chinese authorities claimed but was what I had said I was: a politician fighting for his people's rights. As a result, the CCF decided to cancel the Red Notice against me.

I was in Geneva attending a meeting at the UN on February 21, 2018, when Mr. Min from Fair Trials called me.

"We have good news for you," he said. My heart started beating with excitement. If Fair Trials had good news for me, it was about my Interpol case.

"Did you check your email? We sent you an email four hours ago," Mr. Min said.

"No, I haven't had a chance yet. I've been in a meeting since this morning," I replied.

"We received a letter from the secretary-general of Interpol. The Red Notice against you was cancelled on February 20, 2018. Congratulations!"

"Thank you," I said evenly, holding back. I was in the crowded hall of the UN, but I probably would have screamed if I were somewhere else.

Finally, this heavy burden had been lifted, the chain with which the Chinese regime had shackled me for twenty-one years, had been broken. I had regained my freedom in the free world. Justice had finally prevailed, and my faith was restored. With China's plans exposed, the world finally saw my enemy, believed me, and helped me to defeat them.

This triumph was great news for Fair Trials, too. They worked hard to win this legal battle. A few days later, Fair Trials called a press conference to announce my innocence and the removal of my Interpol Red Notice.

I received the official decision letter from Interpol's secretary-general three days later, through Fair Trials. A certificate that confirmed the cancellation of the Red Notice was attached, as well as the reasons for the decision and an outline of the process that the CCF used to clear my name, consisting of forty-seven clauses.

My friends from around the world congratulated me, and for a while I became a media celebrity. Asked about the difficulties the Red Notice had presented to my activism, I explained everything. I tried to highlight the message that China could turn an honest man into a criminal and terrorist, but that in the end, their corrupt plots would backfire and expose their true nature. I tried to emphasize that the world mustn't trust China, a lying, evil regime.

I was elated to be finally free of the Interpol Red Notice so that I could now freely carry out my activism in free nations, I wasn't going to be kicked out of UN meetings in Geneva and New York. China could no longer pressure those countries and claim I was a terrorist. Many people who wanted to help protect my rights but were constrained due to the Red Notice could now publicly speak for me.

For the final act to end my long ordeal, I had to travel to Washington, D.C. On March 7, with the WUC and UHRP, Fair Trials' U.S. representative Rebecca Shaeffer, UHRP Board Chair Nury Turkel, Human Rights Watch Asia Director Sophie Richardson, and I held a press conference at the U.S. National Press Hall to announce the lifting of my Interpol Red Notice.

THE PRESIDENT OF INTERPOL DISAPPEARS

I knew that China would be infuriated about the removal of my Interpol Red Notice, but especially given the fact that it was cancelled during Meng Hongwei's presidency of the organization. How could Meng Hongwei, a former vice-minister of the Chinese Ministry of Public Security, fail to protect Chinese interests? Why couldn't he prevent the removal of my Red Notice? And why couldn't China—a country that believed in its superior might and authority—have successfully objected when the CCF made the decision and Interpol's secretary-general announced it to the world?

The independence of Interpol's constituent bodies and the separation of powers restricted Meng Hongwei from interfering in my case. As well, the presidency was a symbolic role, without any authority to interfere in daily operations, and as such was required to respect decisions made by the independent experts at the CCF. The president's main role was to represent Interpol at the international level and chair its assemblies. Nevertheless, at the time of Meng's appointment, Human Rights Watch, Fair Trials, and the WUC objected to the election of an official from a dictatorship—especially one who directly managed the brutal security apparatus of China. Many statements were made denouncing his appointment, and it was a heated topic in the international media.

The members of the CCF responsible for deciding on the removal of my Red Notice were principled people, trained with respect for the rule of law and independent of political influence. They were solely motivated by justice.

The Chinese regime didn't share this perspective.

They couldn't accept that twenty-one years of disinformation and abuse directed at me had disintegrated. They made clear in a press briefing that they disapproved of Interpol's decision. Ultimately, China blamed Meng Hongwei for the decision and accused him of incompetence.

Seven months after the removal of the Red Notice, the media was flooded with the news of Meng Hongwei's arrest in China. He had left Stockholm for Beijing on September 20, 2018, and there was no news of his whereabouts until September 25, 2018. When he sent a picture of a knife to his wife in France, she realized that Meng was in danger. She waited a few days, but as time went on, she still couldn't trace her husband's location. Forced disappearance is one of the most wicked tactics used by the CCP. Thousands of Uyghurs have disappeared in this manner, and there is no information to be found about them to this day. The Chinese regime started forcibly disappearing Uyghurs in large numbers after the Urumchi Massacre on July 5, 2009.

Meng's wife informed the French police on October 10, and in that same month Interpol formally requested an explanation for Meng's disappearance from China.

I was attending a UN meeting in Geneva on October 6, 2018, when a BBC journalist called and asked me if I would participate in a live interview with BBC *World News* in fifteen minutes.

"Yes," I said, "But about what?"

He told me that it was about Meng's disappearance and whether it had something to do with the removal of my Interpol Red Notice. I declined the interview as I didn't have an opinion on the matter. But my phone kept ringing. Journalists swarmed around me as the Chinese government announced they had arrested Meng. They all asked if there was a connection between my situation and Meng's arrest. Of course, I couldn't make that claim without proof, but I also couldn't deny it. The vengeful and paranoid Chinese regime was very likely to hold Meng accountable for his failure to prevent my removal from Interpol's list of Red Notices. Although I avoided talking to the media about this incident, some international outlets continued to speculate about the connection.

Six months later, on April 24, 2019, China's Supreme People's Court formally convicted Meng of corruption after he allegedly admitted to receiving 14.5 million Chinese yuan (roughly two million USD) in bribes. It is a fact that there is no Chinese official who isn't corrupt. Purging rivals on claims of corruption is Xi Jinping's favourite tactic. Since he came to power in 2013, he has regularly removed and jailed officials in the Chinese central government and provinces after accusing them of these crimes. Meng is one of countless others.

"Meng jailed himself while trying to jail you." My friends and I said whenever Interpol was mentioned at international gatherings.

Powerful totalitarian regimes are trampling upon international law and trying to make this world an unfair place to live.

But when we stand firm in our struggle for justice, we will prevail. Justice exists in the world and it's our duty to find it. With my twenty-one years of experience, I've been working hard to spread this message.

THE LINGERING GHOST OF THE RED NOTICE

The CCP, with no sense of justice or humanity, couldn't accept that Interpol had lifted my Red Notice. In their eyes, there was nothing above the Communist Party and its will. If anyone or anything—international law, humanitarian policies, rightful verdicts, morals, ideology, society, personal beliefs—contradicted the will of the Communist Party, it became an enemy to be eradicated. Disregard for international law, disrespect for their own law, and abuse of basic human rights are inherent to this regime.

China has always worked to manipulate world politics to suit its interests, using economic power and diplomatic tricks. Relying as it did on the gathering of weak and poor countries under its banner and infiltrating international organizations like the UN, China's loss in the dispute with Interpol was a severe and damaging strike against the regime. China was one of the largest donors to Interpol and had successfully occupied the presidency.

"Interpol's secretary-general is a German and the CCF executives are Americans. They are biased and thus made this case a political issue," China complained at the UN. When UN security removed me from a UN meeting in April 2017 (detailed in Chapter 6), they refused to tell me why, but it was obvious that it was because of my Red Notice. One year later, in April 2018, after its cancellation, I was going to attend the United Nations Permanent Forum on Indigenous Issues (UNPFII) at the UN Headquarters in New York on behalf of the German-based non-governmental organization, the Society for Threatened Peoples (STP). But the Chinese government, refusing to accept

Interpol's decision, repeated its claims, "Dolkun Isa is a terrorist on the Interpol Red Notices." Their lies and persistence prevented me from attending. Although two months had passed since the cancellation of my Red Notice, the UN would not issue me an entrance ID. At the time, I didn't know the under-secretary of the UN Economic and Social Affairs was a Chinese diplomat Wu Hongbo, the man who had ordered my removal from the UN headquarters.

On December 22, 2018, Wu Hongbo proudly boasted on "Hot Topic," a live Chinese-language talk show on the Chinese state television channel CCTV that:

> The principles of the UN require me to be impartial; however, when it concerns my country, I choose to disregard the principle of impartiality and protect my country's interests. For instance, in April 2017, when a Xinjiang separatist and member of a terrorist organization based in Germany was participating in a UN session, I chased him out of the UN. My staff told me it was against freedom of speech, I told them I would take all the responsibility and asked them to do what I ordered.[24]

This was an acknowledgment from Wu Hongbo of his violation of a UN principle and evidence that Chinese officials employed at the UN can and do abuse its principles in their country's interests. This was a testimony that China doesn't respect any law or principle that is not aligned with their own interests. After watching this program on YouTube, I sent a letter to UN secretary-general António Guterres demanding an investigation of Wu Hongbo. I never received a reply.

On April 18, 2018, I arrived in New York to attend the UNPFII meeting that I had been forcibly removed from the year before. The Secretariat refused to give me accreditation, claiming they were verifying my identity. My being prevented once again from entering the UN sparked action from the United States, Germany, and many international human rights organizations. The European Union also got involved. The news eventually reached the office of the UN secretary-general, I did my best to break China's blocking of me, making four trips between the United States and Europe in ten days and enduring great financial loss. But my determination to expose and beat the Chinese regime spurred me on. I wanted to prove to China that I could enter the UN and that justice would eventually prevail over their injustices.

After a week-long back and forth, the Secretariat had to issue me a badge. I spoke at the UNPFII meeting and detailed China's oppression of the people of East Turkistan and my own experiences of China's attempts to harm human rights activists like myself by way of institutions like the UN, in which they had attempted to curb my freedom of speech.

My successful entrance to the UN and my speech offended China. The Chinese representatives at the UN spoke immediately after me and said, "Dolkun Isa is a terrorist on Interpol's Red Notices. He has no right to speak at the UN." Their accusations were shameless.

The Red Notice had been removed from Interpol but not from the Chinese log. It was obvious China wanted to continue playing this card on the international stage. China didn't want to accept this failure, which seemed to belittle their hegemony in institutions like the UN and Interpol, a hegemony from which they benefited greatly. China didn't want to accept the reality that they had been discredited and humiliated by a man like me. Maybe this was the reason China continued fighting me tooth and nail in the UN. To explain more about these battles at the UN, I need to start from the beginning.

CHAPTER 6

CHINA'S HIDDEN HAND INSIDE THE UNITED NATIONS

When Xi Jinping came to power in 2013, he created a "Chinese Dream" and launched a strategic plan, the "Belt and Road Initiative," to realize that dream.

The Chinese Dream is nothing more than a nightmare. It represents China's aim to rule the world, making other countries bend the knee to China, remapping the world, changing ideological frameworks, and ultimately creating a world that is obedient to China. China camouflaged this scheme under the name Belt and Road, disguising their plans as a "project to bring happiness to humanity." This propaganda naturally enticed many countries that hadn't yet learned their lesson from China's lies and deception. Thankfully, many others regarded the project with distrust. China's untrustworthiness and its bad image on the international stage raised alarm bells for them.

Since 2014, China has spent a lot of money to improve its international image. This has been a major undertaking, involving bribing important officials of weaker countries; gaining the support of international organizations like the UN, the Shanghai Cooperation Association, the WHO, and Interpol; and fighting social media opinions against China by spreading propaganda, bribing journalists to praise China, and admonish human rights activists, and waging defamation campaigns on human rights organizations that oppose China and its leaders. China has also spent money creating institutions and fake NGOs using names like "Human Rights Organization," "Research Center," "Humanitarian Relief Center," and others that in fact work for the Chinese government; establishing Confucius Institutes in universities to propagate and spread the CCP's ideology; paying Chinese international students to work for the regime; bribing foreign diplomats, researchers, and writers to advocate for the regime; and doing all they can to get rid of Uyghur organizations and leaders fighting their operation.

Until 2014, there were no "neutral" Chinese representatives who spoke out against Uyghurs, Tibetans, and Falun Gong practitioners—objections always came from the official Chinese representatives at the UN. Beginning in 2014, however, many of the so-called human rights organizations created by the Chinese regime started appearing in the UN and claiming that the peoples of East Turkistan, Tibet, and Inner Mongolia lived happy and peaceful lives, that these regions were experiencing unprecedented development, and that the CCP was taking care of them, not persecuting them.

In the media, Pakistani, Arab, Turkish, even some Italian and other Western journalists joined in the coverup, advocating for China's ethnic policies and justifying its repressive ones. They worked hard to hide Chinese oppression of the Uyghurs and other nations under CCP occupation. They often praised the Belt and Road Initiative and championed the Chinese Dream.

When conferences were held reporting on the state of China's human rights in the parliaments of some democratic countries, professors from renowned universities praised China and justified its policies while belying media reports of the persecution of Uyghurs and other nations under CCP occupation.

At the UN, ambassadors of certain third-world countries started faithfully repeating Chinese propaganda. Totalitarian countries such as Cuba, Venezuela, Iran, Saudi Arabia, Pakistan, and Russia have always stood with China.

Nevertheless, in this atmosphere—in which China was finding new, creative ways to increase public support and regularly denying our cause—we persisted in our fight for the freedom of the people of East Turkistan. The meetings of the UN Human Rights Council, which holds three sessions a year, the Universal Periodic Review (UPR) held every five years to review the human rights records of all UN member states, the Indigenous Forum, Minorities Forum, Human Rights and Business Forum, and UN treaty bodies were all great opportunities for us to raise awareness about the Chinese oppression of the Uyghurs. They were also an opportunity for the international community to assess and judge the Chinese regime. China didn't like this. They didn't want their persecution of Uyghurs and Tibetans—along with the true nature of their dictatorship—to be exposed during these meetings and the Chinese Dream demeaned before the world.

However, China couldn't escape this. To China's chagrin, the Uyghurs, Tibetans, Southern Mongolians, Hong Kongers, Chinese human rights organizations in exile, and international human rights organizations used these forums to continue to speak out about the worsening of China's human rights abuses every year. I always attended these meetings or sent my staff and secured speaking opportunities to expose China's lies, and China regularly tried to prevent me and the WUC representatives from attending. They even tried to pressure the UN secretary-general, in violation of UN principles. A 2017 incident bears testimony to that.

EXPELLED FROM THE UN

All UN Human Rights Council sessions are held in Geneva. I've been attending these sessions since 1999. From April 24 to May 5, 2017, I was in New York to attend the UNPFII for the first time. The WUC didn't have ECOSOC status at the UN, so I applied for accreditation through the Society for Threatened Peoples (STP), which had ECOSOC consultative status.[25] I was a member of the STP for a long time.

I arrived in New York on April 23, 2017. Omer Kanat, the Chairman of the Executive Committee of the WUC arrived too, from Washington, D.C. We went to the Secretariat the next morning and received our IDs without any trouble. We attended the Indigenous Peoples Forum session on April 24. The next day, we went to some of the conferences that we thought were important. However, on the third day of the conference, we ran into trouble at the UN building.

During a break when I went into the hall to get a cup of coffee, three men approached me. One wearing a UN security uniform spoke to me. "Excuse me, sir. Can I see your badge?" he asked. I handed over my card.

"Can I see your ID?" he asked again. I handed over my ID, too.

"Sorry, you need to leave the UN right now," he said, as he looked at my ID.

"Why do I need to leave the UN? For what?"

"For security concerns," the man said.

"What? What security concerns? Can you explain them to me?" I asked.

"I can't explain. But you need to leave the UN immediately!"

As we started quarrelling, two more security officers appeared and people gathered around us. The behaviour of the security police was inexplicable. They acted as though they were arresting a criminal—at least that's what it felt like.

"Sir, please cooperate so that we don't need to force you."

"Of course, I'll cooperate. But please tell me why I need to leave the UN. I won't leave if you don't tell me why," I said, firmly.

"We don't know the reason either. Please talk to your organization and ask them to speak with the Forum Secretariat. It is an order from the top management. We're just doing our jobs," the police said.

I realized that a quarrel wouldn't help. If it was an order "from the top," security had to enforce it. It was better for me to leave myself rather than be dragged out by the police. Omer Kanat brought my bags from the conference hall, and four security officers escorted me from the building. I was extremely humiliated.

I called STP's director, Ulrich Delius, as soon as I left the UN headquarters. He said he would send a letter to the Secretariat of the UNPFII right away.

He sent a letter. He made a call, too. Although the UN said, "We're investigating," nothing came of it. A week later, I still couldn't attend the conference and finally had to return to Munich.

As usual, I think if I had spoken for a few minutes at the UN, I wouldn't have had nearly the amount of news coverage and attention that I received for being kicked out. Every representative had about two to three minutes to speak at the Forum, as there are so many individuals, groups, and nations with complaints to bring to the UN. Three minutes aren't enough to convey the suffering and woes of a nation, but we do our best to present our peoples' situations concisely and movingly. At the conference, Omer Kanat spoke about the grave situation of the Uyghur people, and also about my removal from the UN. Usually, competing with many other speakers at the UN can diminish the attention and spotlight the Uyghur cause deserves. But news of my ouster spread around the world and brought to light the injustice wrought against me and, by extension, the Uyghur people.

On May 19, fifteen international human rights organizations issued a joint statement to demand the UNPFII provide an explanation for the incident. The organizations included China Change, Human Rights in China, Human Rights Watch, the International Campaign for Tibet, Initiatives for China, Minority Rights Group, the Nonviolent Radical Party, Transnational and Transparty, the gaden People's Rights Organisation, the Society for Threatened Peoples, Solidarité Chine, the Southern Mongolian Human Rights Information Center, the UNPO, the Uyghur Human Rights Project, the World Sindhi Congress, and the World Uyghur Congress.[26]

Of course, we didn't stop there. This was about human rights and the struggle between oppression and justice. It was about standing up to China's hegemonic practices in the UN and their exploitation and abuse of UN principles. It was about the battle between the Chinese regime and the Uyghurs on the international stage. If I gave up at this point, it would hurt the Uyghur cause in the UN. There is justice in the world. It is our right to obtain justice, and we must take back our rights, I thought.

I tried to meet officials and organizations related to the UN regarding this incident. The Society for Threatened Peoples (STP), UNPO, HRW, and other organizations worked on this too. On September 19, 2017, I met Michel Forst, the UN Special Rapporteur on Human Rights Defenders, at his office in Geneva. On October 4, 2017, I sent a complaint to Andrew Gilmour, the UN assistant secretary-general for human rights and asked him to investigate. On November 9, I had a telephone interview with his special secretary and assistants. I told them about the incident in New York and how I found it disappointing that the UN had failed to protect the rights of a human rights advocate. I hoped these calls and complaints would make it impossible for UN officials to avoid the matter.

In September 2017, the New York-based Human Rights Watch (HRW) called a press conference at the UN Office in Geneva and published a report titled "The Costs of International Advocacy: China's Interference in United Nations Human Rights Mechanisms."[27]

When preparing this report, HRW Director Kenneth Roth and its Asia Director Sophie Richardson made my removal from the UN premises due to Chinese pressure one of its main topics. It immediately attracted the attention of the international media. The report included descriptions of China's attempts to manipulate the UN, sabotage human rights activists, and cover up its oppressive policies in East Turkistan and Tibet, as well as its intimidation of Uyghurs in the diaspora and use of their family members back home to blackmail them and force their return to China.

This report attracted the attention not only of the media but also of governments and human rights activists throughout the Western world. The European Union, the United States, and Germany intervened, setting off a power struggle between the democratic powers and the totalitarian regimes.[28]

CHINA'S MISCHIEF AT THE UN

In January 2018, I applied to attend the 17th session of the UNPFII. I received a response almost a month later that my application was approved.

Since my expulsion from the UN premises the year before had attracted so much attention from the media, journalists and international organizations wanted to know if I planned to attend the conference again, and if there was any possibility of more newsworthy trouble. Although the conference was several months away, I told them my application was approved and I intended to take part.

The conference was scheduled to run from April 16 to April 27. Before I attended, I would be an invited guest of the International Journalism Festival in Perugia, Italy, ending on April 15, so I booked a flight from Rome to New York for that day. I made a hotel reservation in New York, too. But on April 13 I received an email from the UN Department of Economic and Social Affairs. "Our office has been informed that for security reasons, your registration to the Permanent Forum on Indigenous Issues is pending status before issuance" it said.

I immediately sent an email to Ms. Taryn Lesser in the office of the UN assistant secretary-general Andrew Gilmour and Human Rights Watch Asia director Sophie Richardson, telling them about the letter and asking if I should still fly to New York. I got replies from both of them within a few hours. "Please come to New York, we'll try to resolve this issue here," Ms. Richardson said. Ms. Lesser replied saying she was surprised and would inform the assistant secretary-general.

With this reassurance, I flew to New York on April 15. I landed at 11:00 p.m. and got to my hotel at 2:00 a.m. Omer Kanat arrived from Washington, D.C. at 6:00 the next morning, and we went to the Secretariat to get our badges together. Omer Kanat received his, but the UN staff told me they couldn't issue a badge for me. They couldn't tell me why. Then a UN security officer arrived. "We kicked you out last year. Why did you come again?" he asked, displeased.

"Sir, here is an accreditation letter from the Secretariat that says I can attend this conference." I showed him the first letter from the UNPFII Secretariat.

"Sir, your case is currently under investigation. Please don't come back before you receive an official notice from the Forum Secretariat. You can't enter," the officer said.

We left the badge office and called Ms. Lesser and Ms. Richardson. I informed the German foreign ministry, too.

Ms. Lesser replied right away. She said she would take me inside the Forum with a UN visitor's card and we could talk in detail there.

I had never met Ms. Lesser in person before; we had just talked several times over the phone and by email. However, we met her in front of the UN headquarters and she took us into the building with visitors' cards. Assistant secretary-general Andrew Gilmour greeted us warmly, and I told him everything. He said he was communicating with a related department about it and that he would try his best.

Ms. Richardson contacted the U.S. State Department and the U.S. Mission to the UN and asked for their help. We also met German representatives at the UN, who assured us that they too would be meeting relevant officials about my situation. Three days passed, though, and nothing happened.

On the afternoon of April 18, I received an unexpected email from the UNPFII Secretariat. "Your accreditation has been approved. You can attend the conference now." "Okay, so Mr. Gilmour's efforts and interventions by the U.S. and Germany weren't futile," I thought. Then, I received another email, from the office of Ambassador Kelley Currie, the U.S. Deputy Representative to the UN. It said, "Ambassador Kelley Currie wants to meet you. If you like, please come to the U.S. Representative Office to the UN. We will help you to get your badge." They were obviously worried I could have trouble at the badge office again. I happily accepted the offer.

On the morning of April 19, I arrived at the U.S. Mission to the UN and met Ambassador Currie. After a brief conversation, we went to the badge office with two of her staff. I filled out the relevant form and gave it to the Secretariat staff along with the email saying my accreditation was approved. Once again I was told that my accreditation had been suspended. As Ambassador Currie spoke with the Secretariat staff, the security officer from the other day appeared. "We kicked you out before. Just yesterday I told you not to come back. Why are you here?" he asked, frowning.

Before I could reply, Ms. Currie answered, politely, "We brought him here."

"I didn't ask you, ma'am. I'm talking to this man here," the officer said in a firm voice.

We were all stunned. I felt awkward that the U.S. ambassador was exposed to this mistreatment on my account. Ambassador Currie's assistant, Sevasti Pandermarakis, approached the security officer angrily.

"Do you know who you are talking to, Officer? This is Ambassador Kelley Currie, the U.S. Representative to the UN!"

Now the officer was the one in an awkward situation. He immediately apologized and started defending himself. "We've been told that this man isn't allowed to enter the UN premises. That's why we kicked him out. I didn't know who you were."

"I came here to resolve this issue. Please call your boss," said Ambassador Currie.

The boss arrived moments later. He apologized as he greeted Ambassador Currie, saying, "There is a misunderstanding about this man, ma'am. Sorry, you need to wait a while. There is an investigation going on."

We waited for more than half an hour, but there was still no answer. I felt self-conscious. Here was the U.S. ambassador to the UN sitting, waiting all this time in a security office with me—a man trying to advocate for his people, with no one in the world to care about us.

"I'm really sorry, Ms. Currie. I'm taking up your time."

"Please don't feel sorry, Mr. Isa. You're not the one who should be apologizing," she replied courteously, "I'm an ambassador here to resolve issues like this, This isn't your issue anymore; it has become my issue and it's now my duty to resolve it."

I was touched by these kind words. I wish there were more people like her in the United States and the UN, I thought. We had a meaningful conversation. I told her about the situation of the Uyghurs and the Chinese oppression they faced.

Eventually, Ambassador Currie suggested that we wait at the U.S. Mission, which was only about two hundred metres away, so we went to her office there. However, after two hours of waiting without receiving a reply, I began to feel restless. The security measures meant I couldn't bring my phone or laptop inside the U.S. Mission. I couldn't communicate with anyone or check my email. I told Ambassador Currie that I had some emails to reply to and would like to wait at the hotel. She agreed and told me she would contact me if there was an update.

When there was no answer that day or the next, I began to lose hope. But I knew that the German, U.S. and EU missions were all working on it. The incident was becoming a significant and delicate subject for these missions, the UN, and China. I learned that it had also reached the UN secretary-general, António Guterres, who was tasked with a difficult decision about how the UN would proceed.

I spent a week in New York waiting for an answer from the UN while a diplomatic war raged among the United States, Germany, the EU, and China, and still there was no answer. It was more complicated than I had originally thought.

The WUC's Executive Committee meeting was scheduled to be held in Antwerp from April 23 to the 25th. Members of the Executive Committee and leaders of various Uyghur organizations were gathering to evaluate our work over the past six months and plan for the next six.

The WUC also announced its plan to organize a 5,000-person demonstration in front of the European Commission in Brussels on April 27, after the meeting. Uyghurs from four continents and more than twenty countries were coming to participate.

This demonstration would be one of the largest in the history of the Uyghur diaspora. With this, and members of the Executive Committee arriving ahead of the annual meeting, I had to arrive in Brussels by April 22 at the latest.

When I still hadn't received a reply from the UN, I left New York on Saturday, April 21 and arrived in Brussels on the morning of April 22. Before leaving New York, I met the staff of the German and U.S. missions. "If you could wait a little longer, this issue will be resolved," they said. I told them I had to be in Brussels for the meeting and demonstration, but I would come back if they were able to resolve things. They told me they would be in touch and that I should remain optimistic.

SHAMING CHINA AT THE UN

On Monday, April 23, the WUC Executive Committee meeting began in Antwerp. The schedule was packed, and many things had to be done.

In the evening, I was informed by the German and U.S. missions that my accreditation to the UN had been resolved and advised that the sooner I could get my badge, the better. I hesitated. If I went to New York and encountered another unexpected hurdle, I would have missed the meeting in Brussels for no reason. As the WUC president, I needed to be at the meeting; but winning over China at the UN would prove more important.

I discussed it with the WUC leadership, who all insisted I go to New York. So, on Tuesday, after leaving the city only two days earlier, I returned to New York.

On Wednesday morning, Mr. Koehler Pit from the German Mission accompanied me to the UN Secretariat to get my badge. Nothing adverse happened this time, and I got the badge. We had finally won the week-long diplomatic battle. I entered the

UN headquarters that I had been kicked out of in 2017, proud to have regained my right to speak there.

In my speech, I explained the unimaginable oppression the Chinese regime was inflicting upon the people of East Turkistan. Then I presented my recommendations as follows:

> Some countries, taking advantage of their privileges, are trying to manipulate the UN, harm human rights activists, and abuse their rights. I am an example of that. In 2017, I was kicked out of the UN headquarters. This year, too, I had to wait for one week as my UN badge was suspended. I even left New York. Thankfully, with the help of the U.S. and German missions, I was able to come back and attend this meeting. The UN mustn't lose its founding principles. International organizations, human rights activists and various representatives must be able to speak freely here. Their security must be guaranteed. The voiceless peoples and nations facing injustice must be heard in this forum. And totalitarian regimes like China mustn't be able to abuse UN principles.

Many government representatives welcomed my recommendations. But, of course, Chinese representatives were also present and couldn't hide their displeasure. "This man, although he's here representing the STP, is actually the president of the WUC. His name is Dolkun Isa, and he is a terrorist on Interpol's Red Notices, and the WUC is a terrorist organization. Such a person mustn't be allowed to speak at the UN sessions. He shouldn't have a right to attend any UN meeting," they said, furiously. The hall was abuzz. I raised my hand and asked to reply, but the chair didn't allow me to speak as replies are usually disallowed at conferences. Had I been able to speak, I would have refuted the

Chinese representatives' lie that I was still subject to an Interpol Red Notice. I would have said my Red Notice had been cancelled two months earlier, and that they were clearly lying.

Thankfully, the German and U.S. representatives used their turns to defend me. The German representatives said I was a German citizen and had been living in Germany for twenty years, abiding by the law. They said there was no evidence for the allegations against me, that Interpol had cancelled my Red Notice, and that the Chinese representatives were disregarding this fact.

Although Germany has often dealt carefully and used soft, diplomatic words with China due to their economic ties, it has always stood on the side of justice and protected international legal norms. Germany has also never hesitated to defend its citizens. They certainly played a significant role in protecting me from China.

My year-long battle with China at the UN that started in April 2017 had now ended. I won, and justice prevailed. The Western democratic nations that defended me had the upper hand over the Chinese. Even though China had been able to block me for a time using its economic power and diplomatic pressure, they would now be the ones to lose face.

Later, I learned that the United States, Germany, the European Union, and other democratic countries intervened, and my case reached the UN secretary-general. Under his direct instruction, the UN employees who were being pressured by China were forced to follow UN principles and uphold justice.[29]

I'd like to add something here. China has not only infiltrated the UN headquarters in New York but has even been able to reach the UN offices at Geneva. In 2013, the WUC sent a delegation of five people to Geneva to attend the UN Human Rights Council session. The first two days passed peacefully. On the third day, two UN security officers appeared and told us, "You need to leave the hall, right now. You must leave the UN."

"Why?" we asked.

"We don't know the reason," said the officers, "We're just carrying out the order."

People around us started looking at us, surprised. A woman on the stage was watching us. Noticing the scene, she left the stage and came over to us. "What happened?" she asked the security officers.

"We've received an order to kick these people out of the meeting," they said.

"You can't kick them out! I'm responsible for them," the woman said.

The security officers left. We were stunned, we not knowing what was happening. The woman smiled at us and returned to the stage. Only four years later did we discover who this woman was and why she stood up for us.

After my removal from the UN headquarters in April 2017 had attracted the attention of the media and international organizations, I received an email two months later from Emma Reilly, who said she worked in the Office of the UN High Commissioner for Human Rights (OHCHR):

> I hope this email finds you well. We met briefly during one of your trips to Geneva in 2013—I noticed that UN Security were escorting you and your WUC colleagues from the room, and I intervened to stop them. I am contacting you now on a very serious issue. In February 2013, and many, many times since, I [was told by] my boss in OHCHR to hand over [the] names of human rights defenders to the Chinese government prior to sessions of the Human Rights Council, letting them know who was planning to attend. This was not standard practice and was clearly against the rules. Unfortunately, none

of the OHCHR senior managers were willing to stand up to China and refuse the request. As you no doubt know from the Society for Threatened Peoples, who accredited you for the sessions in 2013, your names were on the list, and were handed over to China. I tried to persuade my boss to at least seek your consent and take measures to protect you from reprisals and intimidation in advance of handing over the information, but to no avail. Even when I pointed out that your colleague, Ms. Kadeer, had children in detention in China at the time, the decision to hand over the names—without even having the respect to let you know in advance—was maintained. I reported this all the way up to the then-High Commissioner for Human Rights, but she decided that politics trumped respecting your human rights. I am deeply sorry that my interventions were not more effective, but I was the only and most junior person speaking out. When the OHCHR took no action, I reported it to the European Union (just after the disappearance of Cao Shunli) and then the Irish government.

Now I learned that the woman who had stopped UN security from kicking us out of the hall four years earlier was Emma Reilly. In September 2017, I had the opportunity to attend a UN conference in Geneva and finally met her properly. We had a long conversation, during which I learned many things from her and found answers to questions that had puzzled me for years. I was astonished to learn the depths of China's infiltration and influence in the UN. Although we had faced some difficulties and were kicked out of the UN several times, I realized it was a miracle that we had mostly been able to attend UN sessions under such circumstances. The pressure China put on UN officials, their bribes, deceptions, and the fabricated claims it had put before the UN to stop our attendance and participation were shocking. And yet, there were principled people within the UN like Emma Reilly who were determined to protect the operations and principles of the organization. Such people have assumed great risk in order to protect human rights and the integrity of the UN and stand up to totalitarian regimes like China that abuse it.

Emma Reilly was a lawyer who had taken a job with the Office of the UN High Commissioner for Human Rights (OHCHR)., where she immediately found unlawful practices that violated the principles of the UN. As noted in her email to me, she personally witnessed, at China's request and pressure, UN officials handing over information to the Chinese government. Unable to keep silent, she alerted her superiors and entreated them to respect UN principles. They didn't listen. At the Chinese Embassy's request, they continued to share information and lists of Uyghur, Tibetan, and Chinese activists with the Chinese government. Emma Reilly did her best to stop this and stood up to those officials and the Chinese government. Unfortunately, her bosses continued to cooperate with China, which she reported to the High Commissioner for Human Rights and even the secretary-general. Despite threats and the risk of losing her job, she never gave up. She took the case to court in 2017 and spoke to the media until the story made headlines and the UN officials were finally forced to admit their wrongdoing. In July 2020, OHCHR spokesman Rupert Colville said, "The practice of revealing names of participants at sessions to governments ceased in 2015 . . . Ms. Reilly's allegations relate to a discounted practice whereby the names of Human Rights Council participants were occasionally confirmed to states in limited circumstances, with care taken to ensure that no action taken by the OHCHR would endanger human rights activists."[30]

A TENSE DEBATE

After China failed to reverse my right to speak at meetings, the Chinese Permanent Mission submitted a Note Verbale to the UN Committee on Non-Governmental Organizations (NGOs) demanding that the consultative status of the Society for Threatened Peoples (STP) be withdrawn and that I be banned from attending meetings. This led to a tense debate between the Chinese and U.S. delegates during the Committee on NGOs session in New York on May 21, 2018. Speaking first, the Chinese delegate said.[31]

> The Chinese delegation formally requests the committee withdraw the NGO consultative status of the STP. We've already submitted a Note Verbale as per the committee's procedure. I believe all the members have seen it. We've outlined the reasons to remove the consultative status of the STP. I don't want to repeat everything now. However, here are three important points. First, the STP has accredited Dolkun Isa, a terrorist working against China, to many UN sessions including sessions of the Permanent Forum on Indigenous Issues. Dolkun Isa was listed as a terrorist by China in 2003. He is also accused of inciting terrorism, organizing, leading, helping and funding terrorists. He was the vice president of the East Turkistan Liberation Organization, a UN-designated terrorist organization. He has led many terrorist incidents that happened in China including explosions, murders and hostage-taking. He is a terrorist by all manifestation. For instance, in the Turkish capital Ankara on December 12, 1995, he publicly declared that he had planned an explosion in the Chinese region of Xinjiang. Second, Dolkun Isa

and his organization call for Xinjiang's independence. He is now the President of the WUC. The WUC's goal is to establish an independent nation of East Turkistan, which jeopardizes the sovereignty and territorial integrity of China. To my knowledge, the STP has jeopardized the sovereignty and territorial integrity of other countries, too. These all prove that the STP violates the principles of the UN. Third, Dolkun Isa participated in the Permanent Forum on Indigenous Issues (UNPFII) on May 5 under the name of STP, but he said he represents the WUC in the session. The WUC has no consultative status at the UN and no right to participate in the forum. Whether it is the STP or Dolkun Isa, they both infiltrated these sessions through lies and fabrication. These actions violate UN principles and standards. Therefore, we request that STP's consultative status be withdrawn.

All the UN member states attended the session, and it was also being live-streamed.

The WUC's efforts to obtain ECOSOC consultative status at the UN had been continually rejected by the Committee on NGOs. China's evil hands in the UN had been telling UN officials that "the WUC is an organization calling for independence," and thus our requests were denied every time. Since the Chinese authorities were unable to prevent me from attending UN sessions, they planned to block me by removing the NGO consultative status of the STP.

A U.S. representative replied as follows:

> Regarding the Chinese delegation's request, I'd like to read the secretary-general's report from May 23,

2017. I'd like to repeat, this is the secretary-general's report, and is not from a state or the media. One chapter of the report reads, 'On April 26, 2017, Mr. Dolkun Isa, a Uyghur human rights activist and a member of the STP was removed from the UN headquarters while he was participating at the annual session of the Permanent Forum on Indigenous Issues (UNPFII) on security concerns, at the request of the Chinese delegation. Mr. Isa's ID wasn't restored again.' This is from last year. It is taken from the UN secretary-general's 2017 report on reprisals against civil society actors. It is clear what is happening here is another reprisal. The committee shouldn't become an accomplice to such actions. We're extremely concerned. As the secretary-general's report reached everyone very late, many people didn't have time to prepare to speak on this. To our knowledge, this man (Dolkun Isa) participated in the session after acquiring the relevant accreditation. If he was a security risk, the UN Security wouldn't have issued him a badge. They take the regulations very seriously. What we request from the chair here is to call the head of the UN Security to give us a report on this man. If this person were a terrorist, the UN Security wouldn't have admitted him to the UN premises to protect our lives, the U.S. wouldn't have let him enter its land. We have to look at the facts and information regarding this person and listen to all sides. We must pay close attention to this matter, more than before, because this is about justice. This is a clear issue. We have the secretary-general's report. We hope everyone in the committee reads this report today.

This response from the U.S. delegation was the start of a heated debate between the two countries' representatives. At that moment, Ambassador Currie entered the hall and sat down with the U.S. representatives and began reading the secretary-general's report, which had been distributed to the representatives just before the session started.

After the U.S. representative's remarks, German and EU representatives asked to speak. The German representative said the following:

> We're astonished to see the request to withdraw the consultative status of the STP at the UN. The STP is an independent human rights organization. They work for threatened ethnicities, peoples, and religions. The organization is based in Germany. It obtained ECOSOC status in 1993 and has since been participating in many international conferences including the Permanent Forum on Indigenous Issues (UNPFII) meetings. Mr. Dolkun Isa registered to the STP to attend the UNPFII and he's been a member of the STP for many years. The STP has many members that comprise of [sic] different ethnic groups and nations. Being a member of several organizations is normal. We see the allegations of terrorism and affiliation with terrorist organizations against Mr. Isa as baseless. Such allegations have been presented many times but have never been proved. If Mr. Isa posed a security threat, the UN Security's top officials wouldn't have issued him the credentials. The UN Security's top officials reviewed Mr. Isa's case last year and didn't find anything that prevents him from participating in the meetings. The evidence presented by a member of this committee

has been found to be irrelevant. The Interpol Red Notice against Mr. Isa has been removed after serious deliberations. Dolkun Isa is a German citizen. The German security authorities have reported that there is no evidence for the allegations against Dolkun Isa. With all of this, there is no basis for withdrawing the STP's UN Consultative Status. The attempt to do so is nothing more than a reprisal against the NGO and Dolkun Isa for speaking out on human rights violations. The UN secretary-general called the moves to block Dolkun Isa from UN sessions last year a reprisal. We call on all the representatives to oppose the motion to withdraw the consultative status of the STP. This committee mustn't take reprisals against NGOs for presenting their worries on human rights issues. We must listen to NGOs as per the relevant regulations. This year, we commemorate the 70th anniversary of the adoption of the Universal Declaration of Human Rights. I demand this committee respect the Declaration's spirit and principles.

These remarks by the German and U.S. representatives provided a legitimate counterargument to the Chinese delegation's accusations against me. Then the EU delegation spoke, expressing their concern over the accusations against me and the request to withdraw the consultative status of the STP, saying the actions of the Chinese side raised serious doubts and that a decision could not be rushed.

Interestingly, neither the Russian, Cuban, nor Pakistani representatives who spoke after the EU representative expressed explicit support for the Chinese motion to revoke the consultative status of the STP and ban me from UN meetings. Those countries had always taken China's side in UN sessions. I wondered if perhaps they recognized the baselessness of China's allegations or whether the secretary-general's report persuaded them to refrain from showing explicit support for China. Nevertheless, they all said the exact same thing, as if they had agreed on it beforehand, "[We give thanks] that the Chinese representatives have been given ample time to deal with this matter until Friday," implying their inclination to the Chinese side.

The Israeli representative spoke briefly, saying he supported the German and EU representatives. The Chinese representative spoke after him and said:

> I'd like to tell the Israeli representative that he shouldn't only listen to the German and the EU representatives. He should listen to us too. We have evidence that Dolkun Isa has not only supported terrorism, but he has also participated in terrorist activities. He has long been involved in activities that threaten and jeopardize the sovereignty and territorial integrity of our nation. While participating in UN meetings, he has violated the UN regulations. He has a serious issue and there is sufficient evidence to revoke the consultative status of this organization. The Chinese motion on this organization has nothing to do with reprisal. What we're trying to do is protect the goals and principles of the UN and to uphold its regulations. We aim to protect world peace and security as well as the security of the UN. The U.S. representative mentioned the secretary-general's report. We're aware of this report and we know who prepared it. Due to such perspective, this man's issue has been classified as 'reprisal.' If you have a nail and a hammer, you look for a hole to nail. This example applies to the people who organized and

prepared this report. Hence, I believe what we did has nothing to do with reprisal. The U.S. representative also said the U.S. has issued this man a visa and this is evidence that he doesn't pose a security risk. If we look back, many terrorist incidents happened on U.S. soil. What about those terrorists who were American citizens or held U.S. visas? Having a U.S. visa doesn't guarantee this man's background. The German representative said this man is a German citizen. But Mr. Isa committed many crimes before moving to Germany. Many of them are linked to terrorist incidents. His German citizenship doesn't mean he doesn't pose a security risk. According to German media, 960 German war criminals joined ISIS in Iraq and Syria. Being a German citizen isn't assurance that someone isn't a terrorist or that they don't pose a security risk. We must also avoid applying a double standard in the war on terror. Some people may not pose a risk to the U.S. or Germany but do to China or other countries. Therefore, we must apply the same standards to judge and fight terrorists. When this man is posing a security threat to some countries, it is unfair to label him a 'human rights activist' in other countries. There is evidence on this man's social media that he preaches Jihad against China. We hope the U.S. and German representatives avoid applying a double standard. We hope you will meticulously review the report and evidence we presented on this man. Finally, the German representative mentioned Interpol has canceled its Red Notice on this man. To our knowledge, this was initiated by the secretary-general of Interpol, who is a German, and the director of the legal department, who is an American. Interpol didn't consult with the member states, let alone China. It was done out of political motivation, it was underhanded, and it was a total dark box operation. As a member of this committee, we've presented our concerns. We've also allowed this organization to respond. With a sense of professionalism and responsibility, I ask the committee not to rush. Let's decide on Friday.

Then Ambassador Currie spoke. She said:

This has been a sad and disappointing day. The members of this committee saw the countries that claim to be the guardians of Islam and the Muslims supporting the Chinese fight against Islam. China is trying to allege that a man who has been working hard to promote the human and religious rights of his people is guilty of terrorism, which is completely baseless. It seems there is an opinion that "the U.S. is not doing its job as the host of the UN headquarters." It seems we've admitted a known terrorist to the U.S., and even to the UN headquarters. We've not considered the safety of our citizens. For years, we've been witnessing China's allegations against Dolkun Isa and the WUC, just like the letter they sent us. We've repeatedly asked the Chinese authorities to provide us with substantiated evidence for their allegations. However, they've so far failed to do so. There is still no evidence today. That's why the U.S. issued a ten-year multiple entry visa to Dolkun Isa, an upstanding German citizen with no criminal record. U.S. officials often meet with Mr. Isa. If Mr. Isa has ever been involved in any terrorist activities, do you really think the United States would allow such a person on U.S. soil to roam freely? Please think about this. Thousands of our young men and women are currently fighting against ISIS terrorists, Jihadists and extremists in Syria. Please don't provoke us! This is in fact an obvious example of China's effort of reprisal taking advantage of its friends in this committee. Let me read to you an op-ed published yesterday in the *Washington Post*. Let's all learn how the Chinese government is treating the Uyghurs in Xinjiang. The headline reads, "China's repugnant campaign to destroy the identity of a minority people."[32] This opinion piece reads, 'China is undertaking a repugnant campaign to destroy the identity of a minority people, the Uyghur Muslims of Xinjiang province in the far northwest.' There is much-documented evidence that backs this. The *Washington Post* and the Associated Press interviewed some former inmates. They found that the Uyghurs are forced to denounce their own culture as backward and renounce their Islamic identity. Uyghurs who prayed, wore long shirts, taught the Quran to children and gave their babies Islamic names are forced to repent. The Chinese government has locked up more than one million Uyghurs in concentration camps. This must be our agenda today. This meeting shouldn't be about the consultative status of the STP but should be about protecting the right of expression of a man who is trying to transmit to the world the voice of his voiceless people. Isn't this the founding goal of the UN? Wasn't the UN founded to protect the rights and self-determination of such peoples? The UN must find out if China's allegations of terrorism against Dolkun Isa are true or not. If they are true, he can no longer participate at UN meetings or enter the U.S. However, they have so far failed to provide such evidence. Besides, it doesn't make sense to allege that a trusted organization like STP is guilty of terrorism. This is *infuriating* and I ask the Chinese delegation to withdraw this unjust request before making any further mistakes.

Ambassador Currie delivered her speech empathetically and with a firm voice and the appropriate body language. She also drew attention to some very important issues. The first was the concentration camps. This was the first time the concentration camps were mentioned at the United Nations. The second was Ambassador Currie's refutation of the Chinese allegation that "Dolkun Isa and his organization have links to terrorism." She powerfully rebutted this, stating that China has never and will never be able to provide evidence for its allegations, and they are just taking reprisal against a man raising awareness and giving voice to a voiceless people. The third was in her saying "U.S. officials often meet Dolkun Isa"—by which she sent a message that the United States doesn't believe in or care about China's allegations against me, and instead is committed to protecting me. Of course, this speech offended China.

The UK representative who spoke after Ambassador Currie expressed his support for the opinion of the EU representative. Then, the Chinese representative spoke:

> I listened to the words of U.S. Ambassador Currie. But I didn't understand why she was speaking so emotionally. I'm not sure if this is true or not, but we are aware that Ambassador Currie participated in a Xinjiang research project in a U.S. think tank

before being named the U.S. Ambassador to the UN. This Xinjiang project aimed to help separatists who want to separate Xinjiang from China and build an independent country. I suspect she has close contact with those people.

During the Chinese representative's comments, the U.S. delegation raised a point of order, and an assistant to Ambassador Currie said:

> Mr. Chair, I think this committee has now hit a new low. The Chinese delegation's personal attack on the U.S. Ambassador is completely inappropriate. They must learn to respect people's opinions. As the chair of this committee, I request that you don't tolerate such behavior in this committee. I've never seen such personal attacks and disrespect in my professional life!

The chair took the point of order and advised the Chinese delegate to "confine himself to concrete aspects of his information about the NGO," and not go into other unrelated matters, cautioning, "We mustn't get into a political discussion." The Chinese representative smiled, feigned calmness, and asked to continue with his comments.

> First, I don't think I attacked her personally. Now I'd like to talk about concrete information. First, the Ambassador mentioned the Chinese government is implementing discriminatory policies against minorities. She used very harsh language. She is using such tactics to show she is politically correct. The Chinese government takes care to protect its

minorities, including the Uyghurs. We respect their religious rights. We respect their freedom of speech. We've made huge investments in the economic development of these minorities. The Uyghurs and other minorities in Xinjiang are experiencing a historic period in which their human rights are better protected than any other period in history. Regarding the op-ed the Ambassador read, the Western media has always been biased against China. They are focused on finding fault in the Chinese regime. When reporting on China, they never report from an objective and unbiased perspective. The facts given in the op-ed are baseless. We've canceled the re-education and re-education through labor programs a long time ago. Second, she demanded the Chinese authorities provide evidence for our claims against Mr. Isa. We've provided much information and evidence. However, as I've mentioned, some countries aren't taking that evidence seriously; they're applying a double standard on terrorism, because they know this man doesn't pose a security threat to them. But this man and his organization have links to criminal activities in China. The facts clearly show that this man poses a security risk to China and many other countries. The critical issue here is that some countries criticize others on issues of human rights and their fight against terrorism while they apply a double standard. When things aren't in their favor, they claim they "stand by the principle." When things are in China and its friends' favor, they distort the facts. We must avoid getting emotional and politicizing this issue.

The chair didn't allow the discussion to continue any further. He said a decision would be reached on May 25, based on the submitted information. He pointed out that everyone had become tired of these exchanges and ended the two-hour session.

Due to more conflict and differences of opinion, the decision was only announced on May 30. China failed, again. Not only was its request to revoke the consultative status of the STP rejected, but its request to withdraw my credentials to participate in the UN meetings was also turned down. We later learned that the Chinese delegation and Western democratic countries had engaged in tense exchanges during the decision-making process.[33]

CHAPTER 7

THE CONCENTRATION CAMPS

In 2016, unprecedented atrocities started happening in East Turkistan. By 2017, the situation had deteriorated drastically: mass murder, arrests with heavy prison sentences, the incarceration of millions of people in closed "re-education" camps, forceful brainwashing, deprivation of their language, faith and traditions—all of these became the new norm the Uyghurs had to accept. These events were happening in the twenty-first century, but in the most oppressive country in the world. We learned that even after the world had witnessed the horrors of Nazi Germany and said, "never again," genocide was unfolding once again, in our homeland. The Uyghur diaspora was horrified, but we were unable to obtain evidence of this genocide to expose China's atrocities. The CCP, with their policy of "not letting even a [single] prisoner flee," suppressed all information and cut off communication channels with our homeland. Our only access to information and news was through intermittent leaks, which made us even more anxious because they were never detailed and always raised more unanswered questions and concerns.

THE CONCENTRATION CAMPS

The WUC leadership decided that to expose China's true nature, we needed to collect evidence about the concentration camps. We started working on a report focused on important thematic issues that were a clear reflection of current Chinese policies.

What exactly happened in East Turkistan in 2017? We could learn about the Uyghurs' situation to some extent from the media, but it became increasingly difficult to understand the exact state of affairs in East Turkistan because the media and information flow were tightly controlled, and as time went on, some news spread more than other stories, clouding our understanding. The world somehow knows Ilham Tohti, a professor at Minzu University of China in Beijing, who has been the recipient of many international awards and was sentenced to life in prison for advocating dialogue to resolve the conflict between the Uyghur and Chinese nations. However, the world doesn't know the hundreds of thousands of other Ilham Tohtis who have been imprisoned unjustly and sentenced to heavy prison terms.

The Chinese constitution and rule of law, including criminal law, do not apply in East Turkistan. The mass arbitrary detention of Uyghurs is proof of that. The tragedies in the "open prison" and "police state" of East Turkistan dramatically increased with the transfer of the former Communist Party Secretary of Tibet, Chen Quanguo, to the so-called "Xinjiang Uyghur Autonomous Uyghur Region" in August 2016.

As soon as he arrived in East Turkistan, Chen began campaigns like Fighting Three Evils, Fighting Religious Extremism, and the Strike Hard Campaign to counter perceived terrorism and implemented a policy of arbitrary detention and heavy punishments for detainees outside the legal system. As he had done in Tibet, he launched police checkpoints in East Turkistan on a large scale. Beginning in October 2016, international flights from Urumchi were suspended. Flights between Urumchi and Istanbul, Urumchi and Astana, Urumchi and Dushanbe and other lines were suspended altogether. Uyghurs' passports were collected on the pretence of being "renewed." Anyone who had travelled abroad until 2017 for whatever reason and anyone who had relatives abroad was taken in for questioning. Later, they became the first victims of the concentration camps. The camps created by Chen would come to torment millions of people in East Turkistan.

Back then, we were unable to prepare the report as we couldn't obtain sufficient evidence and material. But beginning in 2018, everything we knew and wrote about was confirmed by scholars like Adrian Zenz, who published credible reports on the camps using Chinese sources and documents. In 2019, the available evidence was corroborated by camp survivors, who began to testify about their experiences.

PRESIDENCY OF THE WUC

In November 2017, we called the Extraordinary Sixth General Assembly of the World Uyghur Congress. More than one hundred and fifty delegations and observers from twenty countries participated and delivered speeches, including members of the European parliament, the German parliament, former diplomats, and leaders of international human rights organizations. New leadership of the WUC was democratically elected. My long-time friend Omer Kanat and I were the candidates for the presidency. I was elected president with the majority vote.

The Extraordinary Sixth General Assembly meant the beginning of a new era in the history of the Uyghur movement in the diaspora, leading to reform of the WUC's leadership and organizational structure; a review of the WUC's strategies and strengthening of its position in the diaspora advocacy movement; bolstering the WUC's ability to speak for our people under oppression; and finding new ways to win the international community's support and cooperation to stop the severe crimes in East Turkistan.

THE CONCENTRATION CAMPS

At the successful conclusion of the General Assembly, and representing the new leadership of the WUC, I delivered the closing remarks outlining my plans and strategy for the WUC:

> My fellow countrymen, dear delegates, ladies and gentlemen,
>
> I stand before you at a time when East Turkistan has been occupied by the Chinese communist army for sixty-eight years, our people are facing unprecedented oppression, terror and war, and China continues to block our movement using its diplomatic and economic power. And yet, despite all this, we have persisted, and successfully concluded our Sixth General Assembly. Congratulations to everyone!
>
> The Delegation[s], working with determination and striving towards a common goal, ha[ve] participated in the session and placed new responsibility on the shoulders of the next generation of leaders. They have all given invaluable recommendations to the congress to reach its strategic goals. I would like to take this opportunity to thank everyone for their great input and help in the successful conclusion of the session.
>
> The most important thing I need to talk about is unity. Today, we need national unity more than ever before. The WUC, the most representative organization of our movement in the diaspora, derives its strength, lifeblood, privilege, and influence from unity. However, unity isn't achieved through slogans. It also isn't achieved through dictatorship, narcissism, and greed. Whether people have supported the WUC or opposed it, understood us or misunderstood us, joined us or stayed away from us, if

they are Uyghur and from East Turkistan, we have a responsibility to accept and welcome them. The organization of the people of East Turkistan only exists with their support. As the leaders of the WUC, we would like to announce that we welcome every Uyghur in the world. We will make the WUC a perfect organization that meets the hopes of our people and realizes its founding goals. We call on everyone to strive together in this endeavor.

As you all know, this sacred movement was built by forefathers. Our leaders, from Muhemmedemin Bugra, Isa Yüsüf Aliptékin, Ziya Semedi, Abdurup Mexsum, Yusupbeg Muxlisi, Hashir Wahidi, Huseyin Qari Islami, Muhamed Riza Bekin and Ablikimhan Mexsum to Erkin Alptekin and Rebiya Kadeer, have all made immense contributions to this movement. Our movement in the diaspora started from nothing, and today has come to represent the voice of the Uyghur people in the United Nations, European Parliament, and the governments of democratic countries everywhere. We are now able to fight Chinese repression in the international arena. These are the fruits of the selfless labour and efforts of our aforementioned leaders over many years. We are proud of the work of our forefathers and their love for their nation. It is our duty to follow in their footsteps.

The WUC is a democratic organization. The basic principles of democracy include freedom of expression, democratic election, accountability, and respect for different opinions. The WUC must implement a system that welcomes observation, criticism and the suggestions of all people of East Turkistan and accepts competition and differences of opinion. It is in this way only that our people will be able to hold us accountable, convey their disapproval, and tell us our mistakes. This is extremely important for the healthy development of our movement. The WUC and its sister organizations are working in a favourable environment created in democratic nations. The WUC and our organizations' survival and development depend on following international law, the 1948 UN Universal Declaration of Human Rights, the 1966 International Covenant on Civil and Political Right[s], and the laws and regulations of the countries in which we are working. The WUC's constitution and work code reject all forms of violence and terrorism. Violence and terrorism are the basic principles of the Chinese regime in suppressing the people of East Turkistan. The CCP tries hard to eradicate the WUC—a democratic organization striving to protect the rights of its people using peaceful means—and slandering it with claims of terrorism. If we want to effectively raise awareness in the international community of China's state terrorism and extreme repression and bring an end to the oppression of the people of East Turkistan, we need to continually fight for the respect of our rights in a peaceful manner. We must object to the state terrorism of the CCP.

The WUC has received opportunities to speak and bring the Uyghur crisis to the attention of Western democracies, the United Nations and other international organizations. We need to further develop these achievements and build on them to strengthen our sacred movement and representation in the countries and organizations that are increasingly sympathizing with us.

As you are aware, a "Uyghur Friendship Group" has been [*sic*] established in the European Parliament on October 19, thanks to our prolonged efforts. Although China's lobbying activities are strong in those areas, their ploys have failed in the face of rule of law and democratic principles in the countries in which we operate.

These democratic countries and institutions, such as the UN and the EU, are important platforms upon which to strengthen our movement in the future. As our activities in East Turkistan's neighbouring countries are increasingly being restricted by Chinese pressure, it is important to find ways to raise the voice of the Uyghurs in the UN, U.S., EU and other democratic countries and get them to pressure China.

The neighbouring countries to East Turkistan, including Kazakhstan, Uzbekistan and Kyrgyzstan, that share our language, culture and history, are lands in which our movement should have flourished. Unfortunately, with China's pressure, political activities in these countries are facing blockades. It is critical to remember that even though these dictatorships are befriending China and keeping their distance from Uyghur organizations, the people of these countries are our brothers and sisters. We share the same religion, ethnic origin, history, culture and brotherly love that goes back thousands of years. China can never break this bond. China's expansionist agenda and attack on the Uyghurs' language, script, tradition, faith and history—the same values of all the people of this region—is creating a rare

THE CONCENTRATION CAMPS

opportunity to strengthen our national movement and gain their support.

It is now time to enlighten our brotherly nations. I believe, along with enlightenment, we need to emphasize cultivating Uyghur patriotism among our brothers in this region. We should boost cultural and social activities to protect the Uyghur language, culture, tradition and faith. In this region, there are NGOs, and we need to strengthen our relationship with them, cooperate, and find new paths for our movement. Today, these countries may be members of the Shanghai Cooperation Organization (SCO) and face strong political and economic pressure from China, but in the past, these people shared, for better or worse, our history, culture and language. I believe it is crucial to increase and reinforce our relationship with them.

For years, we've focused on strengthening our advocacy mostly in the Western world, but we couldn't do much in the Muslim world. With China's heavy investment in Muslim and Arab countries, it is critical to bring their attention to China's attack on our shared faith and its policies to suppress Islam and eradicate our religion. It is in this way that we might be able to win sympathy for our cause in the Muslim world.

Another important area we need to pay attention to is countries that have territorial disputes with China, including Japan and India; South Asian countries facing threats from China; countries and regions facing direct aggression from China under the pretense of the "new silk road"; and the Baluchis and Sindhis in Pakistan. Cooperating with these people is beneficial to our cause.

The WUC has built a great network with many international organizations around the world. Many organizations working in Asia, Africa, Europe and the U.S. are now aware of the Uyghur crisis. We can continue to further internationalize the Uyghur crisis with the help of these organizations.

Today, Tibetans, Mongols and Hong Kongers who face our same struggles are growing their activities against China. Chinese democracy activists are also fighting the CCP regime. These groups want to cooperate with the WUC and fight the Chinese communist regime together. We believe that we will continue our cooperation with these groups.

Dear countrymen, the East Turkistan movement is prodigious. Our enemy is powerful, but our cause is sacred.

Our freedom struggle isn't just the duty of the WUC, it is the duty of all the people of East Turkistan. Anyone who can contribute to this movement is welcome. Let us try to bring people from all walks of life, experts, youths, and everyone in between to this movement. As a representative organization in the diaspora, let's make our future agenda realistic and efficient, and let us carry out our activities strategically and methodically. Let us welcome anyone who wants to fight with us shoulder to shoulder. We must fight for the same goal together.

My election came at a time when the organization's burden and responsibility had increased considerably. I had been working as the secretary-general and chairman of the Executive Committee since 2004. Now that I was the president of an organization that represented the Uyghur movement, carrying out my duties was immensely difficult in an environment where our political, economic, and diplomatic means and resources were very limited.

FACING A CHINESE AGENT AT THE UN

As one of the five members of the United Nations Security Council and an influential country thanks to dirty diplomacy and economic power, China has made considerable efforts to seize control over the UN and block all dissent within the organization. When the United States left some international organizations, including the UN Human Rights Council in 2018, China took the opportunity to expand its influence in those organizations. As it had already taken the reins of the World Health Organization, China was now turning its attention to controlling the UN Human Rights Council.

After years of failing to impede me using its power at the UN Human Rights Council, to expel me from UN buildings, and ban my right to speak at the organization, China changed tactics. It began using its agents and fabricated human rights organizations to refute and repudiate me at UN meetings. Ironically, these fake organizations earned consultative status in the UN.

On April 29, 2019, when I went to New York to attend a meeting of the UNPFIII, I noticed someone who looked Asian tailing me. If I sat in a coffee shop inside the UN headquarters, the man sat two tables away from me and walked behind me when I left. If I glanced back, he would turn away or pretend to look at his phone. He acted very strangely. "Hmm, a Chinese agent!" I thought. But he seemed like such an inexperienced and stupid spy. When I entered the meeting hall, he sat at the back and watched me. When I returned to the coffee shop after the meeting, he followed right after and continued watching me.

On May 1, when I was scheduled to speak at the forum, I saw the Chinese agent sitting at the front of the hall. I didn't pay much attention to him. In my presentation, supported by the evidence we had obtained, I stated that the Chinese concentration camp system constituted genocide and crimes against humanity. Ironically, the Chinese agent asked permission to speak on behalf of the Chinese government to refute my speech. Okay, so he wasn't just a Chinese spy, he was also a Chinese diplomat at the UN—a Chinese diplomat had been trailing me like a shadow for two or three days. The man repeated China's lies about me: "This man is the president of the terrorist organization, the World Uyghur Congress, Dolkun Isa. He is a terrorist on Interpol's Red Notices. He is exploiting this forum. Everything he said is untrue. The Uyghurs are living a happy life, etc., etc." He repeated the Chinese regime's by-now standard lies about me to refute my speech on China's inhumane crimes against the Uyghurs.

Then, Ms. Courtney Nemroff, the U.S. acting representative to ECOSOC, took her turn to contest the Chinese diplomat's accusations:

> Dolkun is a respected human rights advocate. The freedom of speech of human rights activists and NGOs shouldn't be restricted in this forum. If Dolkun was a terrorist, he couldn't have entered the U.S. If he was a terrorist, Germany wouldn't have given him citizenship. The rights of human rights activists shouldn't be infringed here. It is reported that more than one million Uyghurs are currently suffering in concentration camps. We are closely monitoring this issue.

The German ambassador to the UN, Christoph Heusgen, took a turn after the U.S. representative. He said the WUC was a legal German-based organization and that I was a German citizen. He defended me and said the Chinese diplomat's allegations of terrorism were baseless.

THE CONCENTRATION CAMPS

These demonstrations of respect towards me by the U.S. and German diplomats in front of the Chinese diplomats were noteworthy. Afterwards, Ambassador Heusgen shook my hand, saying, "You spoke really well. We support and defend your rightful activities in the UN." Ambassador Nemroff shook my hand as well and said, "Your speech was great, congratulations!" Normally, diplomats wouldn't shake hands with human rights activists and NGOs, openly showing their support. I had never witnessed such an event in my twenty years of activism at the UN. This scene should have sent China the message, "Your hegemony and shamelessness won't work in the UN. You can't just attack others freely here." But an event at the UNPFII proved they were still slow to grasp the message.

That afternoon, a continental conference was held. I participated in the Asian continental meeting. The theme of the meeting was the development of unrepresented people and protection of their traditions and cultures. Chinese representatives were also present. As people could request a turn to speak, I did so and presented the issues in East Turkistan one by one: that China began their persecution after occupying East Turkistan in 1949 and moving large numbers of Chinese settlers into our lands to make us a minority; that they created ecological pollution in East Turkistan through the erratic management of natural resources; that they made local people homeless and created poverty by robbing them of their lands; and that they were now torturing millions of people and locking them up in concentration camps.

The Chinese diplomats in their turn to speak repeated their by-now standard charges. "Everything Dolkun said is a lie. He is a terrorist; he shouldn't be given a turn to speak. He should actually be kicked out of this meeting." I was not given a second opportunity to speak, despite my request. During the "Protection of the Traditions and Cultures of Peoples" session, I made multiple requests to present the grave abuses of the Uyghur language, culture, and traditions. However, a Chinese diplomat was chairing this meeting. Although he was supposed to be neutral, he deliberately didn't look in my direction or pretended he didn't see me. He used his power to ensure that I was unable to speak.

I prepared a note and sent it to the co-chair, who put the note in front of the Chinese chair. Now he couldn't ignore me and had to give me a turn to speak. In my presentation, I said that although it was recognized as an official language in the Chinese constitution and in the Autonomous Law, as of 2018, the Uyghur language was banned from use and was being driven out of the education system. I explained how the Kashgar Old City had been partially destroyed between 2008 and 2009, causing the European parliament to pass a resolution in 2012 to protect it from further damage and warn China; and how the two- to three-thousand-year-old Uyghur culture and heritage were being obliterated. I stressed that China had launched a war on religion in East Turkistan and had been carrying out a systemic cleansing in the religious arena. I closed with the following:

> I spoke three times today. Each time, this Chinese diplomat tried to refute me and call me a terrorist. He insulted me, trampled on my dignity and disregarded my honour. If I were a terrorist, I wouldn't have been able to sit with you in this forum, I would've been instead sitting in jail right now, either in a prison in Germany or the U.S. I've never seen a bomb or touched a weapon in my life. I've been advocating using my right to freedom of speech as recognized in the UN and international law to raise the voice of my voiceless people. But this is considered a crime by China. For this, China put me on Interpol's Red Notices. Fortunately, this injustice that lasted twenty-one years ended, and today my name is cleared from

the Red Notices. I earned my right. However, the Chinese are still insulting me and alleging I am a terrorist. This forum must be a forum that guarantees the rights of people like me, who are struggling for human rights. This diplomat is attacking me personally. I feel that I'm being discriminated against here. As per the principles of the UN, people must be able to present their opinions here without being restricted and discriminated against. Diplomats must pay attention to what they say, respect the language of the UN and avoid making baseless claims.

My presentation created an uproar in the hall. My words obviously affected the Chinese diplomat and put him in an awkward position. The same fellow who had started his last speech with "Dolkun Isa is a terrorist on Interpol's Red Notices" now had to start with "Mr. Dolkun Isa."

"Mr. Dolkun Isa's claim is untrue. The Uyghur language is still being practised," said the Chinese diplomat, responding to my speech, "Mosques haven't been demolished as he claims, mosques are still there, people can freely go to the mosques and pray. The Uyghur culture isn't suppressed. All the ethnic groups in Xinjiang are living happier lives than any time in history . . ."

CONCENTRATION CAMP DEBATE

The Chinese Mission began its attempts to block me from the UN as early as 2012, but we were only able to obtain evidence of some of these early attempts several years later. The evidence we obtained included correspondence between Chinese diplomats in the UN and the UN High Commissioner for Human Rights.

UN regulations state that the list of NGOs and human rights activists participating in UN meetings must be kept private and mustn't be handed over to third parties. Nevertheless, China has always abused international norms, and UN regulations were no exception. Using various means, China would obtain lists of Uyghur activists and look for ways to stop or impede them. Some UN officials reasoned: "China is a major donor to the UN. If we don't give them what they want, they might stop their funding to the UN." Some officials did it under pressure from China, while others succumbed to China's gifts or were worn down by China's shameless, never-ending requests. Fortunately, people of high moral values and principles have always objected to such actions by China. They insisted it was both wrong for China to request such information and to pressure UN officials and for UN officials to give in to these demands. As can be imagined, the issue caused conflict and debate among UN officials.

Since 2012, China has made many complaints against us [the WUC and the STP] to the office of the UN High Commissioner for Human Rights and other UN committees. Of course, they include complaints against me specifically. The Chinese regime has also made complaints against Tibetan, Hong Konger, and Taiwanese human rights activists and demanded their exclusion from the UN. China has never tired of making such complaints to various UN offices.

The Chinese government went further to stop our activism in the UN and brazenly sent letters to individual diplomats of various countries, demanding that they not meet with me and the other WUC staff. China even pressured diplomats of some developing countries. When I met with some of these diplomats in the UN, I got information and written evidence about China's attempts.

Of course, one might wonder: why does China so fiercely oppose my activities in the UN? Why is China so obsessed with me? The answer is relatively simple. In the early days, when the Uyghur issue was unknown in the international arena, China

THE CONCENTRATION CAMPS

treated Uyghur activities in the UN and the European institutions with ignorance and carelessness. This changed after 2008 when the Uyghurs and Tibetans came together came during the Beijing Olympics to protest China's treatment. The demonstration of the Tibetans in Lhasa in 2008 was fiercely suppressed. Then, after the Urumchi Massacre on July 5, 2009, the Uyghur issue was taken to another level. Recep Erdoğan called the Urumchi Massacre a genocide. Other countries, such as Germany, openly condemned China's use of military force to crack down on the peaceful protesters in Urumchi. With that, the Uyghur crisis started making international headlines. Parliamentarians, human rights organizations, and international media outlets started paying close attention to the persecution faced by the people of East Turkistan.

If China had its way, no one in the world would know about the Uyghur crisis, no one would even know there was a nation of people in the world called Uyghurs, no one would hear the Uyghurs. China would freely carry out its assimilationist policies against our people and quietly erase us from history. However, things *didn't* go China's way. Year after year, magnified by Chinese persecution, the voice of the Uyghurs was getting louder in the UN and the European parliament. The European Union even started passing important resolutions on the Uyghur crisis. China realized they couldn't quietly eradicate the Uyghur nation and decided they had to stop Uyghur activism in the UN or it would continue to grow and become an even bigger headache in the future. To stop this from happening, China wanted to prevent me, the other leaders, and the members of the World Uyghur Congress—the most representative and leading organization of the Uyghurs in the diaspora—from speaking at the UN. After Xi Jinping's election, China began using shameless tactics to prevent the topic of the Uyghur crisis from being raised in the UN and repudiated, hid, and twisted the facts when it came up. It is that simple.

CHAPTER 8

THE PRICE OF ACTIVISM

DEPORTED FROM TURKEY—AGAIN

In previous chapters, I described how I was deported from Turkey in 2008 and refused entry in 2014 when I when I had a stopover in Istanbul on my way from Japan to Germany. After I was removed from the Interpol Red Notice in February 2018, I believed I would not have an issue travelling to certain countries, but I wanted to confirm this. Through my contacts in Ankara, I asked about the possibility of visiting Turkey and found out that the travel ban issued in 2006 was still active. My friends advised me to find a lawyer and fight it in court.

I contacted Professor Dr. Ilyas Dogan, a Turkish lawyer in Ankara. As he had been raising the Uyghur issue in Turkish media since 2019, Dr. Dogan understood our situation well, and we used to talk over the phone. I discussed with him the possibility of filing a lawsuit in a Turkish court to lift the entry ban. He said we could do it and had a good chance of winning the case.

In May 2020, I went to the General Consulate of Turkey in Munich and filed for a power of attorney for Dr. Dogan, which

THE PRICE OF ACTIVISM

I sent to him with other related documents. A month later, he began a lawsuit on my behalf in Ankara's Administrative Court. The case ended on August 5, 2021, when, after many legal battles and a long bureaucratic process, he called to announce that we had won the case: the Court had ruled that the ban on my entry to Turkey had been cancelled. This was a moment of great happiness for me, and I was ready to fly to Turkey as soon as possible. Dr. Dogan told me to wait a while as the court ruling needed to reach the Immigration Department and then the Border Police had to remove me from the system.

On September 5, Dr. Dogan received an official notice from the Immigration Department that the entry ban had been lifted on September 1, 2021. By court order, the travel ban issued in 2006 was finally cancelled sixteen years later, and I could finally go back to Turkey. However, as I had pre-arranged meetings in Europe, I could only travel to Turkey after September 25.

Meanwhile, several of us planned to attend the 45th session of the UN Human Rights Council in Geneva, arriving on September 14. Two days later, I received bad news. The founder and former president of the WUC, Erkin Alptekin, had suddenly fallen ill during his vacation in Ankara and was in critical condition in the hospital. My friends in Turkey suggested that, if possible, I should immediately come to visit him. Dr. Dogan assured me that I would have no problem entering Turkey but suggested that he meet me at the airport and rearranged his schedule to come back to Ankara immediately.

I arrived at Ankara Esenboga Airport on September 18 at 1:30 a.m., excited but also nervous. Sure enough, when I went to passport control, there was an issue with my passport. From long experience and knowing that trouble was brewing, my heart started beating fast. Ten minutes later, I was told, "You can't enter Turkey, you have a travel ban." "I know that," I said, "but the issue is over. Here is the court order and letter from the Immigration

Department." The officer simply asked me to wait in an office. From there I called my lawyer.

At the airport, Dr. Dogan, his son and lawyer Mr. Ahmet Batuhan Dogan, as well as my friends Dr. Erkin Ekrem, Dr. Erkin Emet, Meryem Sultan from Ankara, and Abdureshid Abdulhamit and Dilshat Barisci, who had come from Istanbul, were all waiting for me. Over the next hour, Dr. Dogan had several conversations with the police before being told that a new entry ban had been issued on September 9. We were shocked and planned to appeal, but at 2:30 a.m. Saturday there wasn't much we could do before Monday.

I explained the urgency of my situation, that I had come to visit a very ill friend, but there was no point in arguing with the police. I had no choice but to go back to Germany. After much pleading, however, the friends who had come to meet me were allowed to come inside for a brief ten-minute catch-up. Then I was given my passport and a boarding pass for a flight that departed for Germany at 5:00 a.m.

I had half an hour until my flight, so I took a short video and shared it on Twitter, saying: "Today I am deported again by the Turkish police. I had a travel ban since 2006, but the travel ban was lifted by the Ankara Administrative Court in June. I came to Ankara today to visit Erkin Alptekin, the former President of WUC at the hospital. The court decision is meaningless." Dr. Dogan left me and took a video with my friends at the airport and shared it on social media too.

On September 18, at 5:00 a.m., I flew back to Germany. During the three hours I was on the plane, thousands of people commented on my video, criticizing the Turkish government. As the saying goes, "There is good and bad in everything." Had I been allowed to enter that day, I would have just visited, and not many people except some of my friends would have known about it. But this news made the headlines in the Turkish political scene and the media. Close to 450,000 people viewed the short video I shared on Twitter, and thousands of people commented on it. I also received thousands of messages of sympathy. The incident also sparked debates in the Turkish and international media for several weeks.

Most importantly, the issue of my travel ban made its way onto the Turkish political agenda. MPs from opposition political parties brought it up in the Turkish parliament and questioned the government. Ahmet Davutoglu, former prime minister and the current leader of the "Gelecek" party, and the "Iyi" party leader Meral Akşener made statements critical of the Turkish government on this issue.

After this second deportation, I decided with Dr. Dogan to appeal my case to the Constitutional Court of the Republic of Turkey. On September 20, I sent the following letter to the President of Turkey, Mr. Recep Erdoğan. The letter was delivered to President Erdoğan via his Chief Advisor Yalcin Topcu. To this day, I have not received a reply.

20 September 2021

Mr President of Turkey Recep Tayyip Erdoğan,

First of all, I wish you good health, peace and well-being, and I am writing this letter to personally inform you about the status of my ban on entering Turkey. I am sure you are aware that China's oppressive policies against Uyghurs, Kazakhs and other Muslim peoples in East Turkistan have been described as "crimes against humanity" and "genocide" by the parliaments of the US government, Canada, the United Kingdom, the Netherlands, Belgium, the Czech Republic and Lithuania.

In the last 5 years alone, several million people, whose only crime is to belong to a Turkic and Muslim minority, have been confined to concentration camps. Nearly a million children have been forcibly taken from their families and subjected to brainwashing, women have been forcibly sterilised, raped, and forcibly married to Chinese men and more than 16 thousand mosques have been destroyed, the Holy Quran has been confiscated, Muslim names have been banned, and millions of people have been forced to work as slave labourers, the Uyghur language has been almost removed from education in schools. It has been documented by witnesses, international media organisations, research centres, experts and leaked documents of the Chinese government. These policies aim at nothing but to assimilate the people of East Turkistan by targeting their language, religion, culture and history, and ultimately to fully assimilate them.

While China is doing this and the world is watching silently, I and people like me are paying a high price trying to raise awareness of this genocide to the world and to defend the rights of the people of East Turkistan as much as we can. As the President of the World Uyghur Congress, which is the representative body of the East Turkistan people in the world, if I give only myself as an example, I learned that my 78-year-old mother Ayhan Mehmet was imprisoned in a camp and died a year later, which I only learned months later, and I received the news from the Chinese media that my father Isa Mehmet died. I have also learnt from international media that my brother Yalkun

THE PRICE OF ACTIVISM

Isa was sentenced to at least 17 years in prison and that my brother Hushtar Isa received a life sentence. China not only does these things, but also labels me and many human rights activists as terrorists, separatists, and extremists, and tries to silence and block us with many tools, from travel bans to issuing an Interpol Red Notice. Whatever happens, we will continue this fight.

The main reason why I am writing to you is that I have been banned from entering Turkey for 15 years, even though I was educated at Gazi University, I feel that Turkey is like my homeland, and I defend it on international platforms when necessary.

In 2008, when I was sent back from Antalya for the first time, I was very surprised and disappointed. In 2016, I was once again turned back from the border. Until now, the late Muhsin Yazıcıoğlu and other parliament members had submitted several parliamentary questions to the Turkish Grand National Assembly to lift my ban on entering Turkey. Despite our attempts before ambassadors and some ministers, we could not succeed. I still decided to put my trust in the Turkish justice system to seek my rights and filed a lawsuit through my lawyer, Prof. Dr İlyas Doğan. The Ankara Administrative Court examined the situation and unanimously decided to lift my entry ban based on code G-87. I was very happy that justice was served. My lawyer received the confirmation letter regarding the lift of my entry ban on September 6, 2021, by the Immigration Department. After hearing the news that Mr. Erkin Alptekin, the founding President of the World Uyghur Congress and the son of our late leader Isa Yusuf Alptekin, with whom you were acquainted, was taken to intensive care in Ankara, I immediately flew there on September 18, 2021. Unfortunately, I was stopped again at the airport, and I was surprised to learn that a new ban with the code number Ç-149/Ç-152 was imposed by the Immigration Department without any concrete evidence or justification. I was sent back to Germany,

I know that my travel bans are due to China's pressure and threats against different countries. However, countries with a rule of law do not respond to China's demands to ban me from entering these countries without any concrete evidence, because they find it contrary to international and domestic laws. The fact that Turkey, which we consider to be a state with a rule of law, has re-imposed this ban in a way that we consider to be unlawful has deeply upset me and is contrary to Turkish laws. It is also an indication of how far China's hand has extended and how much its influence has increased over Turkey. I believe that you will stand by your statement that "The world is bigger than five," which you personally expressed at the United Nations General Assembly. It is also time to prove that the world is bigger than China. I would like to personally share this situation with you, given that you are in the highest position in the Republic of Turkey, and I would like you to be sure that I have never been involved nor will I ever be in any behaviour that would prejudice this country, in Turkey or elsewhere.

Finally, I would like to express my gratitude on behalf of the World Uyghur Congress for accepting and hosting many refugees from East Turkistan, and

I respectfully request you to lift this ban against me as soon as possible.

Yours sincerely,
Dolkun Isa
President of the World Uyghur Congress

Although I have been removed from the Interpol list of Red Notices, China's evil ploys that label me a "terrorist" continue in some countries.

MY MOTHER'S DEATH

After I left my homeland in 1994, I never saw my parents again. Although I could sometimes speak to them over the phone, I never met them again in person. Nonetheless, I always lived with the hope that we would one day meet again.

The CCP's assimilationist policies since their occupation of East Turkistan in 1949 failed to assimilate our people. This was why they revised their policies to eradicate my people through genocide. Like millions of other Uyghurs, I was affected by this genocide.

My parents were getting old. When we spoke on the phone, we only talked about our health. We knew the Chinese intelligence agencies tapped our phones, so my parents couldn't tell me about the pressure, intimidation, and other troubles they faced. Sometimes, my mother would sob on the phone, but she would say nothing when I asked what happened. "We're doing good, don't worry," she would say. I couldn't ask again. Any word from them would become their calamity. It's been twenty-eight years since I left them.

In 2008, Dr. Erkin Sidiq travelled to Aksu from the United States and visited my parents. He brought back their greetings, photos, and a short video. That was the first time I had seen my parents' faces since I left China in 1996.

In April 2017, I called my parents. I didn't know it at the time, but this would be my last conversation with them. The call ended after our typical greetings and asking after each other's well-being. One week later, my wife called them. "Please don't call us again," my mom told her. I was shocked to hear this. For the past twenty-four years, my mother had never said such a thing, even when they faced immense difficulties. My mother was a brave woman. When the Chinese regime listed me on Interpol's Red Notices in 2003, the police came to my family. "We're going to bring your terrorist son back from Germany and punish him," they told my parents, intimidating them. "Bring him if you can. Why are you telling me? Do you need my permission?" my mother retorted, without hesitation. Asking us not to call her meant the situation must have become truly horrific.

On June 12, 2018, one of my friends who lived in another country told me the news of the death of my mother, Ayhan Memet. I was devastated. My mother, whom I couldn't see for twenty-four years, suddenly passed away, and how and where she died was unknown.

The media was curious to know these details. However, I had no answer, I knew nothing. I tried in vain to communicate with anyone in the homeland who could tell me what happened. My brothers' phones were all off. I couldn't contact my friends back home; internet communications were completely restricted.

As per our traditions, I held a Nezir (mourning ceremony) in a hall in Munich on June 18. My friends from Europe, the United States, and Australia came for the Nezir and consoled me. Those who couldn't come sent their condolences and phoned me. MPs of some countries sent special condolences too, including the U.S. Ambassador-at-Large for International Religious Freedom, Mr. Sam Brownback, as well as Ambassador Michael Kozak.

THE PRICE OF ACTIVISM

Three weeks after the Nezir, Radio Free Asia's Uyghur Service published the news of my mother's death. The reporters at RFA spent more than two weeks researching and interviewing the police officers and local authorities in Aksu. They found out that my mother died in a concentration camp. According to the report, she was taken to a camp in either May or June of 2017 and died there on May 17, 2018.[34]

In which camp was my mother locked up? What kind of nightmares had she faced? How did she die? Where is her grave? I never found answers to these questions. My mother was seventy-eight years old when she died. China killed a seventy-eight-year-old woman in its concentration camp. This news created a stir in the media for some time and added to the rage against China.

In January 2020, the Chinese regime published a propaganda video forcing my elder sister Arzugul Isa, my sister-in-law Asiye, and her son Zulpikar to speak against me.[35] The fact that the Chinese regime's propaganda campaign only began two years after the reports of my mother's death may have been because my relatives were in concentration camps until then. In the video, I got to see some of my relatives whom I hadn't seen in twenty-six years. Although they were forced to speak against me, I felt relieved to see them alive. They said in the video, "Our father and mother died of natural causes in their old age, but our brother Dolkun Isa has spread lies claiming they died in concentration camps." They were forced to say that; there was no other way they would have said it. It was impossible to refuse the Chinese regime. If you watched the video carefully, you could tell they were reading from a pre-written text. Sadly, this video uncovered another awful truth. I didn't know the fate of my father until that time and learned in the video that he had also died. I still don't know where and how he died. My father, Isa Memet, was ninety years old. I wonder how, in the twenty-first century, many other people live without knowing where the grave of their father is, or when and how he died. Perhaps no one except the Uyghurs face such harsh tragedies.[36]

I knew my younger brother, Hushtar Isa, was taken away at the beginning of 2016 and has since disappeared. When I visited Japan in April 2019, I learned from a neighbour's son who was studying in Japan that my elder brother, Yalkun , was sentenced to seventeen years in prison for allegations of separatism. I still don't have any more details than that. If my brothers Yalkun and Hushtar were alive or weren't locked up in a concentration camp or prison, the Chinese regime would likely have featured them in their propaganda video, so this was an indication that they weren't free.

My elder brother, Yalkun, graduated from the faculty of mathematics at Xinjiang University. He was an intellectual who had worked as a mathematics teacher at Aksu Education Institute since 1984. My younger brother, Hushtar, graduated from Xi'an Gonglu University. When he was studying English in Beijing in 1998, he was arrested by the Beijing Security Bureau for "inciting a protest against the government." When he was brought back to Urumchi, they added a charge for "engaging in national separatism" and he was sentenced to two years in prison. Although he was released from prison in 2000, he had to receive medical treatment for a long time. I assume this was because he faced severe physical abuse in prison, though I never had the opportunity to speak to him about it. He disappeared in 2016. Perhaps my brother Hushtar was among those the Chinese regime first took to concentration camps.

As a German citizen, I sent letters to Angela Merkel and the German foreign minister Heiko Mass several times, asking for their help to learn details about my parents' deaths and the condition of my other relatives. I also discussed this in my meetings with officials from the German foreign ministry and the European External Action Service (EEAS). During my visit to the

THE PRICE OF ACTIVISM

White House, I met with the Deputy National Security Advisor, Matthew Forbes Pottinger. At the U.S. State Department, I met with Scott Busby, Acting Principal Deputy Assistant Secretary, David R. Stilwell, Assistant Secretary, and Rick Waters, Deputy Assistant Secretary. I asked for their help, too. Unfortunately, I still don't have any information other than the propaganda video of the Chinese regime.

My entire family was destroyed. It remains unclear today how many of my relatives were sent to prison, concentration camps, how many were transferred to Mainland China, and how many others were sentenced to forced labour.

Millions of Uyghurs and Turkic people of East Turkistan have faced the same fate. The purpose of the Chinese regime's policies is to destroy families by locking up at least one family member in prison or a concentration camp. In this way, they dismantle family structures, orphan children, and create the hellish, fear-filled lives that dominate in East Turkistan.

CHAPTER 9
THE WORLD RESPONDS

In August 2018, the CERD report announcing the detainment of more than one million Uyghurs drew the attention of the United States, the European Union, and the Western media. Uyghurs in the diaspora became more active on social media and international media outlets, giving testimonies and demanding to know the whereabouts of their relatives in concentration camps. The Uyghurs were realizing that the camps weren't a temporary policy, and their relatives wouldn't be released soon. They became increasingly worried that their relatives would disappear in the camps and prisons without a trace.

During this period, under the leadership of the WUC, the Norwegian Uyghur Committee established the Uyghur Transitional Justice Database. The database gathered the information of close to seven thousand Uyghurs in concentration camps and submitted it to relevant countries and organizations. The WUC, Uyghur Human Rights Project (UHRP), Campaign for Uyghurs, Human Rights Watch, Amnesty International, independent researchers, and the Australian Strategic Policy Institute (ASPI) published many reports on the concentration camps; major media outlets including the BBC, CNN, Sky News, DW, and *Al Jazeera* produced documentaries about the concentration camps; Western researchers published video clips; and the European parliament, the U.S. Congress, Germany, and the British parliament held many testimonial conferences hosting concentration camp witnesses. I testified in the U.S. Congress, the European parliament, and the parliaments of other European countries. The testimonies of Uyghur and Kazakh concentration camp survivors attracted the attention of the international media and became evidence for some countries and parliaments to recognize the Uyghur genocide.

The majority of concentration camp survivors were married to foreign nationals or foreign citizens and thus were released after intervention from their spouses' countries. Before their release, the Chinese government demanded they keep secret what they had seen and gone through in the camps when they left China. They were threatened that if they broke their promise, they would have to think about the safety of their relatives remaining in China. After the survivors left China, they stayed silent for some time, but ultimately, some couldn't resist the call of their consciences and broke their silence to expose the reality of the camps. Omer Bekali, Mihrigul Tursun, Qelbinur Sidiq, Zumrat Dawut, Tursunay Ziyawudun, Sayragul Sauytbay, Gulbahar Jalilova, Gulzire Aulhan, and Gulbahar Haitiwaji are some of the brave survivors who broke their silence, reported their experiences to international media, and testified before parliaments. The biographies of Sayragul Sauytbay and Mihrigul Tursun were published in Germany. The biography of Gulbahar Haitiwaji was published in France. There are many other survivors living in different countries; however, they remain silent, afraid of the Chinese government's threats and worried for their safety as well as the safety of their relatives back home.

In June 2019, twenty-two[37] Western countries published a joint statement demanding the Chinese government close the camps and allow the UN Human Rights Council to conduct an independent investigation. Three additional countries joined later, making it twenty-five countries total. However, fifty countries sided with China in the UN and published a joint statement supporting China one week later, Qatar withdrew from the statement. By October 2020, the number of countries condemning China reached thirty-nine.[38] To counter this pressure, China started a campaign of diplomatic games and pressure in the UN. In September 2020, the number of countries supporting China was reduced to forty-five,[39] and in October 2021, forty-three countries signed a joint statement condemning the human rights situation regarding Uyghurs.[40] In June 2022, during the fiftieth Human Rights Council, the Netherlands delivered a joint statement on behalf of forty-seven countries.[41] In June 2020, fifty Special Rapporteurs issued a statement condemning the human rights situation in China, and more specifically regarding the treatment of Uyghurs.[42] Two years later, on June 10, 2022, forty-two Special Rapporteurs reiterated their call and urged the UN to enable a credible international investigation.[43]

In October 2019, the United States passed the Uyghur Human Rights Policy Act. President Donald Trump signed it. In December 2021, President Joe Biden signed the Uyghur Forced Labour Prevention Act into law. Both acts had gained bipartisan support from Republican and Democrat legislators in the United States.

Five resolutions regarding the Uyghur issue were passed by the European parliament in Strasbourg between October 2018 and June 2022.

The issue of the concentration camps and human rights violations in East Turkistan has been debated many times in different national parliaments and senates around the world.

THE WORLD RESPONDS

Currently, eleven parliaments worldwide (the United States, Canada, the United Kingdom, the Netherlands, Belgium, France, Lithuania, the Czech Republic, Ireland, Taiwan and the European Parliament) have adopted resolutions recognizing that the Chinese government's actions constitute crimes against humanity and genocide or risk of genocide.

On January 19, 2021, the U.S. State Department announced that it had designated China's crimes against the Uyghurs as genocide and crimes against humanity.

This was Mike Pompeo's statement:

> The United States of America has led the world in holding the perpetrators of the most heinous human rights abuses accountable. From the Nuremberg Trials to the creation of the Genocide Convention in 1948, to the declaration of ISIS's recent genocide against the Yazidis, Christians, and other religious minorities in Iraq and Syria, Americans have given voice to those who have been silenced by evil and stood with the living who cry out for truth, the rule of law, and justice. We do so not because we are compelled to act by any international court, multilateral body, or domestic political concern. We do so because it is right.
>
> For the past four years, this Administration has exposed the nature of the Chinese Communist Party and called it what it is: a Marxist-Leninist regime that exerts power over the long-suffering Chinese people through brainwashing and brute force. We have paid particular attention to the CCP's treatment of the Uyghur people, a Muslim minority group that resides largely in the Xinjiang Uyghur Autonomous Region in Western China. While the CCP has always

exhibited a profound hostility to all people of faith, we have watched with growing alarm the Party's increasingly repressive treatment of the Uyghurs and other ethnic and religious minority groups.

Our exhaustive documentation of the PRC's actions in Xinjiang confirms that since at least March 2017, local authorities dramatically escalated their decades-long campaign of repression against Uyghur Muslims and members of other ethnic and religious minority groups, including ethnic Kazakhs and ethnic Kyrgyz. Their morally repugnant, wholesale policies, practices, and abuses are designed systematically to discriminate against and monitor ethnic Uyghurs as a unique demographic and ethnic group, restrict their freedom to travel, emigrate, and attend schools, and deny other basic human rights of assembly, speech, and worship. PRC authorities have conducted forced sterilizations and abortions on Uyghur women, coerced them to marry non-Uyghurs, and separated Uyghur children from their families.

The Chinese Communist Party apparatchiks have denied international observers unhindered access to Xinjiang and denounced reliable reports about the worsening situation on the ground, instead spinning fanciful tales of happy Uyghurs participating in educational, counter-terror, women's empowerment, and poverty-alleviation projects. Meanwhile, they are delivering far darker messages to their own people, portraying Uyghurs as "malignant tumors," comparing their faith to a "communicable plague," and exhorting the Party faithful to implement a crushing blow, telling them "you can't uproot all the weeds hidden among the crops in the field one-by-one; you need to spray chemicals to kill them all."

Since the Allied forces exposed the horrors of Nazi concentration camps, the refrain "Never again" has become the civilized world's rallying cry against these horrors. Just because an atrocity is perpetrated in a manner that is different than what we have observed in the past does not make it any less of an atrocity. Today, I thus make the following determinations:

1. After careful examination of the available facts, I have determined that since at least March 2017, the People's Republic of China (PRC), under the direction and control of the Chinese Communist Party (CCP), has committed crimes against humanity against the predominantly Muslim Uyghurs and other members of ethnic and religious minority groups in Xinjiang. These crimes are ongoing and include: the arbitrary imprisonment or other severe deprivation of physical liberty of more than one million civilians, forced sterilization, torture of a large number of those arbitrarily detained, forced labor, and the imposition of draconian restrictions on freedom of religion or belief, freedom of expression, and freedom of movement. The Nuremberg Tribunals at the end of World War II prosecuted perpetrators for crimes against humanity, the same crimes being perpetrated in Xinjiang. (emphasis in original)

2. In addition, after careful examination of the available facts, I have determined that the PRC,

under the direction and control of the CCP, has committed genocide against the predominantly Muslim Uyghurs and other ethnic and religious minority groups in Xinjiang. I believe this genocide is ongoing, and that we are witnessing the systematic attempt to destroy Uyghurs by the Chinese party-state. The governing authorities of the second most economically, militarily, and politically powerful country on earth have made clear that they are engaged in the forced assimilation and eventual erasure of a vulnerable ethnic and religious minority group, even as they simultaneously assert their country as a global leader and attempt to remold the international system in their image.

The United States calls upon the PRC immediately to release all arbitrarily detained persons and abolish its system of internment, detention camps, house arrest and forced labor; cease coercive population control measures, including forced sterilizations, forced abortion, forced birth control, and the removal of children from their families; end all torture and abuse in places of detention; end the persecution of Uyghurs and other members of religious and ethnic minority groups in Xinjiang and elsewhere in China, and afford Uyghurs and other persecuted minorities the freedom to travel and emigrate.

We further call on all appropriate multilateral and relevant juridical bodies, to join the United States in our effort to promote accountability for those responsible for these atrocities. I have directed the U.S. Department of State to continue to investigate and collect relevant information regarding the ongoing atrocities occurring in Xinjiang, and to make this evidence available to appropriate authorities and the international community to the extent allowable by law. The United States, on its part, has spoken out and acted, implementing a range of sanctions against senior CCP leaders and state-run enterprises that fund the architecture of repression across Xinjiang.

The United States has worked exhaustively to pull into the light what the Communist Party and General Secretary Xi Jinping wish to keep hidden through obfuscation, propaganda, and coercion. Beijing's atrocities in Xinjiang represent an extreme affront to the Uyghurs, the people of China, and civilized people everywhere. We will not remain silent. If the Chinese Communist Party is allowed to commit genocide and crimes against humanity against its own people, imagine what it will be emboldened to do to the free world, in the not-so-distant future.[44]

THE UYGHUR CAUSE IN THE DIASPORA

The Uyghur cause in the diaspora dates to 1949, when the CCP occupied our homeland. Nonetheless, before the dissolution of the Soviet Union in 1990, the Uyghur movement didn't exist in Europe for the most part. The movements in Turkey, Saudi Arabia, and the Central Asian republics didn't yield many results due to the restricted political environment. At the end of the 1990s, particularly after 2000 with the formation of Uyghur communities in Europe and the establishment of the World Uyghur Congress in 2004 in Germany, our national movement started gaining momentum. In 2016, when the Chinese regime established concentration camps and started interning millions of Uyghurs, a worldwide wave against this genocidal policy began and transformed the East Turkistan issue into an international movement.

For many years, we worked tirelessly to bring to the world's attention the Chinese oppression in East Turkistan, to transmit the woes of the people of East Turkistan, and to gain sympathy from the international community for our cause. But we couldn't make it an international issue. After 2018, with the exposure of the Chinese regime's genocide in the concentration camps, the world finally began to take notice. The world started learning about China and its attempts to erase a nation from history with violent repression; realized China's evil intentions to rule the world through genocide; and now understood why China chose genocide after recognizing that it could not continue its expansionist and invasive actions without eradicating the Uyghurs.

One of the duties of our movement today is to create international pressure to end China's genocide against the people of East Turkistan as well as to expose the ways China is threatening global democracies, human rights, and the current international order through investment projects such as the Belt and Road Initiative.

The Chinese CCP is the largest and most evil terrorist organization in the world. They snatched the government from the Kuomintang through violent, amoral military and gangster actions. They killed at least forty-eight million people during the Cultural Revolution from 1966 to 1976. For Western democratic nations to continue cooperating with a government like the CCP is a betrayal of Western values. A nation that has profited from the blood of the people of East Turkistan today cannot escape history's questioning in the future. The Muslim countries that have supported and continue to support China's concentration camps and the genocide of the Uyghurs should pay a particularly heavy price. The Organization of Islamic Cooperation's (OIC) statement that supported China's genocide against Uyghur

Muslims isn't just a betrayal of Islamic values of brotherhood and nationhood, it is also a major sin according to the Quran.

After 2020, the European Union started calling China a competitor in the economy and an adversary in the political system. They used these terms after much difficulty and contention. Then, they marketed them enthusiastically, patting themselves on the back. However, the European Union's objections to China stopped there. The European parliament has adopted five resolutions since 2018 against China's policy toward the Uyghurs, but unfortunately drew a black stain on its image on December 30, 2020, the day Germany ended its presidency of the union by signing the EU-China Comprehensive Agreement (CAI) that has been debated for the past seven years.[45] Although this was part of Merkel and Macron's plan to build a Europe that depended neither on China nor on the United States, this action sacrificed the European values of democracy, human rights, the rule of law, and transparency for economic benefits that it hadn't yet received. It disappointed millions of people, myself included. Although the agreement seemed to bring economic benefits to the European Union, it in fact benefits China in the long run. Most importantly, it disregards the most important genocide happening in the twenty-first century and in fact encourages China to continue its crimes. However, in 2021, the CAI was suspended after the European Union, in coordination with Canada, the United Kingdom, and the United States, imposed sanctions on Chinese officials and one particular group and the Chinese government imposed counter-sanctions on parliament members, scholars, and think-tanks.[46]

The WUC, in cooperation with more than four hundred human rights organizations within the End Uyghur Forced Labour Coalition, have been advocating for governments, companies, and individuals engaging in trade relationships with China not to be complicit in its crimes, not to buy Chinese products stained with the blood of East Turkistan's people, and not to invest in China, but to end their economic cooperation with the country and, most importantly, disbelieve in China, recognizing their lies and distrusting them. We hope that like the United States, all Western democratic nations will impose effective sanctions on China and help limit its expansionist agenda. We're warning the countries that are trampling on human rights for economic gains that China is a disaster to humanity. Those who don't listen to us today will be victims of the woes that China brings them. On June 21, 2022, the Uyghur Forced Labor Prevention Act (UFLPA) came into force in the United States, banning all imports suspected of being made with Uyghur forced labour. This is a major step in eliminating Uyghur slavery, and we hope it will set a precedent for the rest of the global community.

CHINA'S EVIL INFLUENCE IN GERMANY

Over the past years, journalists have frequently asked me, "Do you feel safe in Germany?"

I used to say, "Germany is really a safe country. I don't feel any threat or pressure here." I was aware that the Chinese authorities had been demanding that Germany repatriate me to China since 1998, when its economic and diplomatic relations with Germany started increasing. They made the same demands after 2000 and again after 2010. All these demands were turned down.

When I first learned about these Chinese requests from the German authorities, I had the brief thought, "Will Germany one day give in and extradite me to China for economic gain?" But I was confident in the democracy and rule of law of Germany and never really believed in such a possibility. When I became a German citizen in 2006, my confidence in Germany became even stronger. When I faced deportation to China in South Korea and other troubles in different countries, Germany stood up for me and protected me. Unfortunately, things changed in 2020, when I was suddenly attacked in Munich, a city that I considered my second homeland.

On January 12, 2020, a fellow Uyghur in Munich, Nurmemet Tursun, held a Nezir at his home for his mother who had suddenly passed away in East Turkistan. Nurmemet had been unable to see his mother for many years. Along with the Uyghur community in Munich, I went to Nurmemet's home to express my condolences. Mihriban Zakir, the niece of Shohret Zakir—the number one puppet of the Chinese regime and the chairman of the so-called Xinjiang Uyghur Autonomous Region—and her husband, Ghalip Zakir, also came to the Nezir. They attacked me there, in front of the Uyghur community.[47]

I was coming out of the house after the Nezir ended when Mihriban Zakir suddenly appeared in front of me and started shouting at me. "Don't you say Shohret Zakir's name, never talk about his relatives, don't you dare call him a traitor, think about the future of your relatives back home!" she yelled.

I was in shock. The relatives of a traitor and a criminal directly involved in the torture, killing, and abuse of more than three million Uyghurs in concentration camps were attacking me in Germany. How dare they attack me? Were they doing this on their own or acting on China's orders?

Around thirty people witnessed this exchange as they were leaving the house, and everyone was visibly shocked. "Repeat what you said in front of everyone," I told her. She started shouting again, insulting me, and her husband tried to assault and beat me, but the people around us stopped him.

After failing to stop my activism or repatriate me to China using economic and diplomatic power and abuse of international law, the Chinese regime published many articles through its mouthpiece, the *Global Times*, and other media outlets, slandering the WUC and calling me a terrorist; they posted the

Google Maps location of the WUC to threaten us, and hired professional writers from Turkey, Italy, and other countries to join and support its propaganda. But I never thought a physical attack on me was likely, especially in Germany and in Munich, the headquarters of the WUC. I never thought China would use the relatives of Shohret Zakir to attack me. But then again, the family of Shohret Zakir had been loyally working for the Chinese regime for generations.

Radio Free Asia's Uyghur Service reported on the incident on January 13, 2020,[48] and followed up with another report on January 15:[49]

> The Uyghur community in the diaspora have strongly condemned the actions of Shohret Zakir's relatives in Germany. Uyghurs around the world are denouncing the relatives of Shohret Zakir, the chairman of the so-called Xinjiang Uyghur Autonomous Region . . . .
>
> After the RFA and the WUC published reports on this incident on January 13, the Uyghurs in the diaspora were shocked. Many people took to social media to denounce Shohret Zakir's relatives. People have also expressed their demands to hold them accountable.
>
> We wanted to learn the views of Uyghurs in different countries on Shohret Zakir's relatives' assault on the WUC President Dolkun Isa, in alignment with China.
>
> According to our interviews, the Uyghurs in Kazakhstan have also been outraged by this incident. One of the political activists in Almaty, Qehriman Ghojamberdi, said that he would condemn everyone that wanted to defend Shohret Zakir, the murderer of 20 million Uyghurs."

THE WORLD RESPONDS

Ms. Helchem, a Uyghur intellectual living in Norway said, "This is an attack on the independence movement in the diaspora. Fighting China's puppets abroad is part of our fight with China."

One of the Uyghur elders in the German city of Stuttgart, Abdushukur Haji, expressed his sadness at the incident and called on the Uyghur community to not repeat the mistakes of their ancestors and defend their leaders.

The January 12 incident in Munich hasn't only raised the attention of Uyghurs but attracted the attention of some Western media outlets. On January 13, the "Europeans' Interest," a news website in the EU, published a report with the headline "Chinese government is intimidating the WUC." The news mentioned China's various attacks and threats, the difficulties the WUC and its President Dolkun Isa have been facing in the international community and the incident on January 12 in Munich.

The news report called Shohret Zakir's attack on Dolkun Isa a "serious incident." The Zakir family's demand of Dolkun Isa to stop denouncing Shohret Zakir's crimes against humanity and their threatening Dolkun Isa via his relatives in East Turkistan was written about in detail.

As is well known, in recent months, the Chinese government has been using its propaganda machine including the *Global Times* to attack the WUC and its president. It even forced Dolkun Isa's sister Arzugul to deny her parents' deaths in concentration camps. In fact, Dolkun learned that his mother had died in a concentration camp two years ago and he doesn't know if his 90-year-old father is alive or not.

After Dolkun Isa became the main target of Chinese attacks in recent months, diplomats and media officials of some countries have started becoming concerned for his safety. Dolkun Isa expressed he is prepared to face any kind of attack. Also, he said he would sue Shohret Zakir's relatives in Germany and hold them accountable according to German law.

There were numerous media reports on the incident, and many Uyghur organizations made statements condemning the attack. Social media was full of Uyghurs denouncing Shohret Zakir and his family.

On December 10, 2021, coinciding with International Human Rights Day, the U.S. Department of the Treasury announced that it had sanctioned Shohret Zakir over his complicity in the Uyghur genocide.[50]

At this point, I'd like to outline some of China's ploys against Uyghur activists in the diaspora that I'm aware of.

In 1998, Hashir Wahidi, the president of the Uyghuristan Liberation Organization in Kazakhstan, which had more than 10,000 members, was assaulted and severely beaten by a group of strangers who raided his house. He lost consciousness and fell into a coma after the assault, which left his organs severely damaged. He died a few months later.

During 1995 and 1996, when I visited Kazakhstan, I had long conversations with Hashir Wahidi. This brave man was China's worst enemy in Kazakhstan. He dedicated his life to establishing a Uyghuristan Republic. He never bowed to the threats of China. After his death, Sabit Abdurahman became the president of the Uyghuristan Liberation Organization. Unfortunately, after Sabit Abdurahman's death, the Uyghuristan Liberation Organization—the greatest power against China in Central Asia—disappeared.

THE WORLD RESPONDS

Although it was obvious to everyone that China had murdered Hashir Wahidi, the killers were never found.

On March 28, 2000, the President of The Republic Uyghur Ittipak, the only legal and most representative organization of Uyghurs in Kyrgyzstan, Nighmet Bosakov, was shot dead at eight a.m. His killer was also never found.

Nighmet Bosakov was a wealthy as well as a patriotic man. We shared a close friendship. In November 1998, when we held the 2nd General Assembly of the World Uyghur Youth Congress in Ankara, he brought some Uyghur youths from Kyrgyzstan to participate, and supported us financially and spiritually. In May 1999, a year before his death, when I went to Kyrgyzstan, I was a guest in his house—which had a photo of a blue wolf hanging on its door—and we had many meaningful conversations.

At the beginning of May 2001, Dilberim Samsaqova, the president of the Nuzugum Foundation, an influential organization among Uyghurs in Central Asia, suddenly disappeared. For two weeks, the Uyghurs in Kazakhstan couldn't find her. On May 24, she was found dead.

Dilberim Samsaqova had attended the East Turkistan National Congress in 1999 in Germany. Since then, she supported and participated in our activities until her death. I always kept in touch with her and found her to be a brave and intelligent woman. Her death remains a mystery today as well.

In March 2011, Eminjan Osmanova, the Uyghur department manager of the Uzbekistan Writers Society—an influential organization in Central Asia—was killed. This talented writer's killers were never found.

On December 12, 2016, a renowned Uyghur religious scholar and the founder of the East Turkistan Education and Solidarity Association, Abdulhekim Mahsum Hajim, suddenly died at the age of fifty-four. It was suggested that he was poisoned, but the perpetrator remains unknown. Abdulhekim Mahsum Hajim made great contributions to the development of the Uyghur cause in Turkey. He worked hard to mentor Uyghurs who had been led astray by extremist ideologies and wanted to join ISIS in Syria during 2014 and 2015. He was determined to correct their path. I had conversations with him when he came to Germany in 2015.

These are all tragedies that resulted from the intervention of China in Turkey and the neighbouring countries to East Turkistan, the Central Asian republics. Through such ploys, China wanted to create fear, restrict, weaken, and ultimately obliterate the growing movement against it. Carrying out such physical attacks wasn't easy in Europe and the United States; it was clear, however, that China was daring and determined to extend its evil reach.[51]

After the January 12 assault by the Zakir family, the German police suggested the WUC install surveillance cameras in the office and implement other security measures.

THE UYGHUR TRIBUNAL

Despite the severity of the situation in East Turkistan, most nations outside of the United States have failed to take serious action. Many continue to use ambiguous language when referring to the crisis, most likely to protect themselves against a backlash from China.

The Chinese government has done everything in their power to weaken the response from the international community. They have attempted to discredit voices from the Uyghur diaspora and to deny or hide evidence of their evil actions. They have distorted reality and turned the discussion of the Uyghur crisis into a battle of narratives and geopolitics.

We at the WUC felt that a credible and independent legal assessment of all the available evidence on the Uyghur crisis, China's responsibility, and whether it is a genocide would counter

THE WORLD RESPONDS

China's actions to twist the discussion and could compel governments and international organizations to take stronger action.

We have already seen that a compelling argument can be made for China's actions fitting the internationally recognized definition of genocide. The scale, severity, and intent match those requirements. The report by German academic Adrian Zenz on China's use of mass sterilization and birth prevention measures to decrease the Uyghur population makes the case even stronger.[52]

We began to look at the different legal avenues. I knew that traditional methods, such as bringing China to an international court, would be impossible. Even though China signed and ratified the UN Genocide Convention, they entered a reservation against the jurisdiction of the International Court of Justice (ICJ). China is also a member of the UN Security Council, so they have veto power against the jurisdiction of the ICJ. Also, China is not a member of the International Criminal Court (ICC), making it impossible to bring them before that court.

With all these obstacles in the way, I began networking with other groups to learn from their experiences and see if we might find a different approach.

In September 2018, at the 39th session of the UN Human Rights Council, the Council adopted a resolution (A/HRC/39/L.22) on the situation of human rights of Rohingya Muslims and other minorities in Myanmar. This resolution established an independent mechanism to collect, consolidate, preserve, and analyze evidence of the most serious international crimes and violations of international law committed in Myanmar since 2011, and to prepare files to arrange fair and independent criminal proceedings. This became an international issue, especially after being brought to the ICC.

In December 2018, I invited two activists from the Free Rohingya Coalition, London-based Dr. Maung Zarni, Coordinator for Strategic Affairs and co-author of *The Slow-*

Burning Genocide of Myanmar's Rohingya, and the Campaign and Media Relations Coordinator, Nay San Lwin, based in Frankfurt. They arrived in Munich on December 19, and I invited them to Kashgar, a Uyghur restaurant near my office. Over dinner, we exchanged stories of our experiences in advocacy and the similarities and differences between the Uyghur and Rohingya issues. The Free Rohingya Coalition then explained alternative accountability mechanisms. They introduced me via email to the Rome-based Permanent People's Tribunal.

On January 11, 2019, I met with secretary-general Gianni Tognoni in Milan, where we discussed the Uyghur crisis. He was very interested in the topic and asked me to provide him with evidence. After my return, I sent him our submission to the UN Committee on the Elimination of Racial Discrimination ahead of their review of China and other supporting documents.

From February 8 to 9, 2019, the Free Rohingya Coalition organized the "International Conference on Protection and Accountability in Myanmar" at Columbia University in New York. I was invited to speak about the Uyghur crisis. This international event was attended by many scholars and legal experts working on atrocity crimes. This was a great opportunity for me to network with these scholars working on the Rohingya genocide.

After the conference, on February 11, a WUC delegation, including Mr. Omer Kanat, Dr. Rishat Abbas, Dr. Memet Emin, and I met with Mr. Tognoni again. During this meeting, we discussed ways to hold the Chinese government accountable in the international justice system. Mr. Tognoni explained in detail the process of such an endeavour, as well as the challenges and limitations.

After these meetings, it was made clear to us that it would be practically impossible to bring China before international courts such as the ICC and ICJ. However, there was a possibility to go before a people's tribunal to investigate these crimes.

THE WORLD RESPONDS

At that time, my London-based colleague, Rahima Mahmut, was helping with translation and interpretation at the China Tribunal.[53] She proposed to me that the WUC should meet with their team, as she was well connected to them. I got in touch with Sir Geoffrey Nice and his team. After meeting with them, it was clear that having two tribunals doing the same thing would undermine the efforts of both. The China Tribunal team was quite knowledgeable on the Uyghur issue, having heard testimonies about the Uyghur genocide during the China Tribunal about organ harvesting. It was therefore decided that the WUC should work with Sir Geoffrey Nice and his team.

The Tribunal would remain independent of the WUC to maintain the credibility and neutrality of its final judgment. The WUC would mainly act as a fundraiser and help supply evidence and testimony about the situation in East Turkistan. The bulk of our work would come during Phase II in using the Tribunal's judgment and proceedings in our advocacy efforts.

However, we faced some serious challenges.

The Uyghur movement didn't have the experience for such a bold endeavour. I was unsure about whether it was going to be successful, and this was a worrying thought.

The other challenge was financial. Although the independent tribunal was going to be a pro bono effort, the administrative and logistical costs were high, at least a couple of hundred thousand dollars. This was a considerable cost for the WUC. I agreed to help with fundraising, but this would be a complex and difficult task. I would have to explain the endeavour in detail to the Uyghur community worldwide and convince them of its necessity and benefit. This had never been done before, and it was a daunting task.

I also went to other NGOs to raise funds. Our biggest worry was that these efforts would be stopped halfway through. The Chinese government could interfere and sabotage our plans.

Additionally, collecting evidence from survivors would be difficult. There was concern that the Chinese government would use hostage diplomacy with relatives of the witnesses at the Tribunal or interfere in the process of evidence collection.

These concerns became a reality during the hearings. Beijing took some of the relatives of the witnesses and forced them to speak and denounce their family members in press conferences. The Chinese government also exerted pressure on some of the witnesses, who later withdrew the statements they had submitted to the Uyghur Tribunal.

Since most witnesses spoke either Uyghur or Kazakh, all their testimonies, both written and oral, had to be translated and interpreted. The WUC, the Uyghur Transitional Justice Database, and the Uyghur Academy offered to help with this task. We also gathered many linguists and academics, as well as NGOs, to help with this process. For my part, I formed working groups to address all these issues and received support from different affiliate organizations. Although we were organized and prepared for the Tribunal, it was still intimidating moving forward.

China's arm is long, as we've seen with institutions such as Interpol, the UN, and the WHO, at overseas universities, and with scholars, think tanks and even in the media. China could use many tactics to put the Tribunal at risk, which would have been catastrophic.

It was a very difficult decision to make. But we decided to trust the process and risk everything.

In June 2020, I made a formal request to Sir Geoffrey Nice, QC to establish and chair an independent people's tribunal to investigate "ongoing atrocities and possible genocide" against the Uyghurs, Kazakhs, and other Turkic Muslim populations in East Turkistan. The Uyghur Tribunal was launched on September 3, 2020. Hearings were held in June, September, and November 2021, during which the Tribunal's expert panel reviewed the statements of more than five hundred witnesses and heard live evidence from more than thirty witnesses about their experiences with China's oppressive policies and its concentration camp system, as well as testimony from forty expert witnesses.

After eighteen months of research, collection, and assessment of evidence, the Uyghur Tribunal came to a verdict on December 9, 2021, and published its sixty-four-page summary judgment. Sir Geoffrey Nice, the Chair, read the judgment, which concluded:

> Accordingly, on the basis of evidence heard in public, the Tribunal is satisfied beyond reasonable doubt that the PRC, by the imposition of measures to prevent births intended to destroy a significant part of the Uyghurs in Xinjiang as such, has committed genocide.
>
> In addition to genocide (pars. 176–178), the Tribunal also concluded that crimes against humanity (paras. 167–171) and torture (para. 166) were committed against the Uyghurs and other Turkic people of East Turkistan.[54]

The judgment was based on an evidence database with hundreds of thousands of pages of documents on the situation in East Turkistan. The majority of the witnesses talked about the systematic torture and rape in the internment camps, forced labour, forced sterilization and abortions of Uyghur women, and the surveillance system in the region. These accounts were corroborated by more than three dozen expert witnesses, who detailed their research and investigations, helping to uncover the Chinese government's crimes as well as the structure and the decision-making process of the Chinese Communist Party, and thereby proving the intention of genocide.

After the judgment of the Tribunal, the WUC and its partners attended many advocacy meetings and went on letter-writing, appeals and media campaigns to push the relevant authorities to use the correct terminology when referring to the Uyghur crisis. We felt that calling the crisis a genocide would compel the international community to take action and would lead to even more serious measures. We would raise the findings with the UN Office on Genocide Prevention and the Responsibility to Protect.

Since the Uyghur Tribunal published its summary judgment in December 2021 recognizing China's human rights violations against the Uyghurs and other Turkic people to constitute crimes against humanity and genocide, its impact has been enormous. The Tribunal's work has made crucial contributions to policy debates, prompting parliamentary questions in the United Kingdom, the European Union, Belgium, Germany, and France, and has been referred to in major policy documents such as the EU *Annual Report on Human Rights and Democracy in the World 2021*. Moreover, being covered by more than twenty major outlets worldwide (including the *Washington Post*, Reuters, the *Guardian*, the BBC, *Le Monde*, *Al Jazeera*, *El País*), it has impacted much of the public understanding of the Uyghur human rights crisis.

Overall, the Tribunal also provided a foundation for future efforts of justice and accountability. Now the evidence of the CCP's crimes against Uyghurs is organized and held in one place. We know what crimes have been committed, who the victims are, and who is responsible. This was an important step that will lay the groundwork for all our future efforts.

EPILOGUE

As I wrote this book describing some of the challenges I've faced and the harm that has been inflicted on me because of China, my people were living through the darkest period in our history. Our situation is appalling, it is horrific. Amidst all of this, my job it is to work tirelessly to listen to the woes of Uyghurs, to rescue them from Chinese state terrorism, to free them and bring an end to this genocide.

My goal in writing this book is to warn the world, expose the Chinese communist regime's deep influence on the free world and its great and growing threat to global peace and democracy through my personal experiences and insights. It is to gain the sympathy of everyone who reads my story and learns about the Uyghurs. We need more people to help us. The Uyghurs, who've lived outside the world's spotlight for centuries but today face the death of our nation, need you. The disappearance of the Uyghurs is the fading of a great civilization, the eradication of a beautiful language, and the demise of a nation that has played a marked role in the history of humanity. And this disappearance is only the beginning, a glimpse into the disaster the rest of humanity faces at the hands of China. The threat to democracy, justice, and world peace built with the lives of millions of people is real.

Those who know me and know the Uyghurs frequently ask me: "What can we do in the face of this disaster? How should we help you?" My answer is very simple: Break your silence! To be silent in the face of this genocide is to support it. There is no neutrality in the face of injustice, oppression, and genocide. Silence is the accomplice of genocide."

Yes, humanity witnessed a terrible genocide seventy-five years ago. Although many voiced concerns, the vast majority of the public, organizations, and countries kept silent. As a result, the Holocaust happened. Six million Jews and other innocent people died because of that silence.

Every word you say and every action you take after breaking your silence will be of great help to stop this twenty-first-century genocide. Never underestimate your power. The day you break your silence will be the day you save a Uyghur's life. The day a million people break their silence will be the day a million Uyghur lives are saved. The day twenty-five million people break their silence and announce that they stand with us will be the day that the twenty-five million people of East Turkistan regain their freedom. Your voice matters for the perpetual peace of the world, the health of democracy, and the sustainability of many nations.

APPENDIX A
THE BATTLE CONTINUES FOR FREEDOM FROM TYRANNY

As you have gathered, my story is not just about me but rather about what one government will do at any cost to suppress anyone or any group of people willing to stand up to the Peoples' Republic of China under the tyrannical rule of Xi Jinping. The Chinese Communist Party and its leadership are ideologically bound to a belief set that their form of government is vastly superior to the democratic nations of the West.

As an activist for the Uyghurs, combined with my collective experience in working with all of the groups in the Chinese diaspora, I and others take a much different approach. We seek to hold the regime's leaders accountable to all Chinese citizens and to the global community at large. With our dedicated team of volunteers, community members, and staff at the World Uyghur Congress, we have made some tremendous strides forward for the cause of the Uyghurs as governments, corporations, and citizens are finally realizing that the bargain struck with China for cheap goods has helped not only to empower the CCP economically but has allowed them to subjugate ethnic and religious minorities as indentured slaves to the regime and propagate their false economic model.

There are actual costs to people in turning a blind eye to the brutal and genocidal behaviour of the CCP, and I believe that we are finally turning the corner in alerting all citizens to the actual costs of dealing with Xi Jinping's China. The book would not be complete unless we could highlight some of our great strides forward, although I will remain vigilant in my quest to have our people freed from slavery and released from the concentration camps. Our hope is based on your support, and we thank all those who have helped make the cause one of the most important on the human rights agendas for all democracies.

KEY ACHIEVEMENTS IN 2022–2023

Nobel Peace Prize nomination, 2023

The World Uyghur Congress (WUC) has been nominated for the 2023 Nobel Peace Prize by Canadian Member of Parliament (MP), chair of the Subcommittee on International Human Rights (SDIR), and co-chair of the Canada-Uyghur Parliamentary Friendship Group, Sameer Zuberi, together with Canadian MP and SDIR co-chair Alexis Brunelle-Duceppe and leader of the Young Liberals in Norway, Ane Breivik.

The WUC has been nominated for its contribution to human rights, the advancement of democracy, and bringing the Uyghur genocide to the forefront of the international community. As the leading representative Uyghur organization worldwide, the WUC is dedicated to protecting the rights of the Uyghur people, both in East Turkistan and in the diaspora.

The work of the WUC has made a significant contribution to drawing international attention to the crushing campaign of religious, linguistic, and cultural repression currently being waged

APPENDIX A

by the Chinese Communist Party against the Uyghurs and other Turkic people in East Turkistan.

International Uyghur Forum, Brussels

From November 9–10, the World Uyghur Congress (WUC), HASENE International, International Union of East Turkistan Organizations (IUETO), with the co-sponsorship of the Unrepresented Nations and Peoples Organization (UNPO), Society for Threatened Peoples (GfbV), CCJO René Cassin, FAIR International, and the International Society for Human Rights (ISHR) organized a high-level International Uyghur Forum in Brussels, Belgium. The Forum brought together more than 200 participants from all over the world, including prominent experts in policy, economics, civil society, media, academia, and the legal field, as well as Uyghur and civil society representatives.

The Forum's opening session was held at the European Parliament, hosted by Member of European Parliament (MEP) Ismail Ertug, and was also attended by MEPs Raphael Glucksmann and Miriam Lexmann. The opening session ended with the testimonies of five camp survivors. After that, a panel was held in the European Parliament, hosted by MEPs Engin Eroglu and David Lega, that included the participation of Nury Turkel, the Chair of the U.S. Commission on International Religious Freedom (USCIRF), Uyghur Tribunal Vice-Chair Nick Vetch, and former U.S. Ambassador-at-Large for Global Women's Issues Kelley Currie.

During the remainder of the Forum, key discussions were held about existing avenues for justice and accountability, what the UN and its member states can do against these atrocities, and what role civil society and the media play in the response to the Uyghur genocide. In seeking answers to these questions and identifying best practices, the organizers adopted a resolution based on the Forum's outcomes, which outline the way towards international justice and accountability measures.

Office of the UN High Commissioner for Human Rights Report (2022)

On August 31, 2022, the OHCHR finally published its long-overdue report, just minutes before the end of the mandate of High Commissioner Michelle Bachelet. The delay of the report has drawn widespread criticism from the WUC and others as an indicator that China has attempted to influence the process. Ultimately, the report concluded that the violations against the Uyghurs "may constitute international crimes, in particular, crimes against humanity" but disappointingly stopped short of mentioning genocide.

In the aftermath of the report, the WUC's representatives were quoted by the *New York Times*, the BBC, the *Guardian*, *Politico*, Al Jazeera, and others. Furthermore, the EU, U.S., Germany, the U.K., Canada, Australia, and others released official statements reacting to the publication of the report, highlighting their concerns and calling for urgent attention to the situation.

Global South—LAC advocacy

On May 24, World Uyghur Congress (WUC) President Dolkun Isa and WUC Program and Advocacy Manager Zumretay Arkin, together with UHRP Executive Director Omer Kanat, Hong Kong activist Alex Chow, and ISHR Program Manager Raphaël Viana David arrived in Brazil, where the delegation started their two-week long advocacy in South America. The WUC delegation visited Brazil, Argentina, Chile, and Costa Rica for various advocacy and awareness-raising activities with different stakeholders.

In Brazil the delegation met with the President, the Vice President, and a Member of the Human Rights Commission

APPENDIX A

of the Federal Bar Association of Brazil (OAB) to discuss the current situation of the Uyghurs and the international response, specifically, the UN response to the Uyghur human rights crisis. The WUC team also met with the Ministry of Foreign Affairs of Brazil and Congresswoman Fernanda Melchionna to discuss the existing independent reports on the Uyghur issue, including the OHCHR report.

The delegation met with the Secretary for Human Rights of the City of São Paulo, Soninha Francine, and her team as well as with the Latin America representative of Tibet House, Jigme Tsering, and the Human Rights Watch Director of Brazil, Maria Laura Canineu, to discuss Brazil's human rights priorities. In São Paulo, WUC President Dolkun Isa was interviewed by journalist Maya Paixão for *Folha*, the most influential newspaper in Brazil, on his experience as an Uyghur activist facing transnational repression and the WUC's demands for Brazil's president Lula da Silva. The WUC team was also received by Café de Manhã of Folha de S. Paulo, with whom WUC Program and Advocacy Manager Zumretay Arkin and the International Service for Human Rights' Program Manager Raphaël Viana David discussed Uyghur activism and the broader context of repression faced by human rights activists.

The WUC delegation arrived in Argentina where they met with the President of Centro Islámico de la República Argentina Fabian Ankah and Secretary-General Hasan El Bacha. Shortly after, the team visited former Argentinian Senator Norma to learn about her family's history and to exchange ideas on best practices in countering authoritarian regimes. On the same day the WUC representatives had a productive meeting with the Ministry of Foreign Affairs, International Trade and Worship of the Argentine Republic to discuss the broad range of violations faced by the Uyghurs and Turkic people.

After the successful trip to Brazil and Argentina, the World Uyghur Congress arrived in Chile, where the delegation met with the president and lawyers of the Colegio de Abogados de Chile (Chilean Bar Association) and with students and scholars from the International Relations Institute of the Chile University, as well as professors from the Human Rights Centre at the Alberto Hurtado University to discuss the topics of accountability and documentation of crimes. The WUC was also welcomed to the U.S. Embassy by the U.S. Ambassador to Chile to discuss recent developments in the multilateral negotiations on the Uyghur genocide and met with former President of the Chamber of Deputies of Chile, José Antonio Viera-Gallo.

In Santiago, the WUC's spokesperson, Zumretay Arkin, gave an interview to the Chilean radio station Bio Bio on the Uyghur genocide, and the delegation attended a debrief together with various Chilean non-governmental organizations, which was arranged by Amnesty International in Chile to build solidarity with key partners in the Global South.

The WUC, UHRP, and Lawyers for Uyghur Rights visited San Jose, Costa Rica to attend RightsCon, the world's leading summit on human rights in the digital age to bring the case of the Uyghurs to the attention of global actors. The WUC, together with the UHRP and Lawyers for Uyghur Rights hosted a session titled "Has the International Legal System Failed Us? The Case of the Uyghurs," with contributions from key allies, including U.S. Ambassador for Global Criminal Justice Beth van Schaack, and GLAN, the Global Legal Action Network. On the main stage of RightsCon WUC President Dolkun Isa spoke with Melissa Chan about China's systematic human rights abuses and genocide against the Uyghurs, as well as about Chinese transnational repression through the use of surveillance technology and how it has impacted his life.

APPENDIX A

M-62 (February 1, 2023)

On February 1, the Canadian parliament unanimously passed M-62, the first motion of its kind worldwide, which calls on the Canadian government to leverage Canada's Refugee and Humanitarian Resettlement Program to expedite the entry of 10,000 Uyghur and other Turkic Muslim refugees in need of protection.

The motion was introduced on June 20, 2022, by MP Sameer Zuberi, following the Canadian parliament's recognition of the Uyghur genocide in 2021. The motion responds to the Chinese government's transnational repression against Uyghurs, who are at risk of being forcibly returned to China, where they are at serious risk of persecution. According to research by the Uyghur Human Rights Project (UHRP) and the Oxus Society for Central Asian Affairs, there were 1,546 cases of detention and deportation of Uyghurs across 28 countries between 1997 and 2021, with a dramatic escalation since 2017.

Ahead of the vote, a WUC delegation, led by its president Dolkun Isa, arrived in Canada on January 29 for a week-long advocacy trip and visited Ottawa to meet with Canadian Prime Minister Justin Trudeau, Minister of Immigration Sean Fraser, Minister of Global Affairs Melanie Joly, Minister of Transport Omar Alghabra, and Minister of Housing and Social Development Ahmed Hussen, as well as other high-profile parliamentarians, including Sameer Zuberi who introduced the motion in 2022.

Uyghur Forced Labor Prevention Act (U.S.)

In December 2021, the U.S. government introduced the Uyghur Forced Labor Prevention Act (UFLPA) as the next piece of legislation to encourage resilience, transparency, and equity in post-COVID era supply chains. The policy dictates that goods, wares, articles, and merchandise mined, produced, and/or manufactured in the Xinjiang Uyghur Autonomous Region (XUAR) of China are not entitled to entry into the United

States, and must show a preset of conditions to enter the country. Specifically, the legislation calls out 13 key product categories of focus for the attention of customs agents: apparel, clothing, computer parts, cotton, processed cotton and cotton products, electronics, garments, hair products, polysilicon, rail transportation equipment, silica-based products, textiles, and touch screens for handheld devices and automotives. The legislation effectively introduces a burden of proof for importers to show that their suppliers in the XUAR are using ethical workforce practices—not forced labor. While the policy may seem straightforward on the surface, it is having a rippling market effect as companies scramble to understand not only their primary supply base, but also the unknown and often opaque world of their secondary and tertiary suppliers—their suppliers' suppliers—and so forth.

For most companies, multi-tier supply chain visibility requires an investment in digital tools to enable a deeper understanding than what is obvious in the status quo. This past December, the Customs and Border Patrol estimated that more than 2,200 shipments, worth more than $728 million in inventory, have been stopped at U.S. ports since implementation. Impacted end products were certainly worth billions of dollars.

Companies seeking to understand the UFLPA and how to proactively plan and prioritize for it should follow four core steps:

1. **Conduct a supply chain diligence review to identify immediate, sole-source risks**

Procurement and supply-chain organizations must take steps to identify suppliers operating in Xinjiang at the primary level—seeking to understand their risk level based on labor practices, local law compliance, and direct proximity to local XUAR government. The findings of this preliminary assessment must then be mapped against which components and inventory are not

APPENDIX A

currently being provided by additional suppliers. If sole-sourced components are being actively sourced from the XUAR, immediate actions must be undertaken to mitigate.

2. Build the risk prioritization assessment

After preliminary risk assessment, companies must prioritize the identified risks. A risk matrix that plots the risk level of specific suppliers against risk to the core company operation due to factors such as sole-sourced inventory is key. By clearly identifying which suppliers introduce the most individual and company-specific risk to the core operation, companies can prioritize resources for mitigation efforts.

3. Install supplier protocols to protect against further violations

When inventory is flagged at a Customs checkpoint, companies have 30 days to show a proof-of-ethical-practice notice to Customs to retrieve product and continue sourcing. These practices may include:

- Installing processes to vet potential suppliers for unethical labor practices as part of sourcing, award, and onboarding steps
- Enforcing contract stipulations that require immediate action if violations are found
- Defining contract break violations and guidelines in line with unethical labor practices
- Requiring a supplier code of conduct to promote compliance which explicitly bans the use of unethical labor practices

4. **Install supply chain transparency by enabling digital tools**

In the face of legislative challenges, supply chain risks, and compliance complexity, companies often scramble to answer the call to do everything at once. Fortunately, numerous third-party vendors, digital dashboards, and AI-enabled supply chain visibility tools have entered the market. More often than not, using third-party supply chain risk management (SCRM) tools will be the fastest way to build a deeper visualization of supply chains and associated risks. However, no software tool on the market is a silver bullet. Humans who understand a company's specific supply chain will need to interpret SCRM tools' outputs just like a doctor needs to interpret an MRI image. Moreover, to be truly effective, the sensing and illumination of these buried risks needs to occur on an ongoing and real-time basis, supported by fit-for-purpose processes.

Another key challenge faced by companies is the acquisition of data to support the supply chain illumination. This requires a multi-pronged approach of tapping into commercially available data sources, acquiring data directly from suppliers, partnering with NGOs and industry bodies, and engaging boots-on-the-ground intelligence firms. The Uyghur Forced Labor Prevention Act presents a significant challenge to companies operating in and around Xinjiang. To comply with the law, companies must assess the risks in their supply chain, prioritize mitigation efforts, and implement measures to ensure that their suppliers are not using forced labor. By taking these steps, companies can demonstrate their commitment to responsible sourcing practices, comply with the law, and protect their reputation and bottom line.

Society for Threatened Peoples Award for courageous and tireless commitment to Uyghur human rights (16 October 2022)

On October 16, 2022, WUC President, Dolkun Isa was awarded an honorary membership in the Society for Threatened Peoples

(STP) in Germany for his courage and tireless work defending the rights of the Uyghur people.

UN resolution on Uyghurs (October 7, 2022)

The UN Human Rights Council has voted not to debate the treatment of the Uyghurs and other mostly Muslim minorities in China's northwestern region of Xinjiang even after the UN's Human Rights Office concluded the scale of the alleged abuses there may amount to "crimes against humanity."

The motion for a debate on the issue was defeated by 19 votes to 17, with 11 countries abstaining in a decision China welcomed and others condemned as "shameful."

Many of those who voted "no" were Muslim-majority countries such as Indonesia, Somalia, Pakistan, UAE, and Qatar. Among the 11 countries that abstained were India, Malaysia, and Ukraine.

In a strongly worded statement, Amnesty International's Secretary General Agnes Callamard said the decision protected the perpetrators rather than the victims of abuses.

UK court case

On October 7, the WUC and the Global Legal Action Network wrote to the Irish Revenue Commissioners calling for a ban on the importation of cotton goods from East Turkistan. In the letter to the Revenue Commissioners, the organizations outlined the atrocities perpetrated against the Uyghurs and the irrefutable connection between Uyghur forced labour and Europe's fashion industry. As EU law explicitly recognizes the prohibition of slavery, servitude, and forced or compulsory labour as a fundamental human right, and international law prohibits the importation of goods produced under these circumstances, the groups argue that Ireland is obliged to apply its laws governing imports in a manner that respects that prohibition.

On October 25, the World Uyghur Congress (WUC) and the Global Legal Action Network (GLAN) took the U.K. government to court to challenge Britain's failure to block the import of cotton products associated with forced labour and other abuses in East Turkistan.

From 25–26 October, a WUC delegation attended the official hearing, which is believed to be the first time a foreign court heard legal arguments from the Uyghurs over the issue of forced labour in East Turkistan. The WUC's lawyers, Jenni Richards KC and Tom Forster KC, said there were reasonable grounds to suspect breaches of criminal and civil law under the Foreign Prison-Made Goods Act 1897 and the Proceeds of Crime Act (Poca) 2002, which concerns money laundering.

In 2018, despite enormous challenges, we had a spectacular success at the UN that stunned China, which never imagined it would encounter such a dissenting voice in the UN.

In August 2018, the ninety-sixth session of the UN Committee on the Elimination of Racial Discrimination (CERD) was held in Geneva. The WUC and other international organizations, such as Human Rights Watch, Amnesty International, Human Rights in China, and Human Rights Defenders in China, submitted reports to the committee in advance of the session. They were published on the CERD website and reviewed formally during the session.[55] This was a crucial opportunity to bring the suffering of the Uyghurs, especially those in Chinese concentration camps, to the spotlight. On August 9, I presented a report on the concentration camps, and the committee members asked many questions. On August 10, Uyghurs from Germany, Switzerland, Norway, and the Netherlands demonstrated in front of the UN office in Geneva to protest the Chinese concentration camp system, holding signs with slogans like "Millions of Uyghurs are suffering in concentration camps."

APPENDIX A

From August 10 to 13, the Chinese government's report was examined by the committee. A delegation composed of WUC vice-president Perhat Muhammet, Ekrem Hezim, Abdurehim Gheni, Peter Irwin, and I participated in the session. After hearing the Chinese government's report on the elimination of racial discrimination, the committee's experts questioned the Chinese delegation. The committee's vice-chair and co-rapporteur Gay McDougall asked many questions on the imprisonment of more than one million Uyghurs in concentration camps and demanded the Chinese delegation respond in written format.[56]

China sent forty-nine representatives to this session.[57] Although the Chinese representatives answered the committee's questions, they denied not only that persecution was taking place in the Uyghur region but the existence of concentration camps as well. This provoked a strong reproach from the UN rapporteurs. Kut Gun, a member of the CERD, said, "We're really disappointed. The Chinese delegation deliberately evaded this issue and minced words to avoid answering." Ms. Gay McDougall said she didn't get an answer to her questions. Another member of the CERD, Ms. Yemhelhe Mohamed said, "I couldn't get an answer for my question, so I'd like to ask another question. What is Ilham Tohti's crime?" Nicolas Marugan, the committee's chief rapporteur, said, "The Chinese government denied all the issues raised. Then, is there really an issue in China? What are we debating over?" All the members of the committee expressed their disapproval of the Chinese delegation's responses to the issues raised.[58]

The meeting really heated up. The Chinese representative tasked with responding to the issue of concentration camps in East Turkistan was the Chinese ambassador to the UN, Yu Jianhua. He started by saying:

Some members expressed their worries over the Xinjiang region of China. Let me first present the general situation of Xinjiang. The Xinjiang Uyghur Autonomous Region has been respecting and protecting the rights of all ethnic groups. The freedom and rights of all ethnic groups in China are protected by law. The ethnic groups in Xinjiang, including the Uyghurs, enjoy the same social and political rights as other ethnicities. All ethnic groups are living in peace, their religious freedom is guaranteed. There is no arbitrary detention and restriction of religious freedom in the Uyghur region. Claims like "there are no human rights in Xinjiang" have no basis. There are no "re-education centers" in Xinjiang. We need to reiterate here: Xinjiang is a victim of terrorism. The Xinjiang Uyghur Autonomous Region has taken some actions against terrorism and violence to protect the lives and properties of the people. The government has indicted and sentenced some criminals according to the law. Those among the criminals who have committed minor crimes have been trained and given an opportunity to take the right path. The government has provided them with opportunities to train in law and vocational skills and helped rehabilitate them so they may rejoin society.

The Chinese representative ended his speech by claiming that religious freedom was guaranteed in East Turkistan, that China's fight against terrorism wasn't targeted at a particular ethnic group, and that the high-surveillance systems in the region were also for the benefit of the people. He further stated that the "Three Evils" in East Turkistan carried out violent incidents and represented a serious threat to the region. China was fighting against those powers and was a country ruled by law, he claimed.

This time, the Chinese government brought a Uyghur, Kayser Abdukerim (Kaisaier Abudukerimu), along with the delegation. Kayser was the president of Xinjiang Medical University. When he was given a turn to speak, he said:

> Dear members, I'm most pleased to have the opportunity to come here and talk about the situation in Xinjiang today. Xinjiang is an inseparable part of China and has been since ancient times. Xinjiang is a land where multiple ethnic groups and religions have co-existed throughout history. Without ethnic unity, there can be no development. In recent years, the lives of the people of Xinjiang have improved in many aspects.

Kayser Abdukerim brought examples to prove his claims. He said that tourism had flourished in East Turkistan; that the number of university graduates, medical doctors, beds in hospitals, and even life expectancy had all increased; and that enrollment in schools had reached 90 per cent. He presented many figures. He ended his speech with an invitation. "Today, all the people in Xinjiang are living in unity. I'd like to invite everyone here to visit Xinjiang and see the situation for themselves."

Members of the Chinese delegation from Tibet, Hong Kong, and Macau said similar things, claiming that the rights of the people in their regions were being respected.

After the Chinese delegation's reply, Mr. Marugan, an official of the committee, spoke. He said that the written and oral reports of the Chinese delegation were too extensive to review in the session, and that it would take at least twenty hours to discuss the issues in them fully. He said he was surprised that the Chinese delegation was able to prepare so many reports in a weekend but made clear that regardless of the length of these reports, there remained no answers or evidence for the many questions they raised. He said, plainly:

> I will relay my questions directly and to the point. Please don't think that I'm being impolite. There are no statistics or clear data in the Chinese delegation's response to the issue of ethnic discrimination in China. There are no facts or data on the social welfare, education, housing and employment of the ethnic groups in China. Had you provided us with clear facts, it would have helped us to better learn the reality in China. The concept of separatism isn't clearly defined in Chinese law. In fact, separatism is being widely exploited. We've received reports that the religious freedom, right of assembly and freedom of speech of the Uyghur Muslims in the Xinjiang Uyghur Autonomous Region are being severely abused. We've also received reports that the Chinese government has linked the violent incidents that happened in the Xinjiang Uyghur Autonomous Region and other places to some Uyghurs and used them to justify the strict policies against the Uyghurs in the region. We know that many Uyghur and Tibetan human rights activists and even ordinary people are being accused of terrorism and endangering national security by the Chinese government. I didn't see in your response any information about the legal process that is followed to convict those people and how their rights are being protected.

APPENDIX A

Mr. Marugan said that although the Chinese delegation provided some points from Chinese law about ethnic discrimination and hate crimes, they didn't provide information on whether those laws have been implemented. The questions about the torture of Uyghurs and Tibetans were also left unanswered.

One of the questions put before the Chinese delegation on August 10 was the issue of "bilingual education." Ms. Verene Shépherd said there were reports that the Chinese government was banning the Uyghur and Tibetan languages under a "Bilingual Education" policy and asked the Chinese delegation to explain. The Chinese representative replied that bilingual education was fully guaranteed in the Uyghur and Tibetan regions and meant mother language education and Chinese language education were being conducted equally. Further, it was proven that bilingual education was beneficial to the progress of those ethnicities, and it was therefore welcomed by the people of the region. "The allegation that the Chinese government banned the Uyghur language in Hotan and wants to end mother language education by implementing bilingual education isn't true," the Chinese representative repeated.

However, the Hotan Prefectural Education Authority's document on this issue was circulated on social media and the media verified its accuracy. This government document explicitly stated that from September 2017, all classes in the primary and secondary schools in Hotan Prefecture would be taught in Chinese and use of the Uyghur language in the education system would be banned.

Ms. Shépherd noted that the Chinese delegation had only provided examples of laws pertaining to bilingual education but didn't clarify if those laws were being implemented or if there was supervision in place to ensure that they were being implemented. "Passing and printing laws in the paper is one thing, but actually implementing them is another thing," she said.

In short, the Chinese delegation denied all criticism against them and submitted many documents supporting their claims that there were no human rights issues in China and no ethnic and religious discrimination; that the languages, religions, and traditions of all ethnicities were protected; and that all ethnic groups were living fair and happy lives in China. This CERD session was broadcast live to the world by the UN's webcam.

The Chinese delegation walked away believing the session was a big success. Not long after, however, on August 30, CERD announced its conclusion: "More than one million Uyghurs are locked up in China's concentration camps." On August 31, Radio Free Asia published a news report on the issue:

> The UN human rights experts demanded the Chinese government release the Uyghurs detained in re-education camps. The UN Committee on the Elimination of Racial Discrimination called a session to review the situation of racial discrimination in China on August 10 and 13. During the two-day-session, the Chinese delegation faced intense questioning from the UN human rights experts on the issue of concentration camps in the Uyghur region. According to Reuters, today on August 30, the committee's experts announced the conclusion of the two-day-session and said that the Chinese government has locked up more than one million Uyghurs in re-education camps under the guise of "fighting extremism and terrorism."

The report included other issues: the high-surveillance systems the Chinese government was implementing in the Uyghur region, police checkpoints, subjecting the Uyghurs to collection of their DNA and other private information, restrictions on Uyghurs'

APPENDIX A

freedom to travel and obtain passports, and banning the Uyghur language in the education system.

Furthermore, the committee demanded that the Chinese government provide information on the number of detainees, the reasons for their detainment, and the conditions of the camps and that it immediately end the arbitrary detention of Uyghurs in concentration camps. The CERD report pulled back the curtain that had blinded the eyes of the world and brought an end to our doubts. It had taken two years since the initiation of the Chinese concentration camps in 2016 to bring real attention to this issue in August 2018. We worked hard, running from the UN and the EU to the parliaments and human rights committees of Western democratic nations, but still couldn't get anyone to believe that in the twenty-first century more than one million Uyghurs were locked up and suffering in concentration camps. Everyone was skeptical. But we never lost hope, and we never stayed silent. We organized demonstrations to raise awareness, gain the world's sympathy, and put pressure on China. Our complaints reached many countries. We collaborated with human rights organizations around the world to organize activities, publish reports, and conduct meetings. But until the CERD report acknowledged the millions of Uyghurs imprisoned in concentration camps, our efforts hadn't gone very far. With this report, everything changed. The Uyghur crisis became an international issue. The United States and other Western nations made joint statements speaking out against the concentration camps. In 2019, after denying the existence of concentration camps just one year earlier, China came up with a name for them—"re-education centers." Acknowledging their existence meant the need to justify them with repackaged deception.

This Chinese deception on the issue of concentration camps only pushed the world to further understand the true nature of the Chinese regime. China's crimes against humanity had brought the Uyghur crisis and the issue of East Turkistan onto the international community's agenda. It created polarity between the West and China. Those who didn't believe us before started asking for information. The Western media that had avoided this issue in the past was suddenly heating up; their interview requests were never-ending.

Of course, it's crucial to reiterate the importance of the testimonies given by the concentration camp survivors who were able to escape China in 2019. These personal testimonies given in the parliaments and media outlets of the Western world contributed immensely to the transformation of the Uyghur crisis into a recognized international issue. The tireless struggles of organizations in the Uyghur diaspora, the fearless testimonies of survivors and Uyghurs whose relatives had been imprisoned in concentration camps, endless demonstrations, one-man protests and other activities, and the effective use of the media to expose China's crimes all contributed greatly.

2019 World Democracy Award

The Chinese concentration camps in East Turkistan still exist today, despite pressure from Western democratic nations and criticism by the international community. In fact, the camps are expanding, media reports say. It seems the CERD report and calls from Western governments to close the camps and release the more than one million detainees haven't induced China to change. Initially, as time went on and China didn't respond to calls from the international community, I began to doubt the justice of the world and lose hope for my people who faced the constant, bitter choice—"to live as a Chinese or die as a Uyghur."

At this distressing time, I received news that solaced my grieving heart. I was sent an invitation from the National Endowment for Democracy (NED) in Washington, D.C. The World Uyghur Congress was awarded the 2019 Democracy Award.

APPENDIX A

I was thrilled, but surprised. Although my Interpol Red Notice had been removed the year before, it was still causing problems for me. The Chinese were still shamelessly repeating their old rhetoric, "The WUC is a terrorist organization and Dolkun Isa is a terrorist." Receiving the 2019 Democracy Award from an influential organization in the United States, the leader of the international war on terror, was a historic achievement to me. Will this be a turning point in my political life? Will the obstacles to my advocacy disappear now? Will the rightful struggles of my people facing injustice finally be fully recognized? Many questions occupied my mind.

I arrived in Washington on June 4, 2019, just before the start of the ceremony, which was to take place on Capitol Hill. Famous politicians, including House Speaker Nancy Pelosi, Liz Cheney, Michael McCaul, Tom Suozzi, Jim McGovern, Joaquin Castro, several other members of Congress, senators, officials from the State Department, diplomats, human rights activists, Uyghur activists in Washington, and many journalists would be attending.

The award was given to three organizations together: the World Uyghur Congress, the Tibet Action Institute, and ChinaAid. The ceremony opened with a speech by NED's President, Mr. Carl Gershman. In his speech, Mr. Gershman said:

> On the 30th anniversary of the Tiananmen Massacre, the Americans have come to the realization that China's dramatic economic growth hasn't produced a more liberal and open country, as so many people had hoped that it would, but rather a more closed and increasingly repressive authoritarian state that poses a growing danger to democracy in the world. As the Nobel Peace Prize laureate Liu Xiaobo described, 'the Chinese Communist Party has taken hostage of

[*sic*] the world's largest population' . . . Within that hostage population, the Uyghurs and Tibetans are the most persecuted people.

The hall erupted in applause when Mr. Gershman said he would not refer to the Uyghurs and Tibetans by their usual term, "minority," but would instead be calling them a "people" and "nation."

Further, Mr. Gershman said the Uyghurs and Tibetans face a common existential threat to their culture, language, identity, and faith. He highlighted the fact that the CCP sees everything outside its control as a threat to its power and works to extinguish that threat. He recognized the recipients of the Democracy Award as representatives of three groups that are resisting the pressure to bow down to the CCP, reiterating that the WUC deserved this award for its struggles to protect the rights of the millions of Uyghurs in concentration camps. When he said he was calling the Uyghurs' homeland "East Turkistan" and not by its Chinese name "Xinjiang," the applause erupted again.

Following Mr. Gershman's opening remarks, House Speaker Nancy Pelosi and members of Congress Liz Cheney, Michael McCaul, and Joaquin Castro also made speeches. They said that during the past thirty years, the CCP had been abusing the values of democracy, but the people struggling for their rights would never give up and that China shouldn't forget that the world was watching in that very moment.

After the awards were distributed, each organization had an opportunity to give a speech. Bob Foo, the president of ChinaAid, spoke first. He talked about the CCP's oppressive nature, noting that the regime was built on lies and deception and feared exposure by justice. He also brought up Chinese lawyer Zhang Haitao, who was sentenced to nineteen years in prison for expressing his

APPENDIX A

opinions on social media, highlighting this case as an example of the true nature of the regime.

The director of the Tibetan Action Institute, Ms. Lhadon Tethong, took the stage next to describe the Chinese communist government's oppression of the Tibetan people. This award would bring great hope to the Tibetan people, and she felt proud to be receiving it, she said.

When it was the WUC's turn to receive the award, member of Congress Jim McGovern, who introduced and played pivotal roles in passing into law some important U.S. legislation and was also one of the legislators who introduced the Uyghur Human Rights Policy Act to Congress, took the stage. In his remarks, Congressman McGovern said that the persecution in the Uyghurs' homeland had reached an unimaginable level, especially for the millions of Uyghurs who were locked up in concentration camps facing horrific atrocities and suffering from extreme physical and psychological torture. He noted that orphaned children had become secondary victims and that the Uyghurs outside the camps were living in an "open prison." He reiterated that the WUC had been working tirelessly for the rights of the Uyghurs and, hence, he was conferring the 2019 Democracy Award on Dolkun Isa, the president of the WUC. With that, he invited me onto the stage.[59]

The hall broke into applause when I took to the stage to receive the award on behalf of the World Uyghur Congress. I was exhilarated. My colleagues, who appreciated the significance and historic background of this award, were excited too. It was meaningful to be receiving this award at a time when the Uyghur nation was facing the threat of extinction and more than three million of the people of East Turkistan were experiencing ethnic and cultural genocide.

After eagerly receiving the award, I delivered my speech:

Good evening, ladies and gentlemen and distinguished guests.

The World Uyghur Congress is deeply proud and honoured to receive this award in recognition of our tireless work advocating for the rights of the Uyghur people, despite immense challenges.

I would like to sincerely thank the National Endowment for Democracy. We have made visible progress over the past year, despite huge challenges, and this would not have been possible without the support of the NED. I would like to acknowledge the teamwork of the World Uyghur Congress's leadership, staff and all those in the Uyghur diaspora who have supported us. I would also like to thank all the academics, journalists and activists whose important contributions have made a significant difference.

While we are deeply proud and honoured to receive this award, we cannot lose focus. Despite our best efforts and all the progress, we have made in the past year, the concentration camps [that] arbitrarily detained millions of Uyghurs have not been closed. Despite all our work, Uyghurs in East Turkistan are suffering and are being denied their most basic rights. We are still missing our family and friends who have disappeared into the camps.

At this moment, we can celebrate the great strides we have made over the past year, but our work is not done. In the coming year, we must redouble our efforts. We cannot stop until all those detained in the camps have been freed. We will not rest until the Uyghur people enjoy democracy, freedom, and human rights.

APPENDIX A

House Speaker Nancy Pelosi delivered the closing remarks. Pointing out that one of the brave student leaders of the Tiananmen Square Movement, Orkesh Dolet (Wu'erkaixi), was present in the hall, she expressed admiration for Orkesh's bravery when, at only twenty years old, he stepped up to lead the Chinese people seeking justice. Afterwards, Speaker Pelosi met me and other leaders of the WUC to congratulate us.

I was thrilled with this ceremony. What amazed and excited me was not only the honour the Democracy Award brought, but the change it would bring. I felt this award would clear obstacles from my path, but more importantly, it would symbolically remove the stain China had used to darken my reputation and foist it back on the Chinese regime.

The WUC was different from the other two organizations that received the award. For years the Chinese regime had been slanderously labelling the WUC a "terrorist organization" in the international arena. I, the president of the WUC, had been on Interpol's list of Red Notices for twenty-one years, falsely accused of "plotting murder, robbery and bombing." For the WUC, under the leadership of an alleged terrorist, to be named a notable figure of democracy in the U.S. Congress and by U.S. politicians, was significant. I was being praised for "contributions to freedom and justice." To go from terrorist to freedom fighter was quite an evolution.

The award also sent a signal to China, the second-largest economic and political global power, which had been actively seeking to dominate the world and remove all obstacles in its way. Despite its attempts to obliterate all threats that countered its national interests under the guise of "fighting terrorism," China was failing. It was failing to eliminate me and the WUC from the world. It was becoming a fact that the Uyghur people—who were experiencing the greatest crisis in their history and who had never felt more helpless—were not alone. This award was a sign that justice would prevail, and the East Turkistan national independence movement had won a battle against their Chinese oppressors.

The award not only brought hope and encouragement to my people but was also a comfort for me after the suffering of my thwarted freedom in the free world and violations of my rights in democratic Western nations for more than twenty years.

The Radio Free Asia report on June 7 titled, "Does WUC's Winning of Democracy Award Mean Pressure Against China Will Mount?" wrote the following:

> Since the concentration camps came into the spotlight and as the Muslim and Turkic World are still silent, top U.S. officials have been talking about this crisis consistently. At a time when the Uyghurs and concentration camps have become a usual topic in the Western media including the *New York Times* and the *Washington Post*, the Uyghurs' representative organization in the diaspora, the World Uyghur Congress has received a democracy award in the U.S. Several weeks ago, the Uyghur dissident in Chinese prison Ilham Tohti has won an American freedom award.

The WUC's winning of the 2019 Democracy Award indeed brought great excitement to the Uyghur diaspora. It also attracted the attention of the international media. Major media outlets around the world published reports about the award, describing it as increasing pressure on China and bringing attention to the Uyghur crisis from top U.S. officials.

Before and after the award ceremony, with NED's help, conferences were planned in the U.S. Congress, the Senate, the Department of State, and the Department of Defense. During these conferences, I met Deputy Secretary of State David Stilwell and Deputy Secretary of Defense Randall Schriver and had

APPENDIX A

intense discussions with them about the concentration camps in East Turkistan. I pleaded with the U.S. government to take urgent action to save the Uyghurs from their ongoing genocide.

As well, in collaboration with the Uyghur Human Rights Project (UHRP), the Uyghur American Association (UAA), and George Washington University's Department of Central Asian Studies, the WUC organized a two-day international conference that would take place June 6 to 7, with the theme of "Confronting atrocities in China: The Global Response to the Uyghur Crisis." The opening ceremony was held in the U.S. Congress building, and the discussion part at George Washington University. During the conference, experts from Europe, Japan, Central Asia, Australia, and Turkey, as well as lawyers, researchers, and Uyghur activists engaged in critical discussions about the Uyghurs, the concentration camps, and possible avenues for the world to respond to these atrocities.

APPENDIX B

REBUTTAL TO THE CHINESE PUBLIC SECURITY MINISTRY'S "TERRORIST" ACCUSATION

By Dolkun Isa
20.12.2003
Munich

On December 15, 2003, the Chinese Public Security Ministry published a document accusing four Uyghur organizations and eleven individuals of being "terrorists." The "terrorist" list included the World Uyghur Youth Congress and me.

First of all, I categorically deny the entire "terrorist" accusations brought against me. Those accusations do not have any merit whatsoever. They are nothing but fabricated lies.

For years, the Chinese authorities have labeled all activities carried out by Uyghur people to achieve freedom, human rights and self-determination as "separatism," "fundamentalism" or "extremism" and severely cracked down on them. After the September 11 terrorist attacks, which [were] condemned by the entire world including the Uyghur people, China has taken advantage of the international war on terrorism to portray

APPENDIX B

Uyghur people's peaceful resistance to the Chinese government oppression as "terrorism," and intensified [its] political repression of Uyghurs. Using this new strategy, China has imprisoned thousands of innocent Uyghurs, and tortured or even executed some of them.

The international community has criticized China's practice of hijacking the war on terrorism to crack down on Uyghur Muslims. However, China has disregarded the concerns of the international community and went even further in its campaign to use the war on terror to silence the Uyghur voices. Emnboldened by its success in persuading the US and UN to blacklist the East Turkistan Islamic Movement (ETIM) as a "terrorist" organization last year, China attempted to weaken or destroy the other Uyghur organizations and individuals outside of China by similar slandering tactics, including the statement on December 15, 2003.

The following is my response to the groundless accusations against the World Uyghur Youth Congress and me.

1. The Chinese accusation [referred to], "The World Uyghur Youth Congress (WUYC), also known as the International Uyghur Youths League, the World Uygur Youths League [sic], or the International Eastern Turkistan Youths Congress."

    As a founder and leader of the World Uyghur Youth Congress, I never heard of those other names until this Chinese document mentioned them. The only name the World Uyghur Youth Congress has ever used is "World Uyghur Youth Congress." All the other names mentioned above by China are fabricated out of thin air by the Chinese authorities.

2. The Chinese accusation said, "The World Uyghur [sic] Youth Congress (WUYC) is jointly founded by a band of

Uygurs who have fled abroad from Xinjiang, China, and descendents of Xinjiang people living abroad. It is a terrorist organization aiming at splitting Xinjiang from China."

The World Uyghur Youth Congress was established by a group of Uyghur youths who believed in the inalienable rights of [the] Uyghur people to freedom and self-determination just like any other peoples in the world. It is an organization that uses the international norms as its guiding principle and carries out peaceful activities in line with the laws of the Republic of Germany to promote democracy, human rights and freedom. The World Uyghur Youth Congress has always opposed terrorism in all forms and has been exposing to the world the state terrorism and human rights violations committed by the Chinese government against Uyghurs, Tibetans and even Chinese people.

3. The Chinese accusation listed the following as the major "terrorist activities" of the World Uyghur Youth Congress:

(1) "Major leading members and subordinate groupings of the WUYC have been active in performing violent acts of terrorism. The former chairman of the WUYC, Dolqun Isa, have [sic]has organized criminal gangs in Xinjiang, creating incidents of theft, robbery and explosion, among others. He has also played an active role in terrorist activities."

The Chinese Government is trying to hide the truth by these slanders. They accused me of "robbery, theft, and terrorism," but did not produce any evidence. In fact, they could not possibly produce evidence of something that never has taken place. The Chinese government knows very well what I did in China; all the Uyghur people, especially those thousands of students who attended Xinjiang University during 1987–1988, know it very well.

APPENDIX B

I founded a Student Union for Science and Culture Union in Xinjiang University in 1987. The purpose of the Union was to eliminate illiteracy among Uyghurs by mobilizing university students to offer classes in rural areas during summer breaks. We mobilized thousands of students for that purpose. The Union was a public organization established with the permission of Xinjiang University. I still retain copies of the school permission along with the charter and activities of the Union. In May 1988, a Chinese brochure, which insults the Uyghur people and promotes discrimination against them, was circulated in Xinjiang University. Uyghur students reported the incident to school authorities and government departments and demanded an investigation into the incident and to bring the perpetrators to justice. But no investigation was done. On June 15, 1988, I and another leader of the Student Union for Science and Culture Union had a dialogue with the Xinjiang Uyghur Autonomous Region Party Committee vice chairman Janabil, the Education Committee director Zhang Yang, the Planning Committee director Tohti Ali, and the Finance Committee director Mehmud for 6 hours. We demanded to end the disparity between the Chinese and Uyghur education systems and the ethnic discrimination, and to implement the Autonomous Regions Policy of [the] People's Republic of China. But, they refused our demands. Therefore, we mobilized around 5000 students for a protest rally on city streets. The demonstration ended peacefully without any incident. However, the authorities called the rally [the] "June 15 riot," and placed thirty student leaders including me under close surveillance and questioned us intensely, pressuring us to confess that "we were ethnic separatists." I firmly denied their accusations. On September 27, 1988, all universities and colleges in Urumchi called schoolwide emergency meetings to announce that I was expelled from school. My 4 four years of college life, which lasted from 1984 to 1988, ended that day.

The Chinese accusation did not mention anything about these facts and portrayed my involvement in [the] student movement as "robbery, theft and terrorism." No matter how hard they try to hide or distort the facts, they could not succeed because there are thousands of witnesses both inside and outside of [the] motherland. They probably forgot that they gave me a copy of the 13-page long dismissal notice both in Chinese and Uyghur. I still have the notice and submitted a copy of it to the Germany authorities when I applied for political asylum.

(2) The Chinese accusation said," As vice president of the Eastern Turkistan Liberation Organization at present, Dolqun Isa assists the terrorist organization's leader, Muhanmetemin Hazret, in collaborating with other terrorist groups outside China to engage in violent terrorist activities. He also oversees the operations of the organization's branch in Germany. The first chairman of the WUYC, Umer Kanat, and chairman of the Eastern Turkistan National Freedom Center, Enwar Yusuf, are responsible for the United States branch of the Eastern Turkistan Liberation Organization."

This is very funny. This is the first time I am told that I was the vice president of the Eastern Turkistan Liberation Organization. I know Memtimin Hezret. In fact, all Uyghurs know him, because he was a famous writer and the first Uyghur movie scriptwriter. Several of his scripts were made into movies by the Tangri-Tagh Movie Studio and shown all around East Turkistan. I saw him [for the] first time in Turkey. I read his articles exposing the Chinese atrocities in East Turkistan in Turkish newspapers. But I learned for

APPENDIX B

the first time that an organization called "Eastern Turkistan Liberation Organization" existed and [was] led by Memtimin Hezret only after I watched a CD titled, "The True Face of the East Turkistan Terrorists" that was produced and distributed by the Chinese Central TV Station. The last time I met Memtimin Hezret was either in 1997 or [1998] in Istanbul. All I knew about him was [that] he was making a living by running a small business and writing.

Now, the Chinese authorities are alleging that I am the vice-president and in charge of the Germany operation of an organization I hardly know. They fabricated groundless accusations and fictitious relationships to portray me as a "terrorist."

(3) The Chinese accusation said, "The Eastern Turkistan Youths League (launched in Istanbul, Turkey, in March 1993, and later moved to Switzerland and became part of the WUYC), which clearly advocates in its charter "the development of strong and powerful underground forces to overthrow the existing Chinese regime and realize the independence of Xinjiang." The WUYC has, since its founding, formulated action plans to assassinate Party, government and military leaders of the Xinjiang Uygur [sic] Autonomous Region, destroy railways and bridges, initiate terrorist explosions, attack Chinese agencies stationed abroad, and create armed disturbances at the border areas between China and India, Tajikistan and Afghanistan."

When they fabricated these accusations, the Chinese authorities did not take the legal system and institutions of investigation of European countries into account. They raved as if Switzerland did not have law and investigating institutions and would permit terrorist activities on its territory. I never heard of an organization named "East Turkistan

Youths League" until this Chinese accusation mentioned this name on December 15, 2003. If such an organization existed and carried out "terrorist activities" since 1993, how come no one ever heard about it? The World Uyghur Youth Congress has attended the annual UN human rights Committee meetings in Geneva since 1999 and organized demonstrations in front of the UN with Tibetans. Members of the small Uyghur community in Switzerland also joined us for those demonstrations;, however, we never heard of the existence of an organization named "East Turkistan Youths League." The Chinese government fabricated a fictitious "terrorist" organization out of thin air and linked it to the World Uyghur Youth Congress to make the "terrorist" label stick.

The Chinese government forgot that the activities and programs of the World Uyghur Youth Congress have always been open to the public. If we have to mention the organizations that have [a] relationship or collaboration with the World Uyghur Youth Congress, we may point to the Belgium Uyghur Youth Union, the England Uyghur Youth Association and Kazakhstan Uyghur Youth Union. These organizations have registered with the governments of their host countries and carry out activities allowed by the laws of those countries. No organization other than these is affiliated with the World Uyghur Youth Congress in any way.

(4) The Chinese government shamelessly alleged that, "In 1993, the WUYC masterminded and implemented two explosions in Xinjiang, one in the office building of the Kashi Agricultural Machinery Company and the other in a video lounge in Shache County, which left two persons dead and 22 others injured."

APPENDIX B

When they made up these lies, it obviously escaped from their attention that an organization that was established in November 1996 could not possibly be responsible for an act [that] occurred in 1993. It is self evident that what they are saying about us is false.

4. The government said the following about [the] membership and financial [re]source[s] of the World Uyghur Youth Congress: "Major sources of funds and personnel of the WUYC. The WUYC mainly resorts to theft, robbery or other criminal means for funding. It also receives financial aid from other international terrorist organizations. Most of its recruits are Uygur [*sic*] youths living outside China."

   It is not a secret that the sole financial source of the World Uyghur Youth Congress comes from the donations and membership fees by patriotic Uyghurs living in Europe, mainly in Germany. [The a]ctivities and finance[s] of any legally registered organization in Germany [are] monitored by the German authorities. It is impossible to raise or spend illegal money.

   All the members of the World Uyghur Youth Congress are Uyghur youths living outside China. The organization has no member inside China. However, we do not doubt that there are thousands of Uyghur youths inside China who consider us as their voices and representatives.

5. The Chinese [accusation] said the following in regard to our alleged connection to international terrorist organizations:

(1) "The WUYC is closely tied to other terrorist organizations. Its subordinate [group], the Eastern Turkistan Youths League, maintains a close relationship with organizations in West Asia engaging in violence. It has asked

these organizations many times for help in purchasing arms and explosives."

In a vain attempt to link the World Uyghur Youth Congress with international terrorist organizations, the Chinese authorities made up a fictitious subordinate organization, "East Turkistan Youth League," and alleged that it has ties to international terrorist organization[s].

(2) The Chinese accusation said: "The WUYC also keeps cooperative relations with other "Eastern Turkistan" terrorist organizations. In convening the Third WUYC, it got support from the Eastern Turkistan Liberation Organization, and Muhanmetemin Hazret, leader of the Eastern Turkistan Liberation Organization, has always served as an aegis for Dolqun Isa."

When the Chinese authorities fabricated these groundless accusations, they forgot the fact that the whole world knows who sponsored the Third World Uyghur Youth Congress held in Estonia. The Third World Uyghur Youth Congress was held with the sponsorship of the Unrepresented Nations and Peoples Organization (UNPO) Estonia office in November 2001. In addition to Uyghur youths, members of the Estonia parliament, the mayor of Talin and leaders of Chinese democratic movements also attended the congress and delivered speeches. The congress was covered by international media from the beginning to the end. An Estonia TV network produced and broadcasted a special program on it. During the congress, Estonia['s] foreign [minister] accepted a visit by UNPO general secretary Erkin Alptekin and me. The Chinese government pressured the Estonia government in an official protest letter to cancel the congress. However, even though a small country, Estonia

APPENDIX B

refused to submit to the Chinese pressure and showed the true color of a democratic country.

(3) The Chinese Government alleged, "The WUYC also energetically helps "Eastern Turkistan" terrorists. In 2002, Dolqun Isa, in collaboration with Ahmat Tuhit, sent people to Alma-Ata, Kazakhstan, to take Muhammat Wupur, a terrorist, to a training camp at the border between Afghanistan and Uzbekistan, and later transfer him to Germany to seek asylum."

The World Uyghur Youth Congress has never helped any terrorist. However, it helped Uyghur refugees, through Amnesty International and other international human rights organizations, who fled from China to the neighboring countries in order to avoid persecution for their involvement in political activities inside China and applied for refugee status from the UNHCR offices in those countries. Amnesty International and UNHCR offices in those countries are fully aware of what we did in this regard. Some of the people whom the World Uyghur Youth Congress helped were granted refugee status by UNHCR and sent to democratic countries such as Sweden, Norway and Canada.

The Chinese allegation about an alleged "terrorist" Muhammat Wupur is also a pure fabrication. The alleged incident has never taken place. I am not aware of the existence of a Uyghur named Muhammat Wupur in Germany. I do not think there is a Uyghur with that name in Germany. If the Chinese Government thinks otherwise, they can check with the German authorities.

(4) The Chinese document alleged, "The WUYC and terrorist organizations like the Eastern Turkistan Liberation Organization and the Eastern Turkistan Islamic Movement

support each other, and they are interrelated. Abudu Salam, head of the law department of the first session of the WUYC, is concurrently an assistant to the vice chairman of the Eastern Turkistan Islamic Movement. The key members of the WUYC also take important posts in the Eastern Turkistan Liberation Organization. After the Sept. 11 terrorist attacks against the United States, Hasan Mahsum, head of the Eastern Turkistan Islamic Movement, tried to draw close to the WUYC led by Dolqun Isa for help in whitewashing the notoriety of the Eastern Turkistan Islamic Movement as a terrorist organization. The WUYC also actively collaborates with other international terrorist organizations."

Again, the Chinese government is making up fictitious relationships here. The World Uyghur Youth Congress has never had any relationship or collaboration with the Eastern Turkistan Islamic Movement or the Eastern Turkistan Liberation Organization. The truth is we learned the existence of these organizations for the first time in 2002 from a CD, titled," The True Face of East Turkistan Terrorists," that was produced and distributed by the Chinese government to mislead the international community. The Chinese government is apparently trying to take advantage of the US and UN listings of the East Turkistan Islamic Movement as a "terrorist" organization to fabricate a "terrorist" case against the World Uyghur Youth Congress by linking it to the East Turkistan Islamic Movement (ETIM).

6. The Chinese document said the following about me:

(1) "Dolqun Isa is senior high school graduate, . . . has been head of the World Uygur Youths Congress terrorist organization for many years. Dolqun Isa is now the target of an Interpol red notice."

APPENDIX B

In an attempt to distort the facts, the Chinese government tried to hide the fact that I attended Xinjiang University for four years until I was expelled for my involvement in the student movement that I mentioned above. I have never [been] involved with any terrorist organization, but it is true that I was the head of the World Youth Uyghur Congress, a legally registered organization campaigning for democracy, human rights and freedom [for the] Uyghur people. The truth was my activities in the West to expose the human rights violations committed by China had angered the Chinese authorities[;] therefore they tried to destroy me by fabricating allegations such as "robbery, theft and criminal gangs" and issued a arrest warrant for me through the [sic] Interpol. Fortunately, however, Germany is a country that has a law and, unlike China, respects democracy and human rights. The German authorities investigated the Chinese allegations about me and concluded that I fled China because of my involvement in peaceful political dissent not in criminal activities as China alleged. Therefore, the Chinese authorities failed to materialize their evil scheme to portray me as a "criminal." Now, they are making a second attempt on me using a different label—"terrorist."

(2) The Chinese allegation said, "In 1994, he organized the Eastern Turkistan Students Union and served as chairman and concurrently chief editor of the Eastern Turkistan Youth newspaper. In 1996, he moved to Germany and joined the Eastern Turkistan Union in Europe.... In November 2002, he resigned the chairmanship and became vice chairman of the preparatory committee of the Eastern Turkistan Uygur [sic] Congress. When in Xinjiang, Dolqun Isa formed a gang with several convicted criminals to commit burglary, robbery and other crime[s] and participated in masterminding a

series of bomb blasts in Xinhe County. Since he fled abroad, he has organized and participated in all sorts of terrorist activities launched by the Eastern Turkistan Liberation Organization. At a gathering to mark the 10th anniversary of the so-called December 12 student movement of Xinjiang in Ankara, Turkey, on December 14, 1995, Dolqun Isa claimed, "The uprising against the Chinese tyranny in Hotan Prefecture was organized by us."

The World Uyghur Youth Congress and I do not have anything to do with the alleged "bomb blasts in Xinhe County" or the "uprising in Hotan" or any burglary, robbery, or other crimes. The Chinese allegation[s] about those incidents is a pure slander. The rest of the statements in the above paragraph are true, but they have nothing do with "terrorism." I was only exercising my rights guaranteed by the laws of the host countries. Those activities may be considered "terrorism" by China who is trying to take advantage of the international war on terrorism to label all types of political dissent as "terrorism," but they are perfectly legal in those countries where they were carried out. These allegations show how far China is pushing the definition of "terrorism." It proves that China does not distinguish between peaceful dissent and terrorism and that it classifies everything it does not like as "terrorism" and everybody it does not like as "terrorist."

I would like to emphasize here that the East Turkistan Uyghur Congress Preparatory Committee [was] established to create a stronger organization by merging the East Turkistan/Uyghurstan National Congress with the World Uyghur Youth Congress and headed by Erkin Alptekin, a well-known Uyghur leader known for his peaceful activities for the rights of Uyghurs and other under-represented peoples around the world. He was a retired long-time employee

APPENDIX B

of the U.S. Radio Liberty. The Chinese Government cited my post as the vice-chairman of this committee as part of my "terrorist activities." What China is most worried about is that a unified Uyghur international movement might become a reality under the leadership of Erkin Alptekin. China does not want to see the emergence of a stronger Uyghur organization that can represent the voices of Uyghurs at international forums. Therefore, it has pushed past the limits of decency in its attempt to prevent the unification of Uyghur organizations. That is the main reason why China is slandering the World Uyghur Youth Congress with "terrorism."

In conclusion, the World Uyghur Youth Congress and I have never supported violence or terrorism. On the contrary, we have always been opposed to them. However, we have been carrying out lawful activities to protect the rights of Uyghurs to freedom, self-determination, democracy and human rights, and to preserve the Uyghur language, culture and traditions. All our activities are carried out openly within the scope of the UN charter, the European Parliament charter and the Germany [sic] law. We have nothing to hide.

If any international organization or qualified individual has any questions or wants to know more about our activities, I will gladly accommodate their requests. I trust the World Uyghur Youth Congress will do the same.

At the end, I ask Germany, the United States and all the other democratic countries and international organizations not to take the face value of the Chinese allegations about us but to investigate the allegations thoroughly before reaching a conclusion. I appeal to the international community to condemn the slander campaign launched by the Chinese authorities to silence the Uyghur voices in the free world.

We are being attacked with slanders by the Chinese authorities merely for exposing their atrocities against Uyghurs. All we have done is exercise our rights guaranteed by the UN charter and the laws of the countries we reside in. When our rights are attacked by slanders, I hope the world community will come to our assistance.

ENDNOTES

1. See the website of the World Uyghur Congress for more on the history of the region and its takeover by China: https://www.uyghurcongress.org/en/.

2. For more on the national security law, see https://www.hrw.org/news/2020/05/22/hong-kong-beijing-threatens-draconian-security-law.

3. Austin Ram and Chris Buckley, "'Absolutely No Mercy': Leaked Files Expose How China Organized Mass Detentions of Muslims," *The New York Times*, The New York Times, 16 Nov. 2019, https://www.nytimes.com/interactive/2019/11/16/world/asia/china-xinjiang-documents.html

4. Erkin Tursun was ultimately detained in a concentration camp in March 2018, then later sentenced to nineteen years and ten months in prison.

5. Waris Ababekri died in a concentration camp in China in November 2019.

6. For more information about his life and work, go to https://www.rfa.org/english/news/uyghur/independence-12292020180655.html.

7. The complete text of my statement is reproduced in the Appendix.

8. "Protest Gegen Verhaftung Eines Uigurischen Menschenrechtlers Bei Der UN-Menschenrechtskommission." *Gesellschaft Für Bedrohte Völker E.V. (GfbV)*, 20 Apr. 2005, https://www.gfbv.de/de/news/protest-gegen-verhaftung-eines-uigurischen-menschenrechtlers-bei-der-un-menschenrechtskommission-274/

9. "Deutsche Terrorfahnder Im Reich Der Mitte," *Der Spiegel*, Dec. 2004, https://magazin.spiegel.de/EpubDelivery/spiegel/pdf/38546668.

10. Dave Boyer, "China Protests Dissident's Visit to U.S. during Nuclear Summit," *The Washington Times*, The Washington Times, 31 Mar. 2016, https://m.washingtontimes.com/news/2016/mar/31/china-protests-dissidents-visit-us-during-nuclear-/; "China Angered at Rights Award for Exiled Xinjiang Leader," *Reuters*, Reuters, 1 Apr. 2016, https://www.reuters.com/article/us-china-rights-xinjiang-idUSKCN0WY499; Eli Lake and Josh Rogin, "Xi's Washington Visit Crashed by Unwelcome Guest," *Bloomberg*, Bloomberg, 31 Mar. 2016, https://www.bloomberg.com/opinion/articles/2016-03-31/xi-s-washington-visit-crashed-by-one-of-his-victims.

11. "Türkei Verbietet Uigurischem Menschenrechtler Die Einreise," *Gesellschaft Für Bedrohte Völker E.V. (GfbV)*, 2 Sept. 2008, https://www.gfbv.de/de/news/tuerkei-verbietet-uigurischem-menschenrechtler-die-einreise-4037/.

12. "Urumchi Massacre," World Uyghur Congress, *December 8, 2009, https://www.uyghurcongress.org/en/the-urumqi-massacre/*

13. "VIII UNPO General Assembly—A New UNPO for the Challenges of a New Century," *UNPO*, UNPO, 31 Oct. 2006, https://unpo.org/article/5713.

14. He is now the director of the Uyghur Service at Radio Free Asia.

15. Celia Llopis-jepsen, "Why Did the Nia Bar Dolkun Isa?" *Taipei Times*, 22 July 2009, https://www.taipeitimes.com/News/editorials/archives/2009/07/22/2003449242.

16. *World Bulletin*, "Exile Uighur Rebiya Kadeer Plans to Visit

ENDNOTES

Taiwan," *World Bulletin/News From Turkey and Islamic World*, World Bulletin, 24 Sept. 2009, https://worldbulletin.dunyabulteni.net/archive/exile-uighur-rebiya-kadeer-plans-to-visit-taiwan-photo-h47599.html.

17. Yu Ping, "Exclusive: President Tsai Denied Uyghur Leader Dolkun ISA Entry to Taiwan: Taiwan News: 2019-06-10 23:31:00," *Taiwan News*, 10 June 2019, https://www.taiwannews.com.tw/en/news/3721233.

18. https://www.forum2000.cz/en/homepage

19. "Taiwan Ambassador-at-Large Steps down over Dissatisfaction with Tsai," *Taiwan News*, 4 June 2019, https://www.taiwannews.com.tw/en/news/3717162.

20. "South Korea: Dolkun Isa Release Welcome But Authorities Should Not Have Denied Him Entry," *Amnesty International*, 18 Sept. 2009, https://www.amnesty.org/en/latest/news/2009/09/south-korea-dolkun-isa-release-welcome-authorities-should-not-have-denie/; "East Turkestan: Dolkun Isa Detained in South Korea," *UNPO*, UNPO, 16 Sept. 2009, https://unpo.org/content/view/10070/81/; "Dolkun ISA: UNPO Issues Letter to Meps," *UNPO*, UNPO, 17 Sept. 2009, https://www.unpo.org/content/view/10071/236/; "'China's Long Arm' Threatens Human Rights Activists and Prominent Uyghur Human Rights Activist from Germany Arrested in South Korea—Immediate Release Is Called For," *Gesellschaft Für Bedrohte Völker E.V. (GfbV)*, 16 Sept. 2009, https://www.gfbv.de/en/news/chinas-long-arm-threatens-human-rights-activists-prominent-uyghur-human-rights-activist-from-germ-1/; "South Korea—an Uyghur Activist Denied to Enter, for Being a 'Terrorist,'" *FORUM-ASIA*, 1 Oct. 2009, https://www.forum-asia.org/?p=5345; "South Korean Detention of Uyghur Activist Dolkun Isa Raises Concern over Chinese Influence on Peaceful Uyghur Activities," *World Uyghur Congress*, 18 Sept. 2009, https://www.uyghurcongress.org/en/south-korean-detention-of-uyghur-activist-dolkun-isa-raises-concern-over-chinese-influence-on-peaceful-uyghur-activities/; "South Korea Releases Uighur Activist after Detention at Airport: Taiwan News: 2009-09-19 00:00:00," *Taiwan News*,

Taiwan News, 19 Sept. 2009, https://www.taiwannews.com.tw/en/news/1060950.

21. "China-ROK Relations: Minor Tensions, Positive Overall," *Public Library of US Diplomacy*, WikiLeaks, 12 Feb. 2010, para 13, https://wikileaks.org/plusd/cables/10BEIJING382_a.html.

22. The article is available here: https://www.icij.org/investigations/interpols-red-flag/interpols-red-notices-used-some-pursue-political-dissenters-opponents/

23. Libby Lewis, "Are Some Countries Abusing Interpol?" CNN, Cable News Network, 18 July 2011, http://edition.cnn.com/2011/WORLD/europe/07/18/interpol.red.notices/index.html?hpt=wo_c1.

24. "《开讲啦》我的时代答卷· 前联合国副秘书长吴红波：优秀的外交官要有强烈的爱国心和进取精神 20181222 | CCTV《开讲啦》官方频道." *YouTube*, CCTV, 22 Dec. 2018, https://www.youtube.com/watch?v=pmrI2n6d6VU&t=1496s.

25. The United Nations Economic and Social Council (ECOSOC) resolution allows civil society participation in the work of the UN. The Committee on NGOs oversees its implementation and processes all applications by civil society organisations for ECOSOC status. The status allows NGOs to participate fully in the UN system. Definition taken from the Child Rights international Network (CHIN) website: https://archive.crin.org/en/home/campaigns/transparency/ecosoc/what-ecosoc-status.html

26. "Uyghur Human Rights Activist Expelled from UNPFII," *UNPO*, UNPO, 8 May 2017, https://unpo.org/downloads/2399.pdf.

27. "UN: China Blocks Activists, Harasses Experts," *Human Rights Watch*, 5 Sept. 2017, https://www.hrw.org/news/2017/09/05/un-china-blocks-activists-harasses-experts.

28. "The Costs of International Advocacy," *Human Rights Watch*, 5 Sept. 2017, https://www.hrw.org/report/2017/09/05/costs-international-advocacy/chinas-interference-united-nations-human-rights.

ENDNOTES

29. Robbie Gramer and Colum Lynch, "High-Wire Act Ahead for Trump's New Women's Rights Envoy," *Foreign Policy*, 28 Mar. 2019, https://foreignpolicy.com/2019/03/28/high-wire-act-ahead-for-trumps-new-womens-rights-envoy/.

30. Linda Lew, "What to Do When the UN Human Rights Office May Have Violated Human Rights?" *South China Morning Post*, 13 Dec. 2020, https://www.scmp.com/news/china/diplomacy/article/3113628/what-do-when-un-human-rights-office-may-have-violated-human.

31. A complete video transcript of the session is available at https://www.unmultimedia.org/avlibrary/asset/2157/2157224/.

32. "Opinion | China's Repugnant Campaign to Destroy a Minority People," *The Washington Post*, WP Company, 20 May 2018, https://www.washingtonpost.com/opinions/chinas-repugnant-campaign-to-destroy-a-minority-people/2018/05/20/9fe061b4-5ac0-11e8-b656-a5f8c2a9295d_story.html.

33. Andrea Worden, "China Fails in Its Gambit to Use the UN NGO Committee to Silence the Society for Threatened Peoples and Uyghur Activist Dolkun Isa," *China Change*, 10 July 2018, https://chinachange.org/2018/07/10/china-fails-in-its-gambit-to-use-the-un-ngo-committee-to-silence-the-society-for-threatened-peoples-and-uyghur-activist-dolkun-isa/.

34. "Uyghur Exile Group Leader's Mother Died in Xinjiang Detention Center," *Radio Free Asia*, 2 July 2018, https://www.rfa.org/english/news/uyghur/mother-07022018164214.html.

35. "Reporters From Tianshannet Interviews Dolkun Isa's Relatives Video Clips Expose His Life," *YouTube*, YouTube, https://www.youtube.com/watch?v=cJW3za4taSM. Accessed 29 June 2022.

36. "Targeted by Chinese Smear Campaign, Uyghur Leader Learns of Father's Death," *Radio Free Asia*, 15 Jan. 2020, https://www.rfa.org/english/news/uyghur/activist-father-01152020211855.html; "Relatives of Xinjiang Separatists Condemn Their Lies," *People's Daily Online*, Global Times, 13 Jan. 2020, http://en.people.cn/n3/2020/0113/c90000-9648237.html.

37. "UN Unprecendeted Joint Call for China to End Xinjiang Abuses," *Human Rights Watch, Jul.15, 2019*, https://www.hrw.org/news/2019/07/10/un-unprecedented-joint-call-china-end-xinjiang-abuses.

38. "Statement by Ambassador Christoph Heusgen on behalf of 39 Countries in the Third Committee General Debate," *Permanent of the Federal Republic of Germany to the United Nations, Oct.6, 2020*, https://new-york-un.diplo.de/un-en/news-corner/201006-heusgen-china/2402648.

39. "2020 Edition: Which Countries Are For or Against China's Xinjiang Policies?" *The Diplomat, Oct. 9, 2020*, https://thediplomat.com/2020/10/2020-edition-which-countries-are-for-or-against-chinas-xinjiang-policies/.

40. "Joint statement on the human rights situation in Xinjiang," *Australian Government, Department of Foreign Affairs and Trade, Oct. 21, 2021*, https://www.dfat.gov.au/international-relations/themes/human-rights/unga-third-committee-statements/76th-session/joint-statement-human-rights-situation-xinjiang-21-october-2021.

41. "Joint Statement on the Human Rights Situation in China," *The Netherlands at International Organizations, June 14, 2022*, https://www.permanentrepresentations.nl/documents/speeches/2022/06/14/hrc50_item2_jst_china.

42. "UN experts call for decisive measures to protect fundamental freedoms in China," *OHCHR, June 26, 2020*, https://www.ohchr.org/en/press-releases/2020/06/un-experts-call-decisive-measures-protect-fundamental-freedoms-china.

43. "China must address grave human rights concerns and enable credible international investigation: UN experts," *OHCHR*, June 10, 2022, https://www.ohchr.org/en/press-releases/2022/06/china-must-address-grave-human-rights-concerns-and-enable-credible.

44. "Determination of the Secretary of State on Atrocities in Xinjiang," 19 Jan. 2021, https://2017-2021.state.gov/determination-of-the-secretary-of-state-on-atrocities-in-xinjiang/index.html. Accessed 29 June 2022.

ENDNOTES

45. "EU-China Comprehensive Agreement on Investment: Milestones and Documents," *European Commission*, EU, https://policy.trade.ec.europa.eu/eu-trade-relationships-country-and-region/countries-and-regions/china/eu-china-agreement/milestones-and-documents_en.

46. Vincent Ni, "EU Efforts to Ratify China Investment Deal 'Suspended' after Sanctions," *The Guardian*, Guardian News and Media, 4 May 2021, https://www.theguardian.com/world/2021/may/04/eu-suspends-ratification-of-china-investment-deal-after-sanctions.

47. "Targeted by Chinese Smear Campaign, Uyghur Leader Learns of Father's Death," *Radio Free Asia*, 15 Jan. 2020, https://www.rfa.org/english/news/uyghur/activist-father-01152020211855.html.

48. ئەركىمە ھۆشرەت زاكىرنىڭ مۇخبىرلىرىمىز بىلەن ھۆرگۈت غاقان قىرىلدانىشى د ۇئ ق ھەئىسى دولقۇنئ ھەئاسىيغا ھۆجۇم قىلدى." *Radio Free Asia*, 13 Jan. 2020, https://www.rfa.org/uyghur/xewerler/shohret-zakir-01132020153331.html.

49. مۇھاجىرەتتىكى ئۇيغۇر ئامائىتى ھۆشرەت زاكىرنىڭ مىرگىنامەيدىكى قىرىلدانىشىنىڭ قىلمىشى قاتتىق ئەيىبلىدى. *Radio Free Asia*, 15 Jan. 2020, https://www.rfa.org/uyghur/xewerler/shohret-zakir-01152020213254.html.

50. "Treasury Sanctions Perpetrators of Serious Human Rights Abuse on International Human Rights Day," *U.S. Department of the Treasury* (10 December 2021), https://home.treasury.gov/news/press-releases/jy0526.

51. "Chinese Government Threatens and Intimidates World Uyghur Congress," *European Interest*, 13 Jan. 2020, https://www.europeaninterest.eu/article/chinese-government-threatens-intimidates-world-uyghur-congress/.

52. Adrian Zez, The Jamestown Foundation, Washington, DC, 2020, *Sterilizations, IUDs, and Mandatory Birth Control: The CCP's Campaign to Suppress Uyghur Birthrates in Xinjiang*, https://www.researchgate.net/publication/343971074_Sterilizations_IUDs_and_Mandatory_Birth_Control_The_CCP%27s_Campaign_to_Suppress_Uyghur_Birthrates_in_

Xinjiang. Accessed 2 July 2022.

53. The China Tribunal is an independent people's tribunal established to inquire into forced organ harvesting from, amongst others, prisoners of conscience in China and to investigate what criminal offences, if any, have been committed by state or state-approved bodies, organisations or individuals in China that may have engaged in forced organ harvesting.

54. *Uyghur Tribunal Judgment*, Uyghur Tribunal, 9 Dec. 2021, https://uyghurtribunal.com/wp-content/uploads/2021/12/Uyghur-Tribunal-Summary-Judgment-9th-Dec-21.pdf.

55. World Uyghur Congress, 2018, *Parallel Submission to the Committee on the Elimination of Racial Discrimination (CERD) for the People's Republic of China (PRC)*, https://tbinternet.ohchr.org/Treaties/CERD/Shared%20Documents/CHN/INT_CERD_NGO_CHN_31745_E.pdf.

56. "Consideration of China (Cont'd)—2655th Meeting 96th Session Committee on Elimination of Racial Discrimination," *UN Web TV*, CERD, 13 Aug. 2018, https://media.un.org/en/asset/k1k/k1k9672662. Accessed 2 July 2022.

57. *Permanent Mission of the People's Republic of China*, CERD, 2018, https://tbinternet.ohchr.org/Treaties/CERD/Shared%20Documents/CHN/INT_CERD_LOP_CHN_32040_E.pdf.

58. "Consideration of China (Cont'd)—2655th Meeting 96th Session Committee on Elimination of Racial Discrimination," *UN Web TV*, CERD, 13 Aug. 2018, https://media.un.org/en/asset/k1k/k1k9672662. Accessed 2 July 2022.

59. "Rep. Jim McGovern Presents World Uyghur Congress with the Democracy Award | 2019 Democracy Award," *YouTube*, National Endowment for Democracy, 7 June 2019, https://www.youtube.com/watch?v=PmSxN68_cJ8. Accessed 29 June 2022; "2019 Democracy Award." *NATIONAL ENDOWMENT FOR DEMOCRACY*, https://www.ned.org/2019-democracy-award/world-uyghur-congress/.